Chrysler, Ford, Durant and Sloan

Chrysler, Ford, Durant and Sloan

Founding Giants of the American Automotive Industry

by H. Eugene Weiss

McFarland & Company, Inc., Publishers
Jefferson, North Carolina, and London

LIBRARY OF CONGRESS CATALOGUING-IN-PUBLICATION DATA

Weiss, H. Eugene, 1929–
Chrysler, Ford, Durant and Sloan: founding giants of the
American automotive industry / by H. Eugene Weiss.
p.   cm.
Includes bibliographical references and index.

ISBN 0-7864-1611-4 (softcover : 50# alkaline paper) ∞

1. Automobile industry and trade—United States—Biography.
2. Automobiles—United States—History.
3. Industrialists—United States—Biography.   I. Title.
TL139.W43   2003   338.7'6292'092273—dc21   2003014391

British Library cataloguing data are available

©2003 H. Eugene Weiss. All rights reserved

*No part of this book may be reproduced or transmitted in any form
or by any means, electronic or mechanical, including photocopying
or recording, or by any information storage and retrieval system,
without permission in writing from the publisher.*

Cover images (left to right): William Durant, Alfred P. Sloan, Walter Chrysler
and Henry Ford. *Background image ©2002 Art Today*

Manufactured in the United States of America

*McFarland & Company, Inc., Publishers
Box 611, Jefferson, North Carolina 28640
www.mcfarlandpub.com*

To my supportive family

Contents

Preface 1

1. **Henry Ford** (1863–1947) 3
   Defining an American Industry   3
   The Ford Motor Company   11
   The Piquette Plant   22
   Ford Highland Park   28
   The Ford Dealership   36
   Dodge Brothers Lawsuit   38
   History Is Bunk   42
   H. Ford vs. H. Leland   44
   The Rouge Complex and the Model A and V8   46
   Accounting and Management   56
   The Arsenal of Democracy   59
   Lincoln and Mercury   62
   Summary of a Business Life   63

2. **William Durant** (1861–1946) 67
   Salesmanship   67
   Buick   69
   General Motors   72
   Banker Usury   74
   General Motors Division of Chevrolet   76
   A New General Motors   78
   Durant After G.M.   81
   Summary of a Life   83

3. **Alfred Sloan** (1875–1966) 84
   The Early Career   84
   A Professional Manager   85

United Motors Corporation   88
Reconstruction   90
Marketing and Product   96
Sloan as Head of G.M.   101
Greatness   104
Summary of a Life   107

4. Walter Chrysler (1875–1940) 109
The Railroad Years   109
The Buick Years   113
The Company Doctor: Willys   117
ZSB   118
The First Chrysler   119
The Company Doctor: Maxwell   120
The Elizabeth, N.J., Plant   121
The New Chrysler Car   123
The 1924 Chrysler   130
Chrysler Corporation   133
The Dodge Purchase   138
Plymouth   143
The Depression   148
The Airflow   150
Chrysler Firsts   158
Styling   165
Non-Automotive   167
A Time to Relax   170
Summary of a Business Life   171

Epilogue: Four Business Lives 172
Career Goals and Commitment   172
The Part of Luck   173

Notes 177

Index 185

Preface

The American automobile industry has been called the favorite child of capitalism. It certainly was in that the market has rewarded the automotive industry with exceptional profits for more than four decades, from the early 1900s to World War II. In 1903, the Ford Motor Company was started with a business proposal that had 25 percent pre-tax earnings on sales. In 1906 and 1907, William Durant was making over 25 percent in pre-tax earnings on sales with Buick Motor Company. Later, in the late 1910s he was running General Motors with pre-tax earnings on sales at a level of about 17 percent in spite of heavy investments in plant expansions and acquisitions. Alfred Sloan became president of General Motors in 1923 and ran General Motors with 21 percent pre-tax earnings on sales during the late '20s and an average of 15.5 percent pre-tax earnings for the pre–World War II era, which included the Depression. Walter Chrysler, with a much smaller asset base than General Motors, averaged 6.6 percent pre-tax earnings on sales for the years that he ran Chrysler Corporation until his death in 1940. This is an unrivaled earnings level for any industry and it continued for four decades.

This period of extraordinary earnings allowed these men and their companies to make developments in production, product design, marketing and business organization that have set the standard for consumer products and other industrial firms. Four men, the subject of this book, are primarily responsible for these concepts. Their stories have been told many times. Henry Ford with the Model T put the world on wheels and created a social revolution. He alone lowered the price of the Model T and in 1914 raised the wages in his plant to $5.00 per day, a middle class wage for a job that could be learned in only a few hours. In 1915, the combination of these two actions by Henry Ford resulted in a Ford worker being able to earn the price of a new Model T in only 16 weeks of work at the Ford plant. Only three years earlier, it took a worker 64 weeks to earn the money for an almost identical car. This ratio of hours to the price of a new car became a fundamental of American society for the next 70 years. Wars, depressions, recessions, and inflation cycles came and went, but car prices and factory wages stayed in lockstep. This put America on wheels and bolstered the profitability of the industry.

William Durant and Alfred Sloan were the two leaders of General Motors, which became a profitable industrial giant as the automobile market grew. Walter Chrysler, with the introduction of a well engineered product that was equal to the customer's expectation, brought the automobile industry into the modern era. It is only now, with new research at the Archives of the DaimlerChrysler Historical Collection, that the story of the four giants can be told with a new perspective. Walter Chrysler's life touched on the other three and the contributions of all four can now be viewed together. The stories of all four are told here through events in each business life as they bear on the man's contributions to production, product design, marketing and business organization.

About the Photographs

Many of the sites, objects and automobiles that are important in this automobile history still exist and those in the Detroit area were photographed by the author. There is a notation of the location of each picture if it is accessible to the public.

The majority of the photographs are from the public displays at the following locations.

- Alfred P. Sloan Museum, 1221 E. Kearsley Street, Flint, Mich.
- Henry Ford Museum and Greenfield Village, Village Road and Oakwood Blvd., Dearborn, Mich.
- Walter P. Chrysler Museum, 1 Chrysler Drive, Auburn Hills, Mich.

1

Henry Ford (1863–1947)

Henry Ford is a well known figure but, few are aware of the changes he made that are basic to our modern society. He lived at a time when the United States was a horse-powered, farm-based country. This was an America where people rarely traveled more than 50 miles from their birthplace in their lifetime. The new America that he had a major part in creating would send young people around the world to fight in two major wars.

Henry Ford was the son of a farmer in Dearborn, Michigan, but had no interest in following in his father's footsteps. Early in life he showed a talent for machinery and was fascinated by the wonder products of the day in clocks and watches. Much like a notebook computer today, a watch represented the essence of modern technology at that time and could be held in one's hand. Henry Ford took them apart, repaired them and regulated them for a local store.

One of his early jobs was working as an apprentice at the Flowers Machine Shop. He would also work nights repairing and regulating watches. His knowledge of watchmaking was so complete that he designed a watch and the manufacturing methods to start his own business. He abandoned the project only after he determined that he must sell 600,000 watches at the price he wished to sell them for each year to be successful.

As a young man he met and later married Clara Bryant on April 8, 1888. Their only son, Edsel, was born on November 6, 1893. Henry Ford was successful in building his first automobile, called a Quadricycle, during June of 1896 and it was only the second car to drive on the streets of Detroit. Henry Ford, without the usual business or accounting methods, became capitalism's favorite child by starting with only $28,000 in invested capital and growing his company to be the largest industrial firm in the world.

Defining an American Industry: From the Quadricycle to Oldsmobile to Model A

The automobile market of the 1900s had two general types of cars—the copies of large European cars intended more to convey the importance and wealth of the owner, and an American invention that would provide transportation for the owner. The imported Mercedes, Renault, Fiat or Rolls-Royce cars were copied by the American manufacturers of Packard, Autocar, Pierce, Winton and Peerless as statements of wealth. They were heavy, multi-cylinder cars of low ground clearance to be used at their best on the paved streets of American cities.[1]

American tinkerers and inventors developed a different concept and it sprang up in the towns across America at almost the same time. These were "powered buggies" with a single cylinder engine under the seat, light in weight, and with good ground clearance for the unpaved roads of small town and rural America. The first American car was a Duryea, which in 1896 became the first American production car with a production run of 13 cars. Henry Ford built his Quadricycle that year. During the next 6 years this was followed by production of the Curved Dash Oldsmobile, the Jeffery's Rambler, the first Cadillac, and the first Model A Ford, and all were of this personal transportation type.[2]

No one inventor could take credit for this concept; it just seemed right for an American use of a car for personal transportation in the real world of dirt roads. The success of this concept was proven by Oldsmobile, which sold half the cars in America by 1903, and the second most popular car at that time was a Rambler, which was of similar concept. No one was more outspoken about this design approach than Henry Ford as he compared it to the heavy and complex designs of other cars.[3] The economic basis for the personal transportation type of automobile was well founded. The common alternative at the turn of the 20th century was a horse and wagon. A horse and wagon had an initial cost that was half that of an automobile, but a horse had to be fed each day, whether used or not, and the upkeep cost exceeded that of an automobile that used fuel only when driven. It took 20 minutes to a half an hour to saddle a horse or harness it to a wagon and a similar amount of time after their use. A gasoline car started with the pull of a crank and stopped when the ignition was switched off.

It is easy to see why the first customers for the automobile were doctors; getting to a patient quickly was critical. The market that doctors represented, in fact, had a major impact on the type of car that succeeded in the American market. Electrics would start quickly, but their range was short and unknown. A doctor who extended his rounds to visit an added patient could exceed the battery range and would have to be towed home with a team of horses. Worse, the electric car was then useless for a half a day or more as the batteries recharged—a doctor could not make any calls on patients. It took more time to start a steamer than to prepare a horse, because it needed boiling water to move. While the doctor was visiting a patient, the water in the steamer would cool and there would be a delay before another patient could be visited. Gasoline cars were noisy and dirty, but they started with a pull on the crank. The fuel in the tank was known and the range to visit patients was also known.[4]

HENRY FORD—This photograph was taken in 1915 after he had introduced the moving assembly line at his plants. This lowered his cost and in turn, he lowered his prices to customers. In 1914, he raised the wages in his plants to $5 per day, a middle class salary at that time. These combined events made the time for a Ford worker to earn the price of a Ford car only 4 weeks and a social revolution started. Henry Ford, at the time this photograph was taken, was just beginning to see the revolution in society that he had begun. From the Collections of the Henry Ford Museum & Greenfield Village.

DETROIT IN 1900

The automobile industry started in New England, but the ease of transportation around the Great Lakes for iron ore and coal made it the production center of iron and steel, raw materials essential to the automobile industry. Michigan became attractive because of the fortunes that had been made in the middle and late 1800s in lumber and copper. This money was available for investment. The lumber industry of Michigan, in fact, provided the timber for the massive building projects of row houses and walk-ups in the east coast cities of America.[5]

THE QUADRICYCLE—This car is in a glass case since it is the car that launched the world's first billionaire. In 1896, Henry Ford used his own funds and built the car, the second to drive on the streets of Detroit. With only his own intuition he solved the problems of ignition, carburetion, valve timing, gear ratios, and steering. The car did not have brakes or reverse gear, but it weighed only 500 pounds and could be pushed backward. While others were building one cylinder cars, Henry Ford compounded the challenge by building his first car as an inline two cylinder. This Ford Quadricycle is on permanent display at the Henry Ford Museum in Dearborn, Mich.

Michigan lumber was also the foundation of the shipbuilding industry and steam engine manufacturing, with the related cast iron foundries also part of the Michigan economy. The "lumber barons," as they were called, were self-made men and tended to keep their money and investments nearby in Michigan. They also built their mansions in Detroit as a social center. Samuel Smith was such a man. He had made his fortune in Michigan lumber, investments in copper mines in the upper part of the state, and in Michigan real estate. In 1892, he invested in the Pliny Olds Machine Shop in Lansing, Michigan, that made steam engines for Great Lakes wooden ships. They also made stationary steam engines for manufacturing plant overhead line shafts that were used at that time to drive the machines in a plant. During this time, Pliny Olds' son, Ransom, was experimenting with the newly invented gasoline engines as a safety improvement over steam engines for ships. Steam engines were a serious safety problem because the open fires used to create steam would burn out of control and then burn wooden ships to the waterline. A tank of gasoline was far safer.[6]

The Ransom Olds gasoline engine experiments also extended to building a gasoline powered, three-wheeled wagon in 1896. It was easy to see that automobiles were going to be the "next new thing," to use a more modern expression. In 1899 Samuel Smith made a major investment decision to back Ransom Olds with $200,000 and an agreement to move the business from Lansing to Detroit to be near Smith's home. He also made one of his sons, Frederick, the president and another son, Angus, the treasurer of the new Olds Motor Works. The $200,000 was a huge amount of money and worth about $2 million in today's dollars. Ransom Olds built several prototypes for evaluation but a fire in the new plant burned all the prototype cars except one that had been pushed to safety. That car was the only choice that the new company had as a viable production car, and it proved to be a master stroke. It was the Curved Dash Oldsmobile and from 1903 to 1905 was the largest selling car in America. In fact, over half the cars that were made in America were Oldsmobiles. It was also the subject of the song "In My Merry Oldsmobile."[7]

The Smith family was part of the power structure of Detroit and their new automotive venture was headed for success. Other Detroit leaders looked for similar automotive success. William Murphy, another of the "Barons," approached Henry Ford about Ford's automotive experiments and drove one of Ford's prototypes.

Henry Ford had reached what would have been a career goal. In his late 30s, he was the Chief Engineer of the Edison electrical generating plant in Detroit. He had a staff working for him and the respect of a new industry in Detroit. He had a wife and a young son and rented a nice home (at that time, home ownership was only for the wealthy). Nonetheless, he frightened his wife with experiments on an internal combustion gasoline engine and used his spare time and money to build the "Quadricycle." On June 4, 1896, the car he made was the second automobile to run on the streets of Detroit, and that was only three months after his first car achieved that goal.

William Murphy put together a group of wealthy Detroit investors and offered to back Henry Ford in his automotive design and manufacturing efforts. On August 5, 1899, the Detroit Automobile Company was formed with Ford given a small share of the Company, but no salary because he was still working at the Detroit Edison Company.[8]

THE DETROIT AUTOMOBILE COMPANY

Very little of the Detroit Automobile Company has survived to modern times, but a sales catalog has. It makes a compelling case for the use of an automobile for personal transportation. It showed the following five-year comparison of the Detroit Automobile with a horse and carriage.

People in modern times may question these costs, but the $816 savings shown below must have had some validity with customers in 1900 and would

Table 1. Detroit Automobile Car Costs

Automobile

Original cost	$1,000
Cost of operating, 1/4 cents per mile, 25 miles per day	$114
New tires	$100
Repairs	$50
Painting, four times	$100
	$1,364

Horse and Vehicle

Original cost, horse, harness and vehicle	$500
Cost of keeping horse five years	$1,200
Shoeing the horse	$180
Repairs on Vehicle, including rubber tires	$150
Repairs on harness, $10 per year	$50
Painting vehicle four times	$100
	$2,180

have provided the economic basis for the personal transportation type of automobile. The 1900 catalog went on to point out that the horse might die during the five years while the Detroit car can be well maintained during that time and can always be repaired at nominal cost. The final line pointed out that the automobile will do the work of three horses. Henry Ford was the most knowledgeable person in the company and must have had a hand in writing this catalog. He therefore had a clear understanding of the economic advantages of an automobile.[9]

Ford split his time between the two companies but was most interested in the Detroit Automobile Company. The first Ford product was a small truck. The investors were looking across Detroit to the Oldsmobile plant where the Curved Dash Oldsmobile was making money for the owner, Samuel Smith. It was not long before a major rift developed with Henry Ford over how the company funds should be spent. Ford wanted to generate interest in their truck with success in racing a car, but the investors wanted to build an Oldsmobile competitor and start to make money as Oldsmobile was doing. Later in life, Ford recalled this period as one that was driven by the profit oriented investors vs. his intent to develop a better product through racing. This was a good "spin" on the situation, but it is hard to relate a two cylinder, 30 hp race car to a 4 hp truck. This conflict become so bad that Ford told his workmen not to tell any of the investors that the parts they were working on in the plant were for a race car. Surely he must have known that the investors did not give him their money to use to tinker with race cars.

The facts at the time suggest another motive. Ford was forced by his boss at Detroit Edison to make a decision between the Detroit Edison or Detroit Automobile companies. Ford chose the new automobile venture, but that resulted in the loss of his only salary, which was from the Detroit Edison Company. He also felt that at the Detroit Automobile Company he was doing all the work and for little gain. Henry Ford continued to build parts for race cars and only a few parts for the little truck. Only a few of the trucks were completed and less than that, a handful, were sold. He did have success with the race cars but the situation came to a head in November 1901. The result was that the Detroit Automobile Company made about 10 little trucks and race car fame for Henry Ford, and lost $86,000 for the investors.

The real problem may have been that Ford was simply in "over his head." Henry Ford was a gifted tinkerer and inventor but there is a big difference between a one-of-a-kind car, like a prototype or a race car, and being able to make large numbers of the same parts for production. Ford was to become a leader in the development of breakthroughs in manufacturing methods at the beginning of the 20th century. It is hard to imagine there was a time when Henry Ford was not a master of manufacturing. Writers and historians have had to look through the later manufacturing "halo" to objectively see the abilities of Henry Ford during this earlier time. Ford's background then was that of a beginning machinist with only his experience at the Flowers Machine Shop.

John Anderson, a lawyer and knowledgeable contemporary, said, "Ford was continually engaging in making changes and improvements, meanwhile exhausting the Company's capital with no means of replenishing it with the sale of finished cars; added to which, despite orders from the directors to the contrary he devoted much of his time to designing a race car, instead of concentrating his energies upon the production of a small and more practical vehicle they favored."[10] He was successful in racing and talking about his lightweight race cars that could beat the heavy and complex luxury brands. His racing success convinced most of his investors to reorganize the Detroit Automobile Company into the Henry Ford Company on November 20, 1901, in hopes that he would start to make production cars and make money for them.[11]

THE HENRY FORD COMPANY

To encourage him to settle on a car design, Henry Ford was to receive a larger share of this new company—one sixth. He still felt that he was doing all the work and not being paid what his fame and value were worth. At that time he wrote to his brother-in-law, Milton Bryant, that "My Company will kick about me following racing but they get the advertising and I expect to make $ where I can't make c [cents] at manufacturing."[12] That continued him in an opposite direction from his investors, who wanted him to settle on a car design for production.

That did not happen and in just four more months, after the investors put up $30,000 in new capital for the Henry Ford Company, he was out. He settled with the investors for $900 for his inventions, a bunch of racing parts and drawings that the company did not want, and an agreement to change the company name from that of the Henry Ford Company. His second automotive venture was another failure. He also made his investors, the power structure of Detroit, very angry. He also vowed to never come "under orders" again.

There were more events going on at that time, however. The Leland Machine Shop was the most respected of all the Detroit shops and well known for outstanding precision. Henry Leland himself was a product of the New England precision machine culture. He started as a young boy, during the American Civil War, making rifles with interchangeable parts at the armory at Springfield, Mass. He became the technical head of Brown and Sharpe, a maker of precision machine tools, and held the basic patents for centerless grinders. He came to Detroit near the end of the 19th century and established a machine shop that was known for its passion for precision. The Leland machine shop made the engines for Oldsmobile and Leland made a proposal to Oldsmobile. The Curved Dash Oldsmobile engine was developed for 4 hp. Leland had the valve timing improved and the power increased to 7 hp. He next made the machining more precise and the power increased to about 10 hp. The more precise engine had less internal friction and so greater power output. He was delighted with his new development and offered it to Samuel Smith, the owner of Oldsmobile. To Leland's surprise, the offer was refused. The extra power might break some other part of a car. Why change a car that enjoyed good commercial success?[13]

Everyone in the Detroit automotive circles knew of the Leland proposal and the Oldsmobile refusal. William Murphy was the leader of the Henry Ford Company investors and went to the same church as Henry Leland. Murphy asked Leland what he should do with their chief designer (Henry Ford) who only wanted to use their money to build race cars.

Henry Leland was never tactful in his comments. This is a man who said the following about how his machine shop was run: "It is the foreman's place to know that every piece of work turned out by his department was RIGHT, and it is his work to teach his men how to make it RIGHT. It doesn't cost as much to have the work done RIGHT the first time as it does to have it done poorly and then hire a number of men to make it right afterward."[14] Henry Leland was just as sharp with his comments about the quality of the bearings that were made by Alfred Sloan's Hyatt Bearing Company (See Chapter 3). Henry Leland looked at Henry Ford's design and was not only critical of the design but also of Henry Ford as an inventor. It is easy to see that Leland, a true professional, would see little of value in the "cut and try" methods of Henry Ford and no doubt expressed his opinion very clearly. We know that the Henry Ford Company did not sell any cars and it was reported that it may have made parts for only one or two.

Little is known of the Detroit Automobile Company designs and the Henry Ford Automobile Company designs, but the Detroit Automobile Catalog boasted of a single long lever to brake and make the car go forward. There was a glowing report in the *Detroit Journal* on July 29, 1899, in which the reporter told of a test ride with Henry Ford as driver in the new car (truck). The single lever to accelerate and stop was not mentioned, but if used, it would have been a complex system.[15] We know the weight of the truck was 1100 pounds and about 1600 pounds with a payload. Ford's design intended that the truck would be braked with only the pull of hand strength. This feature alone would have given Henry Leland all the reason he would have needed to criticize the Ford concept. There was a second road test of the Detroit Automobile truck one year later with Henry Ford again as the driver. As reported in the *Detroit News-Tribune*, February 4, 1900, there is a clear mention of a brake pedal and no mention of the single lever control.[16] It appears that Henry Ford was still working out how the single lever feature was to be made.

To the Board of Directors, Leland's comments were as if blinders had been lifted from their eyes and they had a different view of Henry Ford. After some study of the assets of the Henry Ford Company, Leland proposed that the company be reorganized and renamed Cadillac Motor Company. The Board of Directors agreed and the very successful Cadillac Motor Company was born. The first Cadillac car and the 1903 Model A from the soon-to-be-formed Ford Motor Company were almost identical in design. The Cadillac had interchangeable parts and used the Leland 10 hp engine that Samuel Smith had turned down. Most of the members of the Board of Directors and the place of business of the Detroit Automobile Company, the Henry Ford Company and the Cadillac Motor Company were the same.

The fact that the Ford and Cadillac cars were, at one time, almost the same car is an affront to the modern Cadillac Motor Division of General Motors and modern Cadillac customers. The reality is that both Henry Leland and Henry Ford were influenced by the Curved Dash Oldsmobile design that was the industry sales leader at that time. Both were a statement of the industry designs and an acknowledgement of the debt they both owed to Ransom Olds.

At this point in his life Ford was out of work and with few prospects. He had moved his young family in with his father, William Ford, on January 8, 1901, to save money. He was not without physical courage, however. He personally drove in a race car of his design and won, and later, on January 12, 1904, set the land speed record at 91.4 mph. These would be major accomplishments for anyone, and this man would later own the largest industrial firm in the world.

The Ford Motor Company: The Birth of a Giant

Henry Ford was almost out of options for the future. Between The Detroit Automobile Company and the Henry Ford Company he had lost about $100,000 of money from the most prominent citizens of Detroit. While Henry Ford worked at either company, he refused to settle on a car design

1903 CADILLAC—After the failure of Henry Ford's second automotive venture, the investors agreed with Henry Leland to start a new venture. They chose the name "Cadillac" and had immediate success. This photograph is of a 1903 Cadillac and the crowd and smoke are there because the almost 100 year old, 10 horsepower Leland–made engine was just started and was running. This was photographed at the 2002 Meadow Brook Concours d'Elegance. There is a 1903 Cadillac on permanent display at the Henry Ford Museum and Greenfield Village in Dearborn, Michigan.

that could be put into production and refused to do what the Board had told him to do in direct instruction. The most prominent man in manufacturing, Henry Leland, had criticized Ford's designs and his ability as an inventor. At almost 40 years of age, he was as close to failure as possible. He talked about financial success in building race cars and was building two of them as a way to make a living. Later in life he talked about building race cars as though it was possible that his race winnings would support his family, but it had to be more of a dream than reality. While Ford's name was well known in racing, his first two automotive failures eliminated any chance that the usual Detroit area investors would consider any new money for a man who could not focus on the basics of any business.

Help came from an unexpected source. While at the Edison power plant, Ford knew the coal supplier, Alexander Malcomson, and he and Ford formed a company for Ford to develop a new car design. Alexander Malcomson was not part of the Detroit leadership and had invested in a variety of projects and was financially overextended. He was, however, able to raise a small amount of money ($3,000) for Ford's automotive experiments, and if Ford was successful, they would both own the design. Ford designed a very nice two cylinder Model A to be sold at $750. This was about the price of an Oldsmobile or Rambler that had only a one cylinder engine, and they were the two top selling cars in the country at that time. While Ford could design the car, it took someone else to make it a successful business proposal, and of the organizers of the company, that could only be Alexander Malcomson. The following table is from a letter written by John Anderson (the company's lawyer) on June 4, 1903, just before the Ford Motor Company was organized. All the unit costs of the new car proposal were locked in by written contract and the only variable cost that was that of assembly. The business proposal looked very attractive, unfortunately, the reputation of Henry Ford preceded him and the only investors in the new company were friends or business associates of Alexander Malcomson.

Table 2. Cost of the Ford Model A—1903

Machine	$250
Body	52
Wheels	26
Upholstery	16
Tires	10
Assembly	<u>20</u>
Unit Cost	$374
Overhead	30
Contingency	46
FMC profit	<u>150</u>
Wholesale price	$600
Dealer markup	<u>$150</u>
Retail price	$750

The $150 profit for Ford Motor Company was a 25 percent profit margin with no tooling or startup cost, since those risks were borne by the Dodge Brothers. This return compares favorably with the Internet startups of recent times. The profit potential in the early days of the automobile industry was the reason that so many "start up" automobile companies were attracted to the industry. It was also the reason that the companies that did not have a successful product would fail.

The Ford Company was started on June 16, 1903, with $100,000 in capital stock but only $28,000 in "paid in" cash. Unlike the first two ventures, Henry Ford had an ownership position at 25.5 percent and he was now one

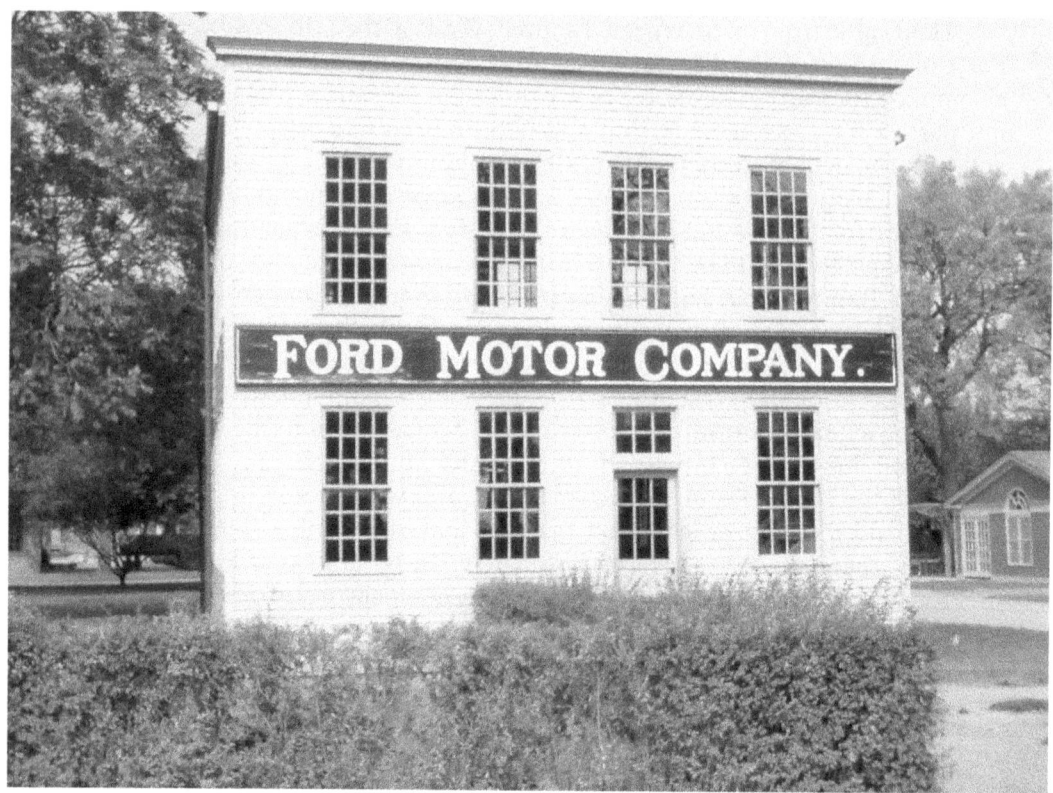

FORD MOTOR COMPANY—Ford Motor Company was formed on June 16, 1903, with only $28,000 of actual cash. The car was an immediate success. The earning power of the company allowed it to grow to be the largest industrial firm in the world with no further addition of outside cash from stock issues, corporate bonds or bank debt. This photograph is of a quarter scale replica of the 1903 Mack Avenue building that was built on the grounds of Greenfield Village at the Henry Ford Museum and Greenfield Village.

of what he had earlier called "profit oriented" investors. Neither he nor Malcomson put any money in the new company, but claimed their share as payment for the car design that Henry Ford had done. Malcomson had the same share as Ford, but Malcomson's business associates and friends had 39 percent and would vote with him. The Dodge Brothers later had a 10 percent share but did not take sides in the future Ford-Malcomson power struggles.

Ford was the luckiest man alive. His two cylinder Model A was a good design for the time. Malcomson came up with the $3,000 to make the prototype, Malcomson's friends came up with $28,000 in cash to start the company and the Dodge Brothers came up with about $70,000 to tool the car and meet payroll until the first cars were sold. This was a total of about $100,000 to launch the Ford Motor Company—but none came from Henry Ford.

THE DODGE BROTHERS

John and Horace Dodge were part of the earlier bicycle boom of the 1890s, but when it turned to a bust at the turn of the 20th century, they started and ran the largest machine shop in Detroit. They made engines, transmissions and various parts for Oldsmobile and other car companies in Detroit. In late 1902, Henry Ford and Alexander Malcomson approached the Dodge Brothers about making all the mechanical parts of the new Ford Model A. The Dodge brothers had been part of the exploding Detroit automobile business and while they knew how to run a very successful machine shop, they knew nothing about how to design an automobile. The brothers made a major decision to support the Ford venture.[17]

They agreed to:

- Drop all existing automotive business even though it was very profitable to them. They would devote their entire shop to the Ford business.
- Sell 650 almost complete running cars to Ford for $250 each.
- Redesign the parts of the Ford car so that they could be manufactured. There is a report that Dodge redesigned the Ford rear axle concept so that it could be made.
- Make all engineering drawings and parts for the Ford car.
- Pay for all tooling for the Ford car.

To accomplish their part of the contract, they had borrow up to $70,000 under the Dodge name for payroll and material until the Ford cars started to sell.

The first Ford was of Dodge production engineering and manufacture except for a wood body, wheels and tires. The Dodge Brothers delivered the first cars under the contract to Ford, but the Ford Motor Company did not have the cash to pay for them. Dodge Brothers took 10 percent ($10,000) of the Ford stock with $7,000 paid in as material and gave a $3,000 note. They were criticized for protecting their investment, in that if the Ford venture failed, then they, not Ford, would own the tools and design for the Ford car. In view of their sizable investment, this was only a prudent action when dealing with someone who had failed twice. The $28,000 in cash that the Ford Motor Company had quickly dropped to $223.65, and it looked as if Henry Ford would have another automotive failure. At that low point, the first Ford car was sold in Chicago.

THE SELDEN LAWSUIT

The next threat to the new automobile company came from the east coast. It has been documented that in February 1899, William Whitney, a Wall

Street financier, looked out the windows of his Fifth Avenue mansion and believed he saw the future of the automobile industry. A blizzard was raging and only the new electric cabs could make headway in the deep, drifted snow. Before the snow melted, he had bought control of the Electric Vehicle Company (EVC), which he formed as a holding company, and created a new organization with the Pope Company that was making Columbia automobiles. With these moves, Columbia became the largest selling car in America by the end of 1899. It was again in 1900. The financier, in spite of his speed, was also cautious. He asked a patent attorney if any patent issues were pending with the new automobile industry. As it turns out, he was told there were. The press was interested in the same subject. The first issue of *Motor Age*, on September 12, 1899, carried the lead story "The Scramble for Patent Control." In the article, William Whitney was mentioned as one of those trying to gain patent control of the automobile industry. Surprisingly, the Selden Patent was not mentioned in this story even though that patent had been in force for four years.[18]

George Selden of Rochester, N.Y., first applied for his patent on May 8, 1879, and in one of the interesting crosses of history, asked a local bank clerk to be a witness. The witness was George Eastman before he became famous for cameras. Selden was a patent attorney by profession. He submitted changes to his patent, which would delay the patent process. It was not issued until November 5, 1895, sixteen years later, and the industry was born during that time. Most attorneys and engineers at the time regarded the Selden Patent as of no import because it detailed an engine that was not practical. Selden had seen a Brayton cycle engine run and it was very smooth. The Otto cycle was very noisy and Selden called it "another of those dammed Dutch engines" in his diary. This would later be a costly mistake.

Whitney's attorneys claimed that the engine detailed in the Selden Patent was not important. What was important, they said, was the new combination of automotive ideas in it and, as such, it was a basic controlling patent and applied to every car made in, or imported into, America. This became an unfolding series of legal steps in the struggle for monopoly control of the American automobile industry which became a reality by 1909.[19]

In 1899, the Whitney forces contracted to become the license holder of the Selden Patent and then devised a simple legal strategy. They started a lawsuit of patent infringement against the Winton Motor Carriage Company. As the case dragged on, the company offered to settle for a nominal fee on each Winton car made. In the fall of 1902, Winton agreed to the fee to forestall a long and expensive lawsuit. The settlement also assured that the legality of the Selden Patent was untested.

In late 1902, other manufacturers were quickly organized into the Association of Licensed Automobile Manufacturers (ALAM). Original members included Olds, Pierce, Peerless, Packard, Searchmont, Hayes Apperson, Knox, Autocar, Locomobile, Winton, International, U.S. Long Distance and Franklin.

By June 17, 1903, Stevens, Cadillac and Thomas also joined. ALAM members paid 1¼ percent of the retail price of every car made or imported in America. Private owners were also included and a potential river of wealth started flowing into EVC, ALAM and the Columbia Motor Company.

Research at the DaimlerChrysler Historical Collection has revealed four ledgers that provide new insight on the Selden Patent lawsuit, the relationship with Ford Motor Company and the impact on the early history of the automobile industry. The ledgers are:

1. A listing of inventors and their inventions that relate to automobiles and wheeled vehicles.
2. A listing of patents that had been issued relating to the automobile industry.
3. A listing of receipts from licensing patents.[20]
4. A listing of the payroll from the Dodge Brothers Machine Shop for 1903.[21]

The DaimlerChrysler Historical Collection archives has such documents in its possession because Columbia Motor Company merged with U.S. Motors, which became Maxwell; then, Maxwell Chalmers; next, Maxwell Motors; and, eventually, Chrysler Corporation. Chrysler Corporation purchased Dodge Brothers in 1928, and merged with Daimler Benz in 1998. The first two ledgers are a complete answer to William Whitney's 1899 original question regarding the patent situation in the automobile industry. The third contains the original accounts of the cash payment to ALAM and Columbia Motor Company for the patents that they controlled. The fourth is the original payroll ledger from the Dodge Brothers Machine Shop and provides an informative insight into the operation of the new Ford Motor Company.

THE FORD MOTOR COMPANY OF 1903

In February of 1903, Henry Ford learned of the settlement of the Selden lawsuit with the Winton Motor Carriage Company. He was planning to enter the automobile business and asked to join ALAM. He was rebuffed because his new company was not yet created. In June, the new Ford Motor Company was formed and he asked again to join ALAM. Ford was rejected again in July 1903, because his company was an "assemblage plant." ALAM was an association of "manufacturers" and felt that Ford Motor Company was not eligible to join until it manufactured some parts and produced drawings of their car. Henry Ford was furious—his "Irish" was up.

The facts about Ford Motor Company (FMC) were correct. They bought wheels, tires, and a small wooden body. The rest of the car came from the Dodge Brother's machine shop that also handled the production engineering and drafting. From a June 4, 1903, letter from FMC attorney John Anderson to his father, we learn that at the Ford Motor Company:

Ten or a dozen boys at $1.50 a day, and a foreman fit the bodies on the machine, put the cushions in place, put the tires on the wheel, the wheels on the machine and paint it and test it to see that it ran "o.k.", and it was ready for delivery. Now this is all there is to the whole proposition.[22]

We know from the contract with FMC that the Dodge Brothers machine shop was required to give up all other business and devote all its efforts to filling the contract. From the Dodge Brothers Machine Shop payroll book we know that Dodge had an average staff of 135 machinists working on the Ford automobile for the last half of 1903, compared to the 12 "boys" that FMC employed. Ford Motor Company in 1903 was an "assemblage plant" as ALAM claimed. FMC was exactly the kind of company that the responsible manufacturers of the ALAM were trying to eliminate. In 1903, for example, 57 companies were founded but 27 failed in what looked like an automobile "game." Ford was not only an "assemblage plant" with little capital behind it, but it was run by a man that had failed in two automotive ventures. There was a report that Henry Joy, the head of Packard Motor Company and who was part of the Detroit power structure, would withdraw from ALAM if the Ford Motor Company was allowed to join.

On October 22, 1903, EVC filed a patent infringement suit against Ford Motor Company among other car makers and importers. The logic was questionable. FMC was not allowed to join in July because it was an "assemblage plant" and three months later it was sued for not being an ALAM licensed manufacturer. With revenue from other car makers continuing each month, ALAM had major resources to bring to the suit. Ledger 3 shows that over $60,000 collected from ALAM members was aligned against Ford and other manufacturers by July 1903. To put this in scale, the Ford Motor Company was formed with $28,000 in cash only a month earlier. When the FMC attorneys Horace Rackham and John Anderson reviewed the lawsuit, they felt their fledgling company was doomed.

Sales for FMC as of September 1903 were 195 cars, a very good first four months for the new company. Ford Motor Company sales continued to increase rapidly and this meant that FMC had the resources to challenge the lawsuit. The increased sales also resulted in a situation unlike that of the earlier suit against the Winton Motor Carriage Company. In that case, the legal costs were high relative to the number of cars that Winton made. In the Ford situation, it was actually cheaper to pay the legal fees rather than a royalty to ALAM.

By 1907, Ledger 3 shows more than $1.6 million had been paid to EVC and ALAM. It was not enough money to keep EVC from going bankrupt in 1907, but Columbia Motor Company continued the case. Later that year, different car companies stopped paying royalties as the suit dragged on. That is reflected in Ledger 3. A 1907 default entry is noted under the Olds Motor Works. On May 28, 1909, the Selden Patent was ruled to be the basic patent of the automobile industry, as the Whitney lawyers had predicted at the turn of the 20th century. The result was a monopoly and every car made or imported in the U.S. had to pay a royalty to ALAM and the Columbia Company. It is rumored that William Durant paid more than $1 million to settle past claims for General Motors. Ledger 3 does not cover that GM entry, but does show more than $800,000 paid in 1909. From 1903 to 1909, Ledger 3 shows a total of almost $2.5 million. ALAM began a complete regulation of the automobile industry as they started to issue their licenses to each manufacturer for set customer prices and maximum sales volume.

It is difficult to project what would have happened to the automobile industry if this monopoly had continued. Each manufacturer would have been locked into the price it can charge for each model and how many of them that could be made. The public demand would have caused the more popular cars to be sold on a black market; other cars that could not fill their volume at the price that was assigned to them would be a drag on the market. It would have been an unmanageable mess with everyone as a loser, but the biggest loser would be the public. Such a restricted industry would never have become capitalism's favorite child.[23]

UNITED STATES MOTORS

United States Motors was formed in 1910 and was the response by Benjamin Briscoe to William Durant's General Motors, which had just been formed. It combined Maxwell-Briscoe, Stoddard Dayton, Sampson Truck, Brush, Gray Motors and Columbia Motor Company. This was a new powerhouse that, with the Seldom Patent victory, would make money from their own automobile business and also from all competitors. Another financier, Anthony Brady, joined Whitney with Columbia Motor Company and arranged the Selden patent revenue so that it was only credited to Columbia and not to United States Motors, where it might be lost in a complex financial structure.[23]

Ford had achieved a very high level of sales and a settlement would have been a financial disaster. There was no choice but to appeal the 1909 decision. Henry Ford had enough practical knowledge, unlike the lawyers, to realize the engine detailed in the Selden Patent was an important element of the patent. On January 11, 1911, the Appeals Court ruled, again, that the Selden Patent was the basic patent for the automobile industry. However, it went on to say that the patent applied only to cars with a Brayton cycle engine. Since FMC and all other car makers had Otto cycle engines, the Selden Patent did not apply to them.

The flood of money to ALAM and Columbia stopped and ALAM collapsed. By 1912, U.S. Motors was bankrupt and Walter Flanders, formerly of the Ford Motor Company, took over the assets and changed its name to the only name that had any presence in the marketplace—Maxwell. All other brands, including Columbia, were dropped. An automobile industry of fixed volume and fixed customer prices controlled by ALAM was not to be. The American automobile industry was free to find its own way. FMC and all other competitors were free to set their own prices and volume, and so they did. Henry Ford was a popular hero in that he stood up to a monopoly and won.[24]

ALEXANDER MALCOMSON

Alexander Malcomson has been dropped to only a footnote to history, but he created the business proposal and a situation in which a flawed Henry Ford could succeed. Ford had a 25.5 percent ownership position, but the company was headed by John Gray, a respected banker, to give FMC a feeling of financial stability that could not be achieved with Henry Ford, a two time loser, as President. Malcomson had the same share of the company as Ford, but could also call on his other friends with shares of the company to outvote Ford at any time. The company did not have any machine shop (it was at Dodge Brothers) and Ford could not tinker on his own projects as he had done in his earlier automotive ventures. Malcomson also placed his own office clerk, James Cousins, at FMC, full time, to check everything that Henry Ford was doing each day. No more parts for race cars or any activity by Henry Ford without Malcomson knowing all the details. There is a report that James Cousins kept Henry Ford from tinkering with production cars and elbowed him out of the way so early cars could be loaded on a railcar.

Henry Ford acted differently with this new venture than he had with the prior companies. Law partners John Anderson and Horace Rackham had Alexander Malcomson as a client and each had invested $5,000 in the new company. John Anderson knew of Ford's reputation from his prior failures. He was pleasantly surprised and said that Ford worked for the success of the company. It may have been because he had a 25.5 percent interest in success, or because he was not required to make the production drawings and run a production shop, or because he realized that living on race car winnings was only a dream or that his new car design would belong to the Dodge Brothers if there was another failure by Henry Ford. We will never know the

Opposite, top: THE FORD MODEL A OF 1903—This car is the first product of the Ford Motor Company. The car was designed by Henry Ford but the production drawings and manufacturing were done by the Dodge Brothers Machine Shop. Ford Motor Company added wheels, tires and a small wooden body to the almost complete car as delivered from Dodge Brothers. This photograph is of a car on display at the Henry Ford Museum and Greenfield Village. *Bottom:* THE MODEL A ENGINE—Henry Ford used a two cylinder opposed engine with his first commercial car design made by the Detroit Automobile Company in 1899. He refined the concept and when the 1903 Model A Ford was introduced it was at the same price as the two largest selling single cylinder cars in America, the Oldsmobile and Rambler. This photograph is of a display at the Henry Ford Museum and Greenfield Village.

1. Henry Ford (1863–1947) 21

real reason. Ford said that he would not come "under orders," but that is what he had to do to get FMC started. Malcomson deserves credit for correctly determining the strengths and weaknesses of Henry Ford and starting a business organized so that Ford could succeed.

In later years, Henry Ford took credit for everything, and an adoring press did not question him closely on the start of the Ford Motor Company. It is true that the company would not have succeeded without his commercial design for the Model A. It would have failed like so many other companies at that time. The Ford Motor Company, however, would not have started without a profitable business plan (see Table 2) and that was done by Alexander Malcomson. The investors in FMC were Malcomson's friends and associates and they were investing in Malcomson, not Henry Ford.

The company was an immediate success. In just six months it made $100,500 and declared a 100 percent stock dividend. With their future assured, on January 26, 1904, they voted to buy an option on 3.1 acres of land that would become the future Piquette Plant. At the end of the first year they showed a $256,000 profit. Malcomson wanted to increase profits and directed Ford to design a 4 cylinder Model B and later an even larger Model K. In later life, Henry Ford said that he hated both cars. They were built only because Malcomson had control of the company stock because of his friends on the Board. When Ford was involved with racing, he belittled the big complex cars that he beat on the track. Now the Ford name was on such cars.

Henry Ford was actually an employee in his own company, but he devised a clever plan to gain control. He formed the Ford Manufacturing Company without Malcomson's involvement.[25] This company was organized to make parts for the Ford Motor Company. The result was that prices to the Ford Motor Company were set so high that Ford Motor Company could not make a profit, but Ford Manufacturing Company would. Added advantages were that FMC could get out from under the complete manufacturing control of the Dodge Brothers machine shop. Henry Ford could run a production machine shop with the fail-safe backup of the Dodge Brothers. Malcomson recognized that he was outmaneuvered by Henry Ford and sold his interest (25.5 percent) to Ford for $175,000 in July 1906. Others of Malcomson's friends left at the same time with similar profits. Ford now had 58 percent of the stock. James Cousins joined the Ford faction and increased his stock holdings from 2,500 to 5,500 shares. Ford would not come "under orders" again. This was a turning point in Ford Motor Company history.

The Piquette Plant: Product Oriented Manufacturing

Now in full control of the company, Ford designed the kind of low priced car that he always wanted. The company had moved from the Mack Avenue "assemblage plant" to a new three story plant on Piquette Avenue in Detroit in 1904. In 1906 Ford also announced a new car to be sold for $500. It was the Model N and as it was developed, the $500 price could not be maintained. However, the $600 actually achieved was still the lowest price of any major manufacturer.

A Ford car required the same level of precision as a Cadillac or Packard car. Leland's standard of precision resulted in a car made with interchangeable parts but at the cost of a machine shop staffed with highly skilled machinists in each department. Increasing production would lower costs somewhat, but the high skill work departments were just replicated over and over to meet the increased production. The conventional machine shop, as at Leland or Dodge Brothers during the early years, was organized around machine tools and skilled machinists in a lathe department or a milling department, for example. Ford production at Dodge started with a batch of 650 cars. By 1905, production was 1,600, then 8,700 in 1906 and 15,000 in 1907. Production was no longer a batch but a flow, with Ford's orders at Dodge growing from 150 per month to 1500 per month.

In 1904 Ford moved to Piquette Avenue, and began to make parts for its own cars. Production methods started to change in 1906. Machine tools were arranged by the operations needed to make the part. As an example, first was a lathe, followed by a milling machine, followed by drill press; with gravity slides between. This might be the order of machine tools in the piston department, for example. These machines were set up by a skilled machinist but the day to day operation was handled by an "operator." The production parts were as good as any made at the Leland Machine Shop but the wage cost was that of an operator, not a skilled machinist. In addition, production increases could be handled with more complex, multiple function precision tools that were run by operators. These new methods swept through the plant. Credit is given to Walter Flanders, who was later involved with the Flanders car, the EMF (Everett, Metsger and Flanders), and the Studebaker cars. He was later the president of Maxwell after the United States Motors debacle in late 1912.[26]

On January 5, 1906, Ford had a press conference on his progress on lowering cost[26] and said, "I believe that I have solved the problem of cheap as well as simple automobile construction. Advancement in auto building has passed the experimental stage, and the general public is interested only in the knowledge that a serviceable machine can be constructed at a price within reach of many. I am convinced that a $500 model is destined to revolutionize automobile construction."[27] Ford also deserves credit because he owned almost 60 percent of the company and the risk of the new manufacturing methods were predominantly his, personally.

When Ford was involved in car racing, he and an engineer who worked for him saw a wrecked race car and to their surprise, the damaged steel parts were twisted before they were broken. This was unusual because the steel

THE FORD PIQUETTE PLANT—The success of the Ford Motor Company allowed the construction of this building at the corner of Piquette and Beaubien in Detroit in 1904. The architecture is a standard "mill design" that had been used since the start of the industrial revolution. The load of the building was taken on interior posts and the exterior brick walls with little consideration for windows or what the building would be used for. On the top floor at the rear, Henry Ford had a room built where the most important automobile product in history was designed, the Model T. This photograph was taken at the corner of Piquette and Beaubien streets facing north.

that they were used to would break first. Ford became interested and found that it was only made in Europe and was called vanadium steel. It was triple the strength of the mild steel they were using and as they later learned, it was much easier to machine. Ford Motor Company wrote letters to American steel companies but received only one positive response. They were also interested in the new steel but the company required Ford to pay for the heat of steel even if the alloy was not successful. The new Ford Motor Company went ahead at their expense, but the heat did not make an alloy and Ford owned scrap. Henry Ford then paid for a second heat and it was a success. Ford started to use strong but light vanadium steel on the suspension parts of the new Model N. At first the steel was very expensive, but as Ford continued to use the steel, first on the Model N and later on the Model T, he was using entire blast furnace quantities and at the same cost as mild steel for the finished part.

Model T

In 1907, Ford closed of the end of the top floor of the Piquette plant and started to design the most important car in the history of the automobile industry. It was a cooperative effort of several people with Henry Ford as the final voice. It was a four cylinder like the Models N, R, and S, but the four cylinders were cast as one piece with a removable cylinder head so the carbon buildup that resulted from the gasoline of the day could be easily cleaned. Competitors said the Ford design would leak water or oil. It would have, if Ford had used the multiple pass milling machines of the day. Ford, however, used a wide machine that made the block and head flat in a single pass. This method is still used today in manufacturing engines.[28]

The Model T was a light, powerful, full featured, five passenger car that was trouble free and easy for the owner to repair. It was a breakthrough consumer product. It was the flood of sales from 1908 to 1927 for the Ford Model T that drove the Ford Motor Company to record production levels. This 19

THE FORD MODEL T—This 1909 Ford Model T is the car that put the world on wheels. This is a "brass era" car that was in production from 1908 to 1915. The "black era" cars were in production from 1916 to the last Model T in 1927. Over 15 million cars were made and society was forever changed. This 1909 Model T is on permanent display at the Henry Ford Museum and Greenfield Village in Dearborn, Michigan.

year span of unlimited demand for one company's product had not happened before, nor after. There was unlimited demand for wartime armaments, but the major wars lasted only 4 or 5 years. There was unlimited demand for TVs in the '60s, color TV's in the '70s, and VCRs in the '80s, but the demand was met by several companies in several countries. At Ford Motor Company, the major problem to be solved each day for 19 years was how to make more and more cars. The result was that any idea to increase production would have an economic payout measured in weeks and months, not in multiple years as was the usual case. Ford was able to improve manufacturing efficiency in ways that other manufacturers could only dream about.

A New Plant

Ford was barely in the Piquette Plant when he started planning for a new location. In 1907, he acquired a huge site in rural Highland Park, Michigan. The Piquette plant was 3.1 acres, and Ford had plans that were as big as the 63 acres he was buying in Highland Park.

Ford had an innovative concept for the new plant. James Cousins handled sales and general business matters and Henry Ford handled product design and manufacturing at the company. Cousins contacted local architects to design this new plant that Ford wanted and was rejected by each one. The problem was that the structure of conventional manufacturing buildings, like the Piquette plant, was carried by the outside brick walls and on wooden posts. A 90 pound per square foot floor loading at the third level was all this building design could support. Ford wanted a four story building and to put the material, and therefore the weight, on the top floor. Completed parts would go down gravity slides to the lower floors and finally to assembly on the second floor. Heavy machinery would be on the ground floor. Local architects said that what Ford wanted was impossible.

Albert Kahn had built an innovative reinforced concrete building for Packard Motor Company in 1905. In 1944, Kahn was quoted about his very clear memory of his first meeting with Henry Ford at the Piquette plant in 1908. When Kahn entered the room, James Cousins and Henry Ford were in a very tense mood and it was obvious that they had been having a major argument, with Cousins repeating the reasons that local architects could not build what Ford wanted. Albert Kahn said he would make a proposal and, of course, he had, in the past, successfully built 4 story reinforced concrete buildings with more than 200 pounds per square foot of floor loading at the top floor.

The Ford Highland Park Plant structure was built with reinforced concrete and with Kahn's design, the load would be carried on the interior structure. The outside walls had no load and therefore could be made of glass. Kahn's design was planned for the work processes that were to take place in the building. The head of manufacturing was William Knudsen, who summarized

CADILLAC AT CASS AVENUE—The Cadillac plant at Cass Avenue in Detroit shows a design concept that was new in 1905 for buildings that housed manufacturing. It was designed by George Mason, mentor of Albert Kahn, and clearly shows the design concept of interior structure and exterior walls of windows. It was built by Julius Kahn, Albert's brother, and used "Kahn Bar" construction methods. Thousands of industrial buildings followed using this concept. This one is still in use today after almost 100 years of service.

the new Kahn concept as first figuring out the machines needed, the order of manufacturing, the flow of material and ensuring they are all going in the same direction. After that was done, then a building was built around it all.

When Kahn finished the proposals for the Ford Highland Plant, he suggested to Henry Ford that the plant be located in the middle of the site. Ford looked at Kahn and laughed. "You still haven't got the most important part of the scheme," he said. "That vacant space is for expansion, by this system we can expand link by link." Kahn later said, "He was a strange man. He seems to feel always that he is being guided by someone outside himself. With the simplicity of a farmhand discussing a season's crops, he made moves as vast, it seems, as geological changes."[29] The Highland Park design effort was a breakthrough in factory construction and Ford never used another architect except Albert Kahn in the more than 1,000 future buildings that he constructed.[30]

At Piquette, Ford made the first step toward greatly reducing the cost of making parts that were as precise as any in the industry. He also made a car with vanadium steel, one of the best materials in the industry. He designed the Model T, a breakthrough concept. He once had said cars should be made "like pins in a pin factory," and so he stopped production of all other cars that he was making, even though they were selling well, and concentrated on the Model T. At the same time, he was planning the largest automotive plant in the world—Ford Highland Park.

The concentration of the automobile industry in Detroit and Michigan is a direct result of three people—Ransom Olds, William Durant and Henry Ford. The first American car, a Duryea, was made in Springfield, Massachusetts, and the largest selling car in 1899 and 1900, a Columbia electric, was made in Hartford. It appeared that the New England precision tool industry would control the automobile industry. The ease of moving bulk iron ore and coal for cast iron and steel changed the automotive center to the Great Lakes basin with Buffalo, Cleveland, Detroit, Indiana and Wisconsin angling for center stage.

It was Ransom Olds and his Curved Dash Oldsmobile that started to settle the issue. The Curved Dash Oldsmobile, made in Detroit, moved into first place in sales with half the market in 1903 to 1905. Automobile suppliers started to locate their plants in Detroit. In 1906 Henry Ford moved into first place with the Model N; Cadillac was in second place, and both cars were made in Detroit. From 1907 to 1910, Ford was in first place in sales and William Durant's Buick, made in Flint, Michigan, was in second place. In 1910, Henry Ford sold 32,000 cars and Buick sold 30,000 to dominate the automobile business with about 40 percent of the market. The question of where the automobile industry would be located was settled. Detroit and Michigan became the "Motor Capital" of the world.

Ford Highland Park: Site of Social Revolution

The Ford Highland Park Plant opened January 1, 1910, and it was the largest automotive plant in the world. It operated on a scale beyond anything that had been seen before.

Ford had been aware that if a large number of parts were made, there would be a variation in quality during the production run that would range from scrap at one extreme to some very accurate parts at the other extreme. After sorting, some parts would be more accurate than the machine could actually make on a consistent basis.

When higher precision was needed, piston to cylinder fit or gear fit, for example, then a method from the watch industry could be used. Waltham Watch Company is the best example because they achieved the highest volume at 4,000 watches per day. Their main business was 10 or 12 watches that

FORD HIGHLAND PARK PLANT—Much of the original Ford Highland Park Plant has been replaced with a shopping center. This photograph shows the Ford intent of 1910. Note the balconies on the fourth floor. There was a facing building to the right with similar balconies, a glass roof and crane way that brought material to these top floor balconies. This is a vestige of Ford's intent to bring material to the top floor and have it move by gravity slides between machines and floors. This was an efficient manufacturing concept before electric powered conveyers and an assembly line. The style of the building is almost a celebration of glass windows. This photograph was taken at the north end of the property, facing north.

were identical except for increasing number of jewels and accuracy. In the 1890s, the watches ranged from $8 to $50 and were made by selecting the tight limit parts from the production run to be assembled with a large number of jewels in the very accurate $50 watches. The $8 watches were the loose limit parts from the same 4,000 part daily production run that were assembled with only a few jewels. It is important to realize that, except for the added cost for jewels, that the cost of all watches was the average for the daily production run, even though the prices varied from $8 to $50. The range of accuracy of the watches and therefore price resulted from the range of quality of a very large production run.

Henry Ford knew the watch business as a young man and no doubt took the basic idea and changed it. He was not trying to make a range of cars at various prices, but a very good car at a low price. He changed the Waltham idea to fit the tight limit parts with the loose limit parts so that all parts of his car were made to a very good clearance and at higher precision than the machine tools could actually make consistently. The added cost for this outstanding level of precision was only that of the selection process.

INTERCHANGEABLE PARTS

Thomas Jefferson was shown the idea of using interchangeable parts to make muskets when he was the American Ambassador to France during Washington's administration. In the early 1800s, Congress determined that the new country must arm itself, and directed that Jefferson's suggestion of interchangeable parts be the basis of manufacture of these muskets.

The marketplace did not demand interchangeable parts; in fact, at the time, it was a high cost method that was only important for repairs. If two parts needed a 0.01-inch clearance to work, then the two parts were simply made to that clearance. To make the parts interchangeable, each part had to be made to fit an intermediate gage at, in this case, to 0.001 of an inch, and then all the parts that were made would fit each other at the required 0.01 of an inch clearance. This was a great deal of extra precision for something that did not actually work any better. Only a government that demanded muskets that were easy to repair under battlefield conditions could specify the requirement for interchangeable parts.

One of the turning points of manufacturing thought occurred in 1807 with the manufacturing methods used on the Terry Clock. Eli Terry was a New England clock maker and agreed to a contract to make 4,000 table clocks. This was a time when a good clock maker could make 2 clocks per week or 100 clocks per year. This contract seemed impossible because Eli Terry was an elderly man and it was not realistic that he could live long enough to fill this contract.

He filled the contract in a new way. The first year was spent in making tools and fixtures to drill holes in the correct place and to make the parts to the correct shape. There were no clocks made. The second year was spent in making the parts needed, but still no clocks. The third year was spent in having Eli Terry's semi-skilled neighbors and friends assemble all of the 4,000 clocks and having them delivered. This cannot be called assembly with what would be the later definition of interchangeable parts, because these were wooden clock movements. Terry's method did show the tremendous increase in production that was possible using special tools and fixtures to do similar operations on a large volume of parts.

During the Civil War, as a young man, Henry Leland learned the lessons of interchangeable parts at the Springfield Armory, where he worked making rifles for the Union Army. At the turn of the century, the same Henry Leland owned and ran a precision machine shop in Detroit. He later founded

THE TERRY CLOCK contract of 1807 represented a major change in manufacturing thought, in that it showed how interchangeable parts would greatly increase production. The contract was for 4,000 clocks. Instead of making clocks, Eli Terry made the tools and fixtures to make clocks during the first year. The second year he then made parts in volume and finally assembled clocks during the third year. This photograph is of a permanent display at the Henry Ford Museum and Greenfield Village at Dearborn, Michigan.

the Cadillac Motor Company. Leland's standard of precision resulted in a car made with interchangeable parts. The new manufacturing methods that Ford was to use also required interchangeable parts.[31]

The career of William Knudsen provides a good picture of the work practices on an assembly line. He advanced through the Ford manufacturing plants until he was in charge of all manufacturing. Henry Ford fired him and he later was made head of manufacturing at Chevrolet. At Chevrolet, he imposed a work rule that he must have had at Ford. The rule was to confiscate all hammers and files in the plant. In fact, the possession of files or hammers on the plant property was cause for that worker to be dismissed. Interchangeable parts were so important to the smooth running of the assembly line that parts that did not fit could not be covered over with a "tap" of a hammer or a "zip" with a file. These parts must be reported and fixed before work could proceed. This illustrates the essential nature of interchangeable parts to the assembly line. It illustrates that an assembly line also forces solutions

Moving Assembly Line

The last step is the most visible and is the one for which Ford is given the most credit. It is important to realize that Henry Ford had to have all the above steps in place before the moving assembly line could be achieved.

It all started in early 1913 when the Flywheel Department was changed over a weekend so that a small number of parts were added at each work station and the piece was pushed to the next operation as it progressed along a work bench. Flywheel production quadrupled. The new method spread to the entire Ford plant by the end of 1913. Some operations improved by 8 times. The final assembly time dropped from 11½ hours to 1½ hours. Ford, himself, said that the man who put in the bolt did not put on the nut. The man who put on the nut did not tighten it. The man who tightened the nut, did them 5 at a time with an automatic nut runner to the correct tightness.

Cost data is scarce and what is available is suspect because Ford was a privately held company without the usual accounting methods. We can, however, get a feel for the scale of cost reduction from the price reduction from 1909 to 1915.

Table 3. Model T Touting Car Price and Ford Volume

Date / Volume	Touring Car Price	Difference
Oct. 1909 / 10,660	$950	
Oct. 1910 / 19,050	$780	$170
Oct. 1911 / 34,858	$690	$90
Oct. 1912 / 68,773	$590	$100
Aug. 1913 / 170,211	$550	$40
Aug. 1914 / 202,677	$490	$60
Aug. 1915 / 308,162	$440	$50

The Ford Touring car was almost identical over all of these years. From other sources, we know that Ford profits were $4.1 million in 1910 and $24.7 million in 1914.[32] These price reductions, manufacturing savings, and pay raises increased, not decreased, Ford profits. The price dropped from $950 to $440, a reduction to 46 percent of the former price, and the cost of a Ford Touring car is believed to have dropped by the same ratio. This was in part because of added volume and in part due the new manufacturing methods. It is not possible to separate the causes because it is a "chicken and egg" question; however, the result was dramatic.

The much lower cost of production resulting from these manufacturing methods and the swell of volume resulting from the customer price reductions and caused a flood of profit to Ford Motor Company.

THE $5.00 DAY

This flood of profit bothered Henry Ford. He saw that his customers were getting the benefits of his new manufacturing methods in lower prices. The swell in profits rewarded him and his fellow stockholders, but the men who actually worked to make the cars that made the profits were getting very little. In 1913, he had the pay structure in his plants reviewed and at a time when $1.70 per day was a typical manufacturing wage, he set the base wage at the Highland Park Plant at $2.35 per day, with most getting $2.50 per day. Much has been written about the assembly line work being so boring that there was a high rate of people absent from work and that Ford created the $5.00 per day wage to solve that problem. That may have been a factor, but most historians agree that Ford's motives were more to share the wealth of the new methods with the workers.

In 1911, Henry Ford met with a reporter and discussed his concern that his Ford workers were not sharing in the wealth that the company was creating. Ford talked of issuing stock to each worker, but it would be held by the company and the worker would get the dividends. His ideas were sketchy, with many details to be worked out. The reporter discussed the story with his editor. The editor asked if the reporter believed in such an extravagant story. He said he did not. The editor said, "Neither do I so let's do Ford a favor and not print it."[33] Ford gave two more years of thought to the matter, culminating with the decision at the January 5, 1914, Board meeting to raise wages to $5.00 a day, actually double the current wage in the plant. The press at the time questioned that the $5.00 wage applied to male workers that were of "good" morals. Given the Henry Ford thought process that he was trying to reward the steady workers who helped him make a fortune, such limits were logical. The press did not go through Ford's thought process and they felt that Ford was some kind of "Indian giver." Further, Ford had to set up a department in the company to determine which workers had "good morals," and that resulted in intrusive questions about a worker's personal life. The result was proof of the law of unintended results. The decision would not be logical to a businessman but was completely logical given Ford's 1911–1913 thought process.

The new pay scale in the Ford plants was at a comfortable middle class level. There are many ways to understand the shift of the tectonic plates of society, but the best way to look at the revolution that Henry Ford created is to compare car prices with monthly wages across the years 1912 to 1915. The Ford Touring car was almost identical between 1912 and 1915. The time to earn the wages to buy that Ford car, for a Ford worker, had dramatically dropped from 64 weeks to only 16 weeks.

Table 4. Time to Earn the Price of a Ford Car

	Touring Car Price	Monthly Wages	Months to Earn the Touring Car Price
1912	$690	$1.70/day x 6 days x 50 weeks / year = $510	64 Weeks
1915	$440	$5.00/day x 5.5 days x 50 weeks / year = $1375	16 weeks

As other manufacturers adopted these methods, this 16 weeks to earn the price of a new car became a societal revolution. Henry Ford said that any man with a good job could afford a car. This 16 weeks to earn the price of a new car held almost constant from 1915 to 1970, a period of 55 years. A Depression, downturns, wars and inflation did not change this fundamental ratio in our society, but it, for sure, changed everything. This ratio became an accepted measure of the economy and was reported as the Automobile Affordability Index by the Comerica Bank in Detroit. The index rose after the 1970s as the typical car had power equipment and air conditioning, and met safety, emissions, and fuel economy standards. It peaked in the late 1990s at 30 weeks and dropped to about 22 weeks by 2001, as pricing pressures caused car prices to drop relative to other products.[34]

People no longer had to work or live near public transportation, but could work or live wherever they wished. Shopping was no longer limited to how far people could walk or what weight they could carry home, because a car could do it all. American society was changed forever and all because of the unprecedented growth in volume of the Model T and new manufacturing methods developed at Ford Highland Park. In the early '20s Ford made 2,000,000 cars per year, or 50 percent of the cars in the world and 60 percent of the cars in the U.S.

The reaction to the $5.00 per day wage was swift in the business press. The *Wall Street Journal* said that Henry Ford should confine his interests to business and not become involved in social issues. Only a private company like Ford could have approved of a $5.00 per day policy because any other would have had study committees before the Board would have considered the matter. Henry Ford did what he thought was best based on his view of an obligation to his employees.

Walter Chrysler was head of production at Buick at that time and was incorporating many of the cost reductions that Ford was pioneering, including a moving assembly line. Buick, a part of General Motors, was run by bankers and the cost reductions made by Chrysler resulted in Buick being the most profitable part of G.M. These similar cost reductions at Buick did not result in lower prices nor higher wages as Henry Ford had done.

Another reaction came from Henry Joy, the head of Packard Motor Company. This is the same Henry Joy who did not want Ford in the ALAM in 1903. Henry Joy sent a letter to Ford saying the $5.00 per day policy would distort the entire working class structure. He had a point—why should a worker spend years in learning a skilled trade and finally be paid $6.00 per day when an unskilled worker could make $5.00 per day at the Ford plant? Ford did change everything, but he was also very open in showing other manufacturers his new methods so they could copy them and make the same major cost reductions and pay increases for their workers.

A side event of the $5.00 per day issue was the large number of workers who came to Detroit for this middle class wage when it was announced in January of 1914. There were no jobs for the new workers at the plant and they became a mob that watched the well paid Ford workers go to work each day. Finally, on January 14, 1914, they surged across the street to get their $5.00 a day jobs and into the Ford Highland Park Plant. They were met by Ford Plant Protection with fire hoses. With a 10 degree high temperature for the day, the water froze on the mob. The mob then went to Ford's home, which was not far away, and terrified his wife and son.

MANCHESTER ENTRANCE AT FORD HIGHLAND PARK—At this entrance to the Ford Highland Park plant, on January 14, 1914, the crowd watched the well-paid Ford workers as they went to work. They then surged across the street to try to get high-paying jobs. As they rushed through this employee gate, they were met by Ford Plant Protection with fire hoses. Water was sprayed and froze on the ill-dressed mob.

Henry Ford immediately bought 55 acres of lakefront property in Grosse Pointe, Michigan. Ford later thought more carefully of moving to Grosse Pointe. He did not feel that he would fit in the Detroit social structure that lived there. He then bought 1,500 acres of land in Dearborn and used a portion for his new mansion, Fairlane. The house would be finished a year later and it would be 1 mile from the front gate and public roads.

Almost all businesses have cash flow as an expense, meaning that the company must pay workers and suppliers before they receive revenue from sales. At Ford during the teen years, something remarkable happened. Ford Highland Park made cars in only 3 or 4 days from receiving the order. Workers were paid weekly or 2 days after the car was made and suppliers were paid, like all other commercial paper, 30 or 60 days same as cash, or 26 or 56 days after the car was built. Dealers pay for new cars as they are shipped, FOB Detroit, and so cash flow for Ford was an income to the company. This was a new and unexpected revenue source that resulted from the Ford manufacturing methods.

This faster rate in making cars revealed a bottleneck. The car bodies were wood and were varnished. The varnish process had four to six coats of "rough stuff," two ground coats, four to six color coats and two clear coats. There were about 12 coats of paint, with sanding or polishing between each coat. Even with all this care, the varnish would crack with the movement of the car body and craze with sunlight and require repainting in less than two years. The total time to paint a car body varied from three to eight weeks depending on color and striping. A body supplier that could meet Ford's production of a thousand cars a day might have 20,000 bodies, in various stages of waiting for paint to dry, stored on floor after floor of their plant. Of all the colors, black would cover the best and would absorb heat best so drying time was the shortest. In 1914, Ford said, "A customer could have any color he wanted as long as it was black." The number of bodies in inventory was cut in half by using only black paint.

The Ford Dealership: A Unique Way to Sell a Consumer Product

Henry Ford's dream of a low priced car for everyman resulted in establishing a market with the starting point of a customer buying his first car. It was important that the dealer that represented Ford provide a low priced entry in the form of good used Fords. James Cousins developed this idea and Henry Ford supported it completely. It became one of the basics of the Ford dealership.

From the start of the Ford Motor Company, Henry Ford stressed that Ford dealers must be able to service their products. Few dealers knew the workings of an internal combustion engine, much less how to repair it. Ford established "road men," factory service representatives, to visit their assigned dealers and teach them how to service cars. Before long, dealers were required to maintain an inventory of parts and a place to service new cars. Henry Ford also used the dealer to assemble final parts to the car to save shipping costs. During the Model T era, the interchangeable parts on all Model T's allowed the Ford dealer to repair used Model T cars during the slack time at the service department. The Ford dealer's used cars were the best in any given market area. This resulted in the four parts of a Ford dealership—new car sales, used car sales, service and parts. The typical Ford dealership was run so that used car sales, service and parts would make enough money for the dealership to break even. New car sales were always a "boom or bust" cycle and a good year would result in good profits for the dealer. A bad year would allow the dealership to survive until a good new car market returned.[35]

Dealership franchises involve the manufacturer's responsibility to sell a product at a discount to the dealer and to provide national sales and marketing support. The dealer's responsibility is to provide a local place of business, at his expense, and to develop the local new car market. With the success of the Model T, Ford had grown to 7,000 dealers by 1913, or an average of three dealers in each county of the United States. The Ford four-part definition of a place of business became the practical requirement for an automotive dealership. The Ford requirement to develop the local used car market became the practical basis of how to develop the local new car market. The Ford dealership became the legal model of an automobile franchise and that, in turn, became the automotive franchise law in every state.[36]

The Model T was an industry leader in the early years. It had a 20 hp engine, as did the Buick Model 10. The Model T, however, had a weight of 1200 pounds compared to 1500 pounds for the Buick. The Model T was an excellent car for performance and cost about $600 during this time, compared to about $1,000 for the sluggish Buick.

Most car dealerships at that time sold several brands, as most appliance or electronics dealerships do today. A low priced product would get customers into the Dealership and the salesman would sell up to the brands with more features. Henry Ford would have none of that idea. He knew that his car was made of the best materials (vanadium steel) and to the highest standards of precision with methods developed in his factories. He was not going to have salesman sell up to a more expensive and more profitable car that was no better than his Ford. A good example would be a Ford-Buick dual dealership. Neither company would have allowed it, but it would be an example of what the car dealer would have wanted and the way most modern dealers in appliances and electronics are organized. The Ford would be the entry car at $600 and the dealer would move the customer up to the $1,000 Buick. There is no doubt that the $1,000 Buick was not a superior car to the Ford during the early teen years.

Ford dealerships were required to be exclusive. The number one reason that Ford dealers were terminated was that the dealer tried to have another car franchise and the Ford field sales force found out about it.

A Ford dealership was an assured way to wealth. Ford demanded and got Ford dealers to have a used car sales department. Ford dealers were required to service and stock parts for new and for used Ford cars. Other car companies wished to do the same thing, but only Ford had the economic power to make it happen.

Ford dealers were wealthy and politically active, and before long this setup became the legal definition of a new car dealership under state franchise laws. Local dealers wanted these laws to protect them from the car companies that would establish a new dealership in an existing dealer's sales area. These laws required a new dealer to have a similar capital investment as the existing dealer and limited the car companies to a high level of investment for any new dealer that they might establish. This was soon the law in all 50 states and even today, automobiles are sold this way.

Dodge Brothers Lawsuit: Ford Buys Complete Control

The Dodge brothers had grown very wealthy with the Ford business. They were the sole supplier of all Model T engines and transmissions and were shipping 1,000 per day to the Ford Highland Park plant. By 1913, however, they felt that they were a detail in Henry Ford's lapel, as they expressed it. Further, they felt that the Model T was becoming dated and that they could build a better car. They gave Henry Ford a one year notice that they would no longer provide engines and transmissions and in 1914 Ford must find another source.[37]

Dodge was a respected name in automotive circles and the Dodge announcement resulted in a flood of dealer requests for their car, sight unseen. The first car was in production in November 1914. It was superior to the Model T in every way. It had a 35 hp engine rather than 20 hp, a 3 speed transmission rather than a 2 speed planetary unit, and an all steel body. The price was $785 and was a real value over a Model T.

Ford's need to start making his own engines and transmissions in 1914 resulted in a major expansion at Ford Highland Park. In the usual Henry Ford fashion, it was to be financed out of current earnings. He began to realize that a multi-story plant like Highland Park was inefficient because of space taken by elevators and crane ways and the labor cost to operate them. He had acquired 1,500 acres in Dearborn but used only a small amount to build his home. He began to plan a new super plant on that property even bigger than Highland Park. He bought 500 more acres and conceived of a huge complex that would make steel, glass, tires, cast iron, and all the parts of a car, as well as assemble it. But first, he had to raise the funds to finance this gargantuan project.

1915 DODGE—In 1913, the Dodge Brothers felt that they could build a better car than the Model T. They had been making major parts for the Model T, such as the engine and transmission, and wanted to make a car of their own design. The new Dodge had an all steel body, a 35 horsepower engine and a three speed transmission. The Dodge was an immediate success in the market. This car is on permanent display at the Walter P. Chrysler Museum, Auburn Hills, Michigan.

His view of investors was only slightly better than that of bankers, so he began to look at the other stock holders of his company. In 1901 and 1902 he had called the investors in the Detroit Automobile Company or the Henry Ford Company profit oriented, millionaires, or parasites. He had the same view about the Ford shareholders in 1915.

He took two actions. First he announced that the dividends on Ford stock would be reduced. For the Dodge Brothers, the dividends would be reduced from $6 million to $120,000 per year. The Dodge Brothers started a lawsuit to make the Ford Motor Company pay reasonable dividends to the stockholders as required under corporate law. The second action, after the ink was dry on the Dodge lawsuit, was to say that Ford and his son, Edsel, would withdraw from the Ford Motor Company and form the Henry Ford and Son Company and make the Fordson tractor and maybe other automotive products. This was an exact repeat of the 1906 action to form the Ford Manufacturing Company to get rid of Alexander Malcomson. The rest of the Ford stockholders were in panic as they saw their bountiful Ford dividends coming to a halt with a company that did not have Henry Ford to run it.[38]

THE FORDSON TRACTOR

Ford had a concept of applying the same kind of design and low cost manufacturing methods of the Model T to manufacturing a farm tractor for the American farmer. He started in 1906 with a design that used a Model K engine mounted crosswise on the farm tractor prototype. His next prototypes used a Model T engine and in fact, a Model T in a cut down chassis was widely used as a homemade farm tractor by farmers throughout America. Ford envisioned a light tractor in a similar role as the Model N or Model T, the light cars for everyman.

Farm tractors have a serious design problem in that if they hit a big rock or obstruction with the plow underground, then the tractor driving wheels will continue forward and flip the tractor up in the air and over on its back. This was a cause of death and injury to tractor drivers. Most farm tractor manufacturers tried to solve this problem with as heavy a design of the tractor as they could make. The Fordson tractor that Henry Ford designed had the plow attachment points and the weight distribution such that his tractor was as resistant as any of the heavy designs. The Fordson introduced the basic design approach of having several castings bolt to a single unit to serve as the engine block, transmission case, rear axle and frame. This was original and all later tractor designs followed this concept. The 1908 Model T and the 1917 Fordson tractor represented the peak of Henry Ford's technical skill.

The Fordson started production and its value to American farmers was immediately recognized, but world events soon intervened. It was priced at $750, or $300 more than a Model T touring car. There is no question that Henry Ford lost a great deal of money on each Fordson tractor, but he regarded it as a way he could help the everyday life of a farmer.

World War I had started and the Europeans had not paid attention to the experience of the American Civil War. Entrenched, massed, defensive rifle fire by either side in the latter part of the American Civil War caused staggering losses to advancing troops. The generals of Europe had their own concept of the power and spirit of advancing troops, "elan" as the French called it. Massed rifle fire and machine gun fire proved that the experience of the American War was correct. Unfortunately, it was not until a generation of young French, British and German troops were killed or wounded that the futility of the "elan" tactics was proven. The Fordson tractor was a solution to extend the limited English manpower that remained so the farm crops could be planted and maintained. Britain became the best customer for the Fordson tractor. Henry Ford would later move the tractor operation to Ireland to meet the demand.[39]

THE FORDSON TRACTOR—This is the first Fordson tractor, and in 1917, Henry Ford gave it to Luther Burbank to aid in Burbank's experiments. Ford and Burbank were good friends and Ford admired Burbank's plant experiments in hybridization that improved taste, color and aroma. Burbank improved more fruits, vegetables, grains and trees than anyone before or since. Tractor is on permanent display at the Henry Ford Museum and Greenfield Village in Dearborn, Michigan.

THE LAWSUIT AND BANKERS

The Dodge lawsuit, about requiring FMC to pay reasonable dividends, had to be settled and as would be expected, Dodge won. The stockholders were awarded $19 million in 1917. This settlement was for dividends that should have been paid in prior years. During the trial Henry Ford testified and expressed unique views about the purposes of an American company. Ford said that a company had an obligation to spread its benefits to the greatest number of employees, and to the public at large. The court, in the final decision, ruled that the Board of Directors is organized and carried on for the profit of the stockholders. Mr. Ford's means to that end, by doing a public good, does not change the Board's primary obligation to the stockholders under law. Ford's thinking was original but had no basis in law.

This stiffened Henry Ford's will to buy out all stockholders and he had a third party negotiate with each. They were completely shaken by the possibility of Henry Ford and Edsel Ford leaving the Ford Motor Company and reducing the value of their stock. The Dodge Brothers received $25 million for their stock, the two lawyers Horace Rackham and John Anderson received $12.5 million each, John Gray had died but his estate received $25 million, and James Cousins received $30 million. The cost to Henry Ford was $105 million for total control and, of this, Ford needed $75 million in new funds.[40]

Henry Ford was a laundry list of Midwestern farmer beliefs and his later life did nothing but further solidify them. All farmers have a healthy dislike for bankers. From their viewpoint, bankers do nothing useful. They loan money for seed in the springtime, sit in their offices all summer during floods and drought, and want to be the first paid when the crop is harvested in the fall.

Henry Ford needed to borrow $75 million to buy out all shareholders and that kind of money could only come from the east coast bankers. Henry Ford would not deal with, in his view, the devil, and he devised another plan. He cleared his plant inventory of Model T parts and shipped them as unordered cars to his dealers around the country. The dealers yelled, but they had made a great deal of money with Ford and so they just went to their banks for loans to pay for the unwanted cars. This "high handed" action by Ford solidified local dealers into getting state franchise laws passed all across the country. There was still not enough money and Ford not only laid off almost all his workers, he also closed offices, sold desks and file cabinets and even company stationery. Finally the $75 million was raised and Henry Ford owned the entire company. In 1919, one man owned the largest industrial firm in the world. This was unprecedented in business in that other leaders had only a quarter of the companies that they dominated. Rockefeller, for example, had 27 percent of his company. Only someone who wanted total control would have not rested until he owned it all.

History Is Bunk: A Museum of What is Really Important

In 1919, Henry Ford took the *Chicago Tribune* to court because they referred to him as an "ignorant idealist." During the libel trial, the *Tribune* lawyers hammered at Henry Ford's lack of knowledge of history and at one point Ford burst out "the history of wars and royalty as taught in school is largely bunk." This was shortened by reporters to "history is bunk" and the press had a field day. He later said, "I will start a museum to show people what real history was all about."

Henry Ford's ideas were further solidified when he asked well known historians of his acquaintance if they had knowledge of the importance of a harrow. They had no idea what he was talking about. That convinced him that a museum was needed to show how the lives of ordinary people were changed

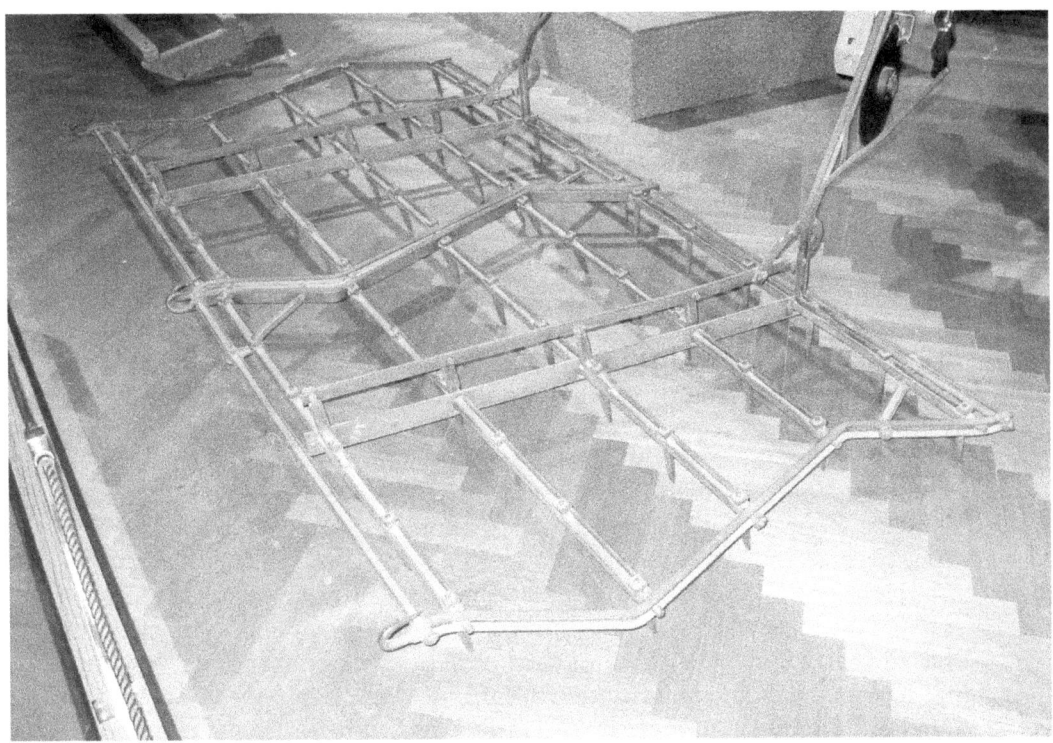

A HARROW—Henry Ford won a libel lawsuit but during the trial he was reported to have said that "history is bunk." He was referring to textbook history. When he asked historians about the importance of the harrow to mid–American history, they had no idea what he was talking about. The harrow allowed the soil of the Mid–west to be broken and planted so a crop could be harvested before winter. This was important history to Henry Ford, the son of a farmer, and he founded the Henry Ford Museum and Greenfield Village to preserve the history of what was important to ordinary people. Spring tine harrows, disk harrows, the spike harrow pictured here and others are on permanent display at the Henry Ford Museum in Dearborn, Michigan.

by technology. That was real "history" to Henry Ford and more important to Midwesterners than the history of "wars and royalty" of Europe. Ford was right, for, as the son of a farmer, he realized that the history of the harrow was more important. Europe had been successfully plowed and planted for thousands of years. The soil of the Midwest, however, broke into big clumps when it was plowed for the first time, which then had to be broken up quickly so a crop could be planted and harvested before winter. This was a matter of survival in the most basic form. The development of the harrow resulted in survival, thereby allowing the Midwest to be settled.

Ford won the libel suit—he was not an "ignorant idealist," but he was awarded only six cents. The six cent award did not stop him from going ahead with his dream of a museum of what was important. The Henry Ford

Museum and Greenfield Village is an odd legacy from the man who said that "history is bunk." It is a gift to future generations from a man who lived during the birth of the automotive revolution that he started, and the advent of aircraft, helicopters, radio aircraft beams, electric lighting, electric motors, electric generation, radio, television, photography, railroading, plant hybridization—in other words, the entire foundation of our modern way of life.[41]

This lawsuit marked the beginning of a new and dangerous part of Henry Ford's life. He was the sole owner of his company, one of the wealthiest men in America and in fact would soon be the world's first billionaire. He soon liked his press coverage and bought a newspaper to be able to express his opinion on any subject. If other people were so smart, why weren't they as rich as he? He took credit for everything within Ford Motor Company. Inventions at Ford Engineering were in Henry Ford's name regardless of the real inventor. Contacts with the press were only made by him. In such a large company, someone else might attract the attention of the press. That was reason to be fired and they were.[42]

He became vague about how the Ford Motor Company was started but took credit for it all. There was no mention of Alexander Malcomson and that the entrepreneurial spark of the business proposal (see Table 2) could not have come from Henry Ford, with his lifelong disdain for accounting or investors. He made no mention of the Dodge Brothers and the engineering and financial investment that they made toward the success of FMC. It took the Dodge lawsuit in 1917 to reveal the $60,000 to $70,000 that the Dodge Brothers had spent to launch the Ford Motor Company. Only then, in the testimony of Henry Ford under oath, did he acknowledge the importance of the Dodge brothers at the start of the company. He developed a total reliance on his own feelings, took credit for all ideas and would not listen to other viewpoints. This new aspect of Henry Ford's character would affect his thinking on replacing the Model T and his technical judgment in future designs.

H. Ford vs. H. Leland: Remember 1902?

After Henry Leland reorganized the Henry Ford Company in 1902, it became the very successful Cadillac Motor Company and in turn became one of the cornerstones of Durant's General Motors in 1908. Leland ran the G.M. Division with great success. In 1917, the United States Government asked each of the car companies to bid on making a new high powered aircraft engine that had been designed at Packard. It was a "state of the art" V-8 and V-12 engine with more than 400 hp and was called the Liberty engine. The U.S. government was asking Cadillac and therefore Leland to manufacture a precision engine that would be the culmination of Leland's lifelong obsession with making precision products. William Durant was a pacifist and did not want G.M. or Cadillac plants to be used for war material. They argued and Leland left Cadillac to form a new company that would make the Liberty engine. The new company was named for the man that Leland had voted for to be president when he had turned 21, Abraham Lincoln. As WW I started, Durant changed his mind and both Cadillac and Buick made the Liberty engines, along with Lincoln, Packard and Ford.

Leland was successful making Liberty engines but when the war ended, the former head of Cadillac turned to what he knew best, making a luxury car. The Lincoln car was to be introduced to a waiting public in early 1920, but production delays made timing later and the recession of 1920–1921 made it difficult to sell a luxury car, especially a new and untested one.

The Federal bookkeepers also said that Leland had made $5.7 million in excess profits on the Liberty engine contract and that it had to be repaid. The number was revised downward to $4.0 million, but it was too late. The

THE LINCOLN MOTOR CAR COMPANY—Henry Leland started this plant to make the Liberty V8 and V12 aircraft engine for World War I. After the war he began to make the Lincoln luxury car. Production barely started when the recession of 1920–1921 forced Leland into bankruptcy. On February 4, 1923, on the front steps of the front administration building, Henry Ford bought the company for $8 million. This picture was taken at the corner of Livenois and Warren Streets in Detroit, Michigan.

Lincoln Motor Company was bankrupt. On February 4, 1923, the assets of the company were sold at public auction by the Wayne County Sheriff in Detroit, Michigan. There was only one bidder, Henry Ford. He bought the Company for $8.0 million, which would have been "pocket change" for him at that time. The Federal bookkeepers later determined that their claim was in error and Leland owed only $500,000 in excess profit on the sale of Liberty engines to the U.S. government. The new owner and Leland did not agree on anything and Leland was out of the company within months.

Henry Ford's motives for buying Lincoln were suspect, because the Lincoln represented the kind of car that was everything Ford had been opposed to. It was a complex and expensive car that he had argued against all his life. Getting "even" for the 1902 Henry Ford Company events and criticism by Henry Leland must have felt good to Henry Ford. Henry Ford showed that, as the world's first billionaire, he did not accept the criticism of the *Chicago Tribune* nor the 1902 comments about his ability by Henry Leland.[43]

The Leland Lincolns were good cars but the Lincolns made by Ford were better. Henry Ford used his manufacturing staff to change the way the Lincoln car was tooled. Machine tools that actually made no sense from the economic standpoint were designed for the Lincoln. Leland could not have considered such methods, but Ford did because it was just the way he did things and he had resources that Henry Leland did not have. Edsel Ford took control of Lincoln Division and was responsible for some of the best designs of the classic car era of the early thirties.[44]

The Rouge Complex and the Model A and V8: Behind One Fence

Henry Ford's concept for the Rouge manufacturing complex in Dearborn, Michigan, was staggering in scope. The idea was that Ford would own the entire production process, from raw material to ship or rail transport to the Rouge and finally to a finished car. Rubber plantations in South America, iron mines in the Midwest, a glass plant, steel mill, foundry—in short everything would be under Ford control. The remarkable part was that it was funded from Ford earnings.

The Rouge complex started by making a small patrol boat for the Navy for WWI. The next item was production of the Fordson Tractor, as discussed earlier. A steel mill, foundry, and a glass plant followed and then Model T engines and parts. Highland Park and the regional assembly plants started to achieve volumes in the range of a million and a half to two million cars per year.

The Model T was almost a religious experience for Henry Ford. On returning from a trip in 1912, the engineering staff had built an improved Model T car and when it was presented to Henry Ford, he was so angry that he tore

1919 MODEL T CLOSED CAR—The Model T was advertised as the "Universal Car." By the late teens and 20s it certainly was. There were millions of them like this "black era" 1919 model. Period photographs of the 1920s or '30s showed that Model T cars were everywhere. They were parked on urban streets, driving on the roads, in front of houses and farms. They were truly a part of every American scene. This car, with the bulky closed body, looks ungainly, and it had only a 20 horsepower engine for power. This car is on permanent display at the Henry Ford Museum and Greenfield Village at Dearborn, Michigan.

off a wooden door and had the car destroyed. That was the last attempt to make any change to the Model T. The world's first billionaire would not listen. The Ford dealers in 1916 warned that the lack of a more "up to date" car was causing them a loss of sales.

What Henry Ford could not control was the marketplace. By 1926, a decade later, he no longer had the sales to run his Highland Park Plant for five and one half days each week and had to drop to a five day work week. He explained it as a desire to give his employees a two day weekend, but the truth was obvious. In May of 1927, he had to announce that after over fifteen million cars for nineteen years, the production of the Model T would stop.[45]

An immediate cause was that the public was demanding more and more closed cars. At the start of the 1920s, 90 percent of the cars were open tour-

THE LAST MODEL T—The public was stunned when Henry Ford announced that the Model T production would come to an end. This is the last of 15 million cars. In 1926 the formerly all black Ford cars came in colors and the radiator was nickel plated to respond to the pressure of a very handsome Chevrolet. The car still had the 20 hp engine. This photograph is of a permanent display at the Henry Ford Museum and Greenfield Village in Dearborn, Michigan.

ing cars. Closed cars grew in popularity until at the end of the 1920s, they were 90 percent of the market. In northern states, a closed car could be driven during the winter months and the usefulness of a car was increased by 25 percent. The 20 horsepower Model T engine that was so lively in 1908 was hopelessly burdened under the weight of the steel and glass of a closed car. Ford could not make the Model T price low enough to interest customers anymore. There was a new marketplace and it did not include a Ford Model T.

THE MODEL A AND CHEVROLET

The tragic part of the Model T announcement was that Henry Ford did not have a replacement car in mind and he just sent his workers (about 100,000) home, without pay. The Detroit area and the state of Michigan were thrown into economic depression.

Ford retained a small group of men and set about to start to design a new car. It was to be called the Model A because it was a new beginning of the company, as the first Model A in 1903 was at the start of the firm.[46]

One of the requirements of the new design was a 40 hp engine to power the new closed bodies that the public was demanding. The engine development was going badly and, try as they might, the designers could not make the new engine reach the 40 horsepower goal. Out of frustration, the engineers tried a Zenith carburetor and it worked. The problem was that Ford had always used Holley carburetors and George Holley was a personal friend of Henry Ford. The engineers had a meeting with Ford to update progress on the new car and expected to be told not to use the Zenith carburetor. Instead, Ford listened to the report, examined the parts and declared, "too many screws"; there were 12. The engineers were dumbstruck but redesigned the carburetor over the next month and had another meeting in which Ford could examine the models of the new parts. He again said, "too many screws"; there were two. He continued that if you move this and change that, you need only one. Ford was right and all of the 3.5 million Ford Model A's had only one screw holding the carburetor together. Every product design from Ford Motor Company was approved by Henry Ford, personally. The Model A carburetor design was typical of all Ford designs in that they were simple, rugged, low in cost, and easy to repair.[47]

William Knudsen was head of all Ford production when he was fired by Henry Ford. He was hired by Alfred Sloan and soon ran Chevrolet Division of G.M. He had the goal of outselling his old boss and did so in 1927 and 1928. Knudsen also knew that Chevrolet could compete with Ford at a slightly higher price in the market because of the GMAC financing plan that made the car price to the customer not the whole price, but rather a price per month as a time payment plan. Henry Ford was opposed to a time payment plan for his customers and Ford was the last company to offer them. Chevrolet introduced a new car in 1928—a four door sedan priced at $675. The new Ford Model A was introduced that year at $585 for the four door sedan. The new Chevrolet was unusual in that the engine compartment was very large.[48]

The Model A was not fully developed and there were monumental production problems. In 1928, volume was only one third of the usual level for Ford. The Ford accounting department was not capable of determining the cost of the new Model A in advance and it was only after the year ended that it was obvious to everyone, including Henry Ford, that every Model A was costing him money. There was no choice but to increase the four door sedan price to $625 in 1929.

In 1929, everyone found out that the large Chevrolet engine compartment was designed for a six cylinder engine. The 1929 Chevrolet six cylinder, four door sedan was $675 and the four cylinder, four door Model A was $625. The 1929 Chevrolet six cylinder, at $675, was about the same price as the prior 1928 Chevrolet four. A six for the price of a four. Chevrolet had trumped Ford. The Model A was shown up for what it was. It was an "up to

THE 1928 MODEL A FORD AND 1926 CHEVROLET—This Chevrolet shows the early influence of Harley Earl. One of his goals was to tie the hood and body together into a long, low form. Chevrolets of the later '20s had the hood and body look of one unit with a strong form and accent stripe running the full length of the car. The new 1928 Model A Ford made no such styling attempt and in fact had a vertical post at the cowl to separate the hood from the body. The G.M. styling office of Harley Earl had complete design control of the 1929 Chevrolet. This photograph is of two cars on display at the 2002 Old Car Festival at Greenfield Village, Dearborn, Michigan. There are similar Model A cars and a 1929 Chevrolet on permanent display at the Henry Ford Museum.

date" car of the early '20s, but not competitive for the late '20s or the '30s. Ford's plan to create a Model A that would last for decades as the Model T had done was not to be, and the resulting four years of the Model A showed it was a bad business decision.[49]

THE FORD V8

Most companies have a research or product development department that tries to have new product alternatives under development for any change

THE 1929 CHEVROLET ENGINE—The 1929 Chevrolet six revolutionized the American low priced automobile market. It made four cylinder cars, such as the new Ford Model A, cars of the past. The engine, known as the cast iron wonder, was named because it retained cast iron pistons long after the rest of the industry used aluminum. The engine was durable and stayed in production in various forms until 1954. Note the water pump mounted with the fan on the block to draw the coolest water from the radiator and force it to cool the top of the pistons and the valves and to the end cylinders of the engine. This Chevrolet engine is on permanent display at the Henry Ford Museum and Greenfield Village.

that might occur in the marketplace. Henry Ford did not have any such function, but rather chose to trust his feelings about any new products. An unusual program for Henry Ford was the building of a 60 degree bank angle V8 prototype in 1928. He had a 90 degree V8 bank angle prototype made in 1929. Neither was a smooth engine, but they did represent his thinking during the Roaring '20s as to future automobile development. As the country sank into the Great Depression the V8 that Ford had planned for the Roaring '20s was the wrong car for 1932, yet it was the only new product he had. If there ever was a consumer product that defied the logic of the marketplace, it was the

Ford V8. It was introduced in 1932 at the depth of the Depression. Unemployment was at 25 percent. Household income and car sales were at 40 percent of that of 1929. Economic activity had dropped to 25 percent of the 1929 level. Who could afford to buy anything, much less a V8 car with poor fuel economy? Ford persisted with this concept in spite of any logic. He could not use a six cylinder design because Chevrolet had done that and Ford would not copy Chevrolet. In 1932, Plymouth would also introduce a very good six cylinder car.

In September 1931, the drawings for the 1932 Ford Model B were complete and it was a facelift of the 1931 Model A. Even Henry Ford had to recognize that a Model A/B four cylinder was not competitive with either the six cylinder Chevrolet or six cylinder Plymouth. He was in a corner. The last Model A came off the assembly line on October 31, 1931, and production workers were laid off. On December 1, the Purchasing Department was told to start to buy parts for 1,000 Model B cars per day. On December 7, 1931,

1930 FORD MODEL A—The 1930 Model A was restyled to have the hood shape flow into the body for a modern appearance such as the Chevrolet had. The 1929 Chevrolet changed the market by adding a six cylinder engine as standard at the Ford four cylinder price and Ford was again behind the market. This is a photograph of a 1930 Ford that is on permanent display at the Henry Ford Museum and Greenfield Village in Dearborn, Michigan.

THE FORD V8—While the Ford V8 was not driven by the needs of a Depression era market, it was a breakthrough product in the kind of performance that was available in the low priced market. Unfortunately, the engine was developed on the buying public. There was a never ending series of overheating problems. Note that Henry Ford persisted in having the water pump mounted on the cylinder head rather than on the cylinder block, as was industry practice. Ford did not make this change until 1937 after five years of marginal cars had been made. This is a 1932 Ford V8 engine that is on permanent display at the Henry Ford Museum and Greenfield Village in Dearborn, Michigan.

Henry Ford brought everything to a halt. What to do? The only product that had any development was a V8, but this was the Depression, not the Roaring '20s. He had only one choice and on March 12, 1932, he announced that the new Model B four cylinder car would have a V8 engine as an added model.[50]

A V8 engine has two more cylinders and pistons and four more valves than a six, which was used by competition. Henry Ford had a challenge to keep the V8 cost as close to a six as possible. Essential to this cost goal was to cast the engine block as one piece of iron. This was never achieved before in high volume. Prior V8s were cast as multi-pieces that were bolted together, a very costly method. In 1929, Oldsmobile tooled a V8 with a one piece cast iron block but the volume was 4,000 per year, whereas Ford was planning on that number per day to achieve a "Ford" kind of price. The solution that

Henry Ford chose would have been rejected by any engine engineer. This was an L head engine with six exhaust passages cast in the block with each passage traveling a very long 7 inches to the outside of the two banks of the engine. These exhaust passages were in front of the front cylinder, between the middle cylinders and to the rear of the last cylinder in each V8 engine bank. The result was that the 21 inches of exhaust passages were water jacketed in each bank and were therefore heating engine water rather than being air cooled with a manifold that is outside the engine, as in a conventional design. The Ford V8 would run very hot and was prone to overheating, and worse, the hot passages would distort the top side of each cylinder to an egg shape and the round piston rings would wear excessively. The Ford V8 was known for ring wear, oil consumption, and early repair.

These same long passages were a casting nightmare because the casting cores nested within each other and were subject to shifting when the casting was made. The tight fit of the exhaust passages, and the water jacket around it on the Ford V8 engine caused engines to be junked as many "hot rod" engine modifiers tried to polish and enlarge these exhaust passages but instead cut through to the water passages. For the 21 years that the engine was cast at the foundry, the scrap rate was at an acceptable level only because of extraordinary manufacturing methods. In a sense, the poor cost control from Ford's accounting methods solved the engineering problem. The artificially low customer price of the V8 plus several ring replacements was still less costly than a more durable competitive engine.

Ford's feeling for simple, low cost designs usually served him well. There were times that his authoritarian control prevented people, in this case his engineers, from correcting his poorer designs. He insisted that the new V8 have the distributor driven from the front of the camshaft. This was a simple and direct way to drive the distributor. However, it placed the distributor on the front face of the engine in the way of front tire splash and a flood of rainwater through the radiator, which was driven into small spaces by the force of the speed of the car. Wet ignition was a result. In addition, the distributor was fixed and could not be rotated to set spark timing as with a more conventional design.

Engine cooling was another area in which he would not listen to his engineers. The Model T had a thermosyphen system that circulated hot water for cooling without a water pump. It was simple and low in cost and no doubt appealed to Henry Ford. In fact, it did not work very well because the hot water would take the easiest route across the engine and leave the ends of the engine to run hot and boil. The only reason that it worked on the Model T was that the engine had very low power output. With the Model A, the power output was increased and a water pump had to be used. It seemed to Henry Ford that there was no difference between pumping hot water out or pumping cold water into the engine. Henry Ford used the pump to move hot water out of the engine and that seemed to be using the pump to aid the natural flow of the water. With the new V8, he again used this seemingly simple system at the start of development.

During the V8 development, his engineers could have explained, if he would have listened, that the direction of the water flow was of vital importance. The hottest part of an engine was at the exhaust valve and it is cooled only when the valve is on the valve seat where the heat can be conducted away. The valve can be made with expensive alloys but the seat is gray iron because it must be cast to be made. Gray iron will "ablate," i.e., disappear molecule by molecule, when hot. The theory was not understood during the '20s, but the practical aspects of burned valve seats were. Engineers had known since that time that engines with the coolest water from the bottom of the radiator directed to cool the exhaust seats would have longer valve and valve seat life. Chevrolet and the new Plymouth in 1928 had such a system. To cool an engine like a Ford V8, which tended to run hot, the coolest water must be directed, under pump pressure, at the water jacket side of the valve seats. Henry Ford did not listen and the Model A system of pumping hot water out of the engine was doomed to failure on the new V8. The water pump in the head, like the system that was used on the Model A, was used on the V8 until 1937. Each year during the '30s, the Ford announcement for the new model year would have some engine cooling system improvement. In 1933, it was better engine cooling and a larger grille opening to help engine cooling. In 1936, it was a higher capacity radiator and larger hood louvers for better airflow to help engine cooling. In 1937, it was a higher capacity water pump to help engine cooling and the water pump was relocated to bring cool water into the block.

The Ford Accounting Department was no better at estimating the cost of a V8 Ford than it was at estimating the cost of the earlier Model A. When the costs were completed for 1932 it was obvious to everyone, including Henry Ford, the $50 (about 10 percent) price increase for the Ford V8 was costing money for every car made. In 1934 and beyond, the V8 Ford would be 20 to 30 dollars more than a Chevrolet on a model to model basis. Henry Ford had convinced everyone that a Ford was the lowest priced car, and now a very nice, roomier, and full featured Chevrolet was cheaper. A very durable Plymouth with hydraulic brakes was about the same price as the Ford V8.[51]

The engine, the V8-85, that was wrong for the 1932 Depression market had a newly tooled option added in 1937. It was the V8-60, but it quickly established itself as a poorly developed alternative to larger V8-85. Sales for 1937 with two V8s was almost the same as 1936 with only the V8-85. Ford continued well behind Chevrolet in 1938, 1939 and 1940 when the Ford V8-60 was replaced by an in-line six cylinder.

A properly engineered V8 could have been designed for 1932 if Henry Ford had listened. It would still have been wrong for the market, but at least it would not have been an embarrassment, as an increasingly sophisticated public learned to expect more from Henry Ford. He was a beloved icon in American culture but he was selling V8s that were showing an increasing number of basic engineering problems with each passing year. Except for 1935 when Ford was in first place, the marketplace had spoken and Chevrolet was the winner. After thirty years in the business, the V8 was Henry Ford's last challenge; however, as a technical and business decision, it was even worse than that of the Model A.

Accounting and Management: All We Need Is Cash at the End of the Year

Henry Ford had a total blind spot on accounting. He could not understand that some money was for capital expense and the cost must be spread (depreciated) over the useful life of the capital item. Other money was used for current operations and that money generated a profit or loss during the current year. There is a story that Ford was in one of the bookkeeping departments and scooped up the ledgers on the desks and threw them out the window. He then said that none of that stuff was necessary. Just look in the cash drawer at the end of the month or year and if there is any money there, then that is how much the company made.

Edsel Ford was President of the company and he and Henry Ford had agreed to expand the Sales Department to a fourth floor location. As luck would have it, the first department to move in was an Accounting Office. Henry Ford saw this happening and ordered that the furniture be moved outside and that everyone in the office be fired. This was not only Henry Ford's view of accounting, but in a perverse act, he then told his son that now there was "plenty of empty room on the fourth floor." Edsel Ford saw to it that everyone was rehired but placed in a location away from where Henry Ford could see them. Henry Ford's practice of countermanding Edsel's orders destroyed Edsel Ford.

The Henry Ford "shop owner" approach to accounting was present at all levels of the company. When Henry Ford II took over in 1945, he knew that the major problems were in management and accounting. He hired Earnest Breech from General Motors to apply the G.M. system to Ford. When Breech arrived in 1946, he found the company books were "like a country store." He tried to determine some costs and found, to his horror, that they did not know if a steering wheel cost $1.00 or $1.50. He asked the highest ranking financial officer, the treasurer, about this, and he replied that it made no difference since the company was solidly in the black. Breech could have explained, but did not, that no one knew if there was a profit because capital costs were not properly expensed against those apparent earnings.

Breech realized that Henry Ford's method of accounting was not just the odd thinking of a favorite grand uncle but a fundamental business blunder. The Chevrolet financial comparison, which follows later, shows what a competent business manager could do in the same market environment.[52]

The Rouge steel mill, glass plant, and other capital items were paid for out of cash in the '20s and '30s and with the Ford accounting system there was little effort to expense them against earnings for their useful life. This was a wholly owned company that didn't need to use "generally accepted accounting practices." It was only necessary to maintain a set of books for the federal and state governments so that taxes could be paid.

In the postwar period, Henry Ford II hired a group of Air Force officers to develop a system of financial control so that the complex business of the Ford Motor Company could be managed like that of General Motors. This group of ten, "the whiz kids," also had to develop "generally accepted accounting methods" so that Ford Motor Company could someday be a public corporation and sell stock in the open market. The head of the "whiz kids" was Tex Thornton and in 1947 he did a detailed study of the big three car companies using the same accounting practices from 1927 to 1939. He discovered: "Ford wound up close to break-even. General Motors made more than a billion dollars, Chrysler, organized along the same pattern as G.M. made over $700 million." The basic report, if it still exists within Ford Motor Company, is not available to researchers, but this is a revelation of major import. What is available suggests that the careful study by Tex Thornton was correct.[53] The following Chevrolet Division information is from a Federal Trade Commission Report, as are the Ford data. The Ford figures are not comparable, however, because they include Lincoln Division. This is probably not a major issue, but it does make the comparison inexact. The following table shows the net profit made by Chevrolet and Ford.

Table 5. Net Profit of Chevrolet and Ford Motor Company—1928–1931

	Chevrolet Division	*Ford Motor Co. w/Lincoln*
1928	$92,435,300	($79,624,100)
1929	$104,361,000	$84,094,300
1930	$66,798,600	$28,229,600
1931	$63,584,200	($48,611,000)
Total	$327,179,100	($15,911,200)

It is true that there was a depression, but Chevrolet was in the same depression. Chevrolet introduced a new car in 1928 and a new 6 cylinder engine in 1929 with a product program easily as large as the Ford Model A. The Chevrolet changeover was made in 45 days of careful planning. The most conservative estimates place the Ford changeover at about one year. From the business standpoint, the Model A was a disaster in that it lost money for Ford during the four years that it was sold.

The same comparison is made for the V8 era with the same source of data and the same difficulties of comparison. The following chart shows the net profit for both Chevrolet and Ford including Lincoln.

Table 6. Net Profit of Chevrolet and Ford Motor Company—1932–1937

	Chevrolet Division	Ford Motor Co. w/ Lincoln
1932	$17,850,200	($80,353,600)
1933	$40,584,700	($12,796,900)
1934	$39,097,300	$17,929,500
1935	$60,446,900	$9,250,600
1936	$76,972,300	$19,689,500
1937	$55,714,500	$2,573,800
Total	$290,665,900	($43,707,100)

Chevrolet was in the same market as Ford and while Ford tooled the V8-85 and the V8-60 engines that Chevrolet did not, it is obvious that the pair of V8 engines did not pay off for Ford. Had Henry Ford not owned the company, he would have been replaced by someone that would have "increased shareholder value." Ford did not make money after the Model T era as the Tex Thornton report states, so there were no reserve accounts set up to replace the major capital items at the Rouge or at any part of the company.

The size of the financial crisis at the Ford Motor Company came to light in the 1953–1955 time frame. The "cost plus" profits of WWII contracts gave Ford Motor Company the funds to retool a new car for the 1949 model year.

The 1953 cars were a success, but there was not enough production capacity to meet market demand. The Ford assembly plants were of the Model T era with aisles that were too narrow for material delivery with forklift trucks. The paint ovens were too short for the cars of the 1950s and were not hot enough for the 1950s paint systems. The cost to modernize the plants was $1 billion, or the entire net worth of Chrysler Corporation at that time. That total did not include the cost of modernizing the manufacturing base that was required to support the assembly plants because it was not even estimated.[53]

Ford Motor Company considered the billion dollar problem. Bank debt was believed to be a good alternative because it would force discipline that the cash system used by the Ford family did not have. With a cash system, the profits were huge and unlimited for the family, but in reality they were small in comparison with the cash needs of the huge company. After much discussion, the billion dollar modernization was cut in half to avoid bank debt, but that did not solve the problem. The needed funds could only be generated by Ford becoming a public company. In November 1955, the Ford Company sold an initial pubic offering at $64.50 per share. This raised $640 million in one day, a Wall Street record. It took another 15 years of careful debt management of the now public company to modernize the Ford Motor Company capital structure.

The Rouge Steel Plant was "state of the art" when built. However, it must have been a poignant lesson for Henry Ford II. In 1920, at age 2½, he sat on his grandfather's knee as the first heat of steel was "blown out" of the new steel plant. In 1947, Henry Ford II learned from Tex Thornton that his grandfather, whom he adored, had made a major financial blunder by not accumulating cash reserves for the future. This became critical in the late '60s when other steel mills modernized to galvanized steel for body stampings, which was excellent for resisting rust. The Rouge Steel Plant did not have the funds to modernize and was still making the same kind of rust-prone rolled steel for Ford cars that they had been making for 40 years.

MANAGEMENT

Henry Ford's management style was that of a "control freak." Capable people would sometimes attract attention away from Henry Ford. That was reason to be fired, and they were.

Henry Ford was asked why he fired William Knudsen. Ford responded that "Mr. Knudsen was too strong for me to handle. You see this is my business. I built it up and as long as I live I propose to run it the way I want it to run. Mr. Knudsen wanted it run his way. I woke up one morning to the realization that I was exhausting my energy fighting Mr. Knudsen to get things done the way I wanted them instead of fighting the opposition. I let him go not because he was wasn't good but because he was too good—for me."[54]

Ford's approach to management assured that Ford Motor Company had no more talent than he possessed, personally. The idea that the Ford Company could put together the talents of several people never occurred to him. The company would always be limited by his talents and faults. By 1945, he had eliminated all the company talent around him, and his son, Edsel, had died in 1943.

The Arsenal of Democracy: Huge Scale Production

In addition to the social revolution that Henry Ford created, the manufacturing methods became the basis of the WWII "arsenal of democracy." Fundamental to the "Fordism" methods is the concept of interchangeable parts. The "Fordism" approach of having the precision in the machine tools and using semi-skilled operators to run the machines was the heart of how American industries could greatly expand production in only a few months. European manufacturers relied on precision machinists to make war material, and that took years of training to learn their trade. American tool designers and machinists designed and made the precision machines but designed in such a way that the work piece was loaded into the machine in only one way and the operations were performed automatically without handling by an operator. In this way, the buildup for war material could be quickly expanded with multiple machines and staffed by operators with a minimum of training.[55]

Many have argued that Henry Ford borrowed the ideas of other people. That was certainly true. Interchangeable parts came from the French by way of Thomas Jefferson and the American arms industry. In 1806, Eli Terry changed the interchangeable parts idea by noting that tools that make interchangeable parts would also make parts in high volume. Arranging tools in order of the matching operation and run by operators was done in the sewing machine industry in the 1850s and watch industry in the 1890s before Henry Ford used this technique at the Piquette plant in 1906. Select fit of parts to greatly improve accuracy was used in the watch industry in the 1890s. Conveyers to move material to the worker rather than the other way around were used at an automatic grain mill built by Oliver Evans in 1783. The meat packers of Chicago in the 1860s used a conveyer as a "disassembly" line for hog carcasses before Henry Ford used it as an assembly line in 1913.[56]

Henry Ford created the Model N and Model T, which had a limitless market demand that made all of the above ideas and any other proposal have an economic payout measured in weeks and months. While he did not invent the ideas, he did invent the combination. He also had at least 58 percent control of the company and could approve of an idea in minutes. He also had at least 58 percent of the financial risk. This was "Fordism" and it revolutionized American manufacturing.

A good illustration of this method is from WWI. The French had an excellent weapon in the 75 millimeter gun. The secret of its success was the recoil mechanism that could absorb the full recoil and still hold the aim. The guns of the day would recoil and had to be re-aimed with every shot. The French 75 could fire as fast as it could be loaded and one French 75 had the firepower of a four gun German battery. The recoil mechanism was a very precise machining task. With the French machining design and methods of production it could only be increased by training more skilled machinists. The Germans were at the gates of Paris and something had to be done to make more of the French 75 guns.

A French delegation came to Washington, D.C., to see if any American manufacturer would make these difficult parts. The usual weapons manufacturers looked at the design and refused. The automobile industry was approached and the Dodge Brothers looked at the design. They were as knowledgeable as anyone about the manufacturing methods at Ford and no doubt were a part of developing them. Horace Dodge was a particularly skilled tool designer and he saw a way to make the recoil mechanism. The Dodge Brothers took the contract and had a plant running within 4 months and production in 6 months. After the War, the French general, Foch, came to the Dodge Plant near Detroit, Michigan, where the guns and recoil mechanisms were made. After a speech of congratulations about the contribution to the war effort, Foch went on to wonder how so may skilled machinists could be trained so quickly. The answer was that these workers were not skilled machinists but were semi-skilled workers that were trained in a few days. The exceptional precision was in the machine tools designed by Horace Dodge and the Dodge tool engineers.

World War II put the American and European manufacturing system in clear contrast. Chrysler Corporation was fully converted to war work for World War II and one of their projects was to make the Bofors "pom-pom" anti-craft gun. The archives of the DaimlerChrysler Historical Collection has a file on the project. The Swedish production blueprints have notes to "fit at assembly" and "drill to fit at assembly." These methods are not allowed at an American plant in that all parts must be made to fit from the machine tools that made them. Other parts shown on the Bofors blueprints simply could not be made to the shape as shown except by hand. The engineering rule at Chrysler was that the drawing and the part had to match. Such indefinite language on the drawings was unacceptable because design intent was not clear. Either the part or the drawing had to be changed until they were in agreement. These Bofors parts had to be redesigned to accommodate what production machine tools could make. When these changes were made, Chrysler became the highest volume supplier of Bofors "pom-pom" guns in the world.[57]

Everyone is familiar with the Lend Lease Act before WWII. The U.S. government realized that war production could be expanded with "operators" under the Fordism or American manufacturing system, as it was then called. The basis of the system was skilled tool makers and machinists to make the precision tools and their training was as slow as ever. The archives of the DaimlerChrysler Historical Collection has a very good section on the Educational Orders Act of 1938. It details how educational orders could be placed with selected manufacturers (including Chrysler) for them to buy machine tools for munitions to be owned by the government This was a five year program and six items were selected for 1939 machine tool orders and training. They were gas masks, recoil mechanisms for a 5 inch gun, semi-automatic rifle, anti-aircraft search light, forgings of a 75mm shell and machining a 75mm shell. These were judged the most critical of a list of critical items. Training to man the "Arsenal of Democracy" started in 1938, long before Pearl Harbor on December 7, 1941.[58]

The automobile industry was at the forefront of WWII production. About 15 percent of all the machine tools in the United States was controlled by the automobile industry, and the Great Lakes Basin had 615 of the 941 automotive plants in the country. Of these 262 were in Michigan alone. The biggest industrial firms in the world, G.M., Chrysler and Ford, were the Arsenal of Democracy.

Lincoln and Mercury: The Ford Car Will Not be Upstaged

The Great Depression hit the luxury car market very hard and Lincoln saw sales drop from 6,000–7,000 to 2,000–3,000 per year by 1934. Even people who could still afford a luxury car would not buy one because of social pressure. There were so many people out of work, about 25 percent, that it was just not right to display wealth in such an open manner as to drive a Lincoln. Lincoln dealers were going out of business and something had to be done. Henry Ford was finally convinced and a new Lincoln body was tooled and a 75 degree bank angle V12 was also tooled. The new Lincoln V12 engine was a typical Ford 90 degree bank angle V8 set at a 75 degree bank angle with 4 more cylinders. It had all the overheating problems of the original V8 and a new problem of a weak lower bearing structure. The engine was a constant problem to the owners and to Ford Motor Company. The car, however, had the packaging and weight distribution advantages of the Chrysler Airflow.

The car, called a Lincoln Zephyr, was beautiful. It had all the grace and style of a contemporary aerodynamic car. While the Chrysler Airflow left the viewer wondering if there was a hood, the Zephyr had a hood and it flowed into a total of a well executed design. A variation of the Zephyr design was the Continental of 1940 and it is recognized as one of the most beautiful cars ever created. Edsel Ford deserves all the credit.[59]

The Zephyr was introduced for the 1936 model year and the custom Lincoln continued at the $4,000–$5,000 price range and 2,000 per year volume. The Zephyr, at $1,300, sold 14,000 cars the first year and in spite of the weak engine, the Lincoln dealers were back in business with about 20,000 cars per year for the rest of the '30s.[60]

MERCURY

The market of the '30s continued to develop after the depths of 1932 and it became obvious that every Ford sale was to be a ripe market for future Buick or Oldsmobile sales. The Ford customer that wanted a car with more room or features or just to be part of the Alfred Sloan move up to a "car for every purse and purpose" had no place to go in the Ford Motor Company offerings. Henry Ford was convinced by his son, Edsel, that a new brand was necessary to meet this market and tooling for a new car was planned. It had unique sheet metal and was to be priced several hundred dollars over a Ford and the same amount under a Lincoln Zephyr.[61]

Edsel Ford understood the need for the car and it was unique in tooling from the Ford of 1939. Henry Ford had a way of being perverse with his son. While he allowed all new tooling, he did not allow the new Mercury to look different from the Ford. There was a Mercury model, the coupe, that did not have a matching Ford model but that was not enough to establish a different position for the Mercury. Henry Ford could not bear the thought that there was a better car than a Ford, even if it was made by the same company. The Ford and Mercury were twins in appearance and only someone with a ruler could tell that the cars were actually completely different. Edsel won the battle but lost the war to his father. The entire reason an existing Ford owner would want to move to another car was to get something different from the Ford that he was driving. The Mercury was not it. Henry Ford saw to it that the Mercury was "a big Ford" and the whole market purpose was lost. The car sold 80,000 or about 14 percent of the Ford Motor Company sales during Henry Ford's lifetime. Buick and Oldsmobile continued to sell about one third of the G.M. cars during the same period, which was about the same rate as prior to the Mercury introduction. The existing Ford cars continued to be a rich source of business for future Buick and Oldsmobile sales.[62]

Ford was in his seventies and in total control of his company. He was stubborn and would not allow any functional change to his cars. Hydraulic brakes were a particular problem. The public was demanding them as were the dealers, but Ford refused. Perhaps he did not understand, or maybe Ford did not feel comfortable with liquids as opposed to solid steel rods. In any case, he had his first stroke in 1938 and it was only then that 1939 model Ford cars had hydraulic brakes, 3 years after Chevrolet and 11 years after Plymouth. In 1940, he had his second stroke and the giant of an industrial firm floundered. There were some capable managers and there was an important contribution to the war effort by Ford Motor Company. In 1945, his grandson, Henry Ford II, took control. Henry Ford died in 1947.

A Summary of a Business Life: Stunning Hills and Valleys

Lowering the cost of precision manufacturing, the moving assembly line, and coupling these with the $5.00 day wage were monumental achievements and fundamental changes to society. This alone qualifies Henry Ford as one of the giants of the century.

The Ford manufacturing system of the teen years became the American Manufacturing System of World War I and the Arsenal of Democracy in World War II. This would also qualify Henry Ford as one of the giants of the century.

Ford's simple, rugged and easy to repair engineering designs influenced several generations of engineers. The inexpensive used Ford cars were how any young man would have first learned the way machines were made. It may be an overstatement to give too much credit to Henry Ford, because his design approach was also very much a part of the American character. For whatever reason, American designs were very precise, rugged and easy to repair as compared to more complex European designs. WWII armaments are a good example in that European designs required the final touch of the file of a skilled "fitter" to work properly. American designs followed the "Fordism" approach of being simple and made with extreme precision by semi-skilled operators.

In the 1920s and '30s Ford became the "big boss" and would not listen to some basic facts. He trusted his own instincts, which were often wrong. The V8 was an example of his technical failure.

Automotive Franchises and Management

The American automotive franchise laws are an unintended Ford invention. His dealers made it the law of the land and Ford's shipping of unordered cars in 1920 reinforced his dealers' drive to see that it was the law in every state.

The franchise laws are of importance to the manufacturers in that each manufacturer does not face direct competition from another manufacturer at the point of sale. Each dealer is also protected from a manufacturer that might want to set up a competing dealer in a nearby location.

From the public and customer viewpoint, the franchise laws keep the customer from making direct comparisons across brands or across automotive trades. An automotive trade is very complex. It involves the new car price and features, the used car value, and the financing terms of the new car against the trade-in car financing terms. The franchise laws require that this comparison be made between two dealerships that were in different locations rather than at a single point of sale as it is done at electronics and appliance stores.

There have been attempts to change the way cars are sold, but to date, the state franchise laws have prevented any change.

Ford's testimony at the Dodge lawsuit gives an important insight into his thinking. He said that the Board of Directors had an obligation to the employees and to the general public as their primary responsibility. He was wrong, as the court's decision points out. He could not have discussed this testimony with his lawyers at the time of the trial or if he did, he ignored their advice because he thought he was right. He was not. Over time, he must have formed his ideas about American business, but he could not have discussed his ideas with anyone nor have read or studied the subject. His thinking does much to explain the fact that he constantly lowered car prices for the public and why he doubled factory wages to $5.00 a day for the employees.

His company was his and he could not envision that it could have any more ability than he himself had. He and the company were one, for better or worse, and toward the later years, it was for worse. His ideas that his company had a social obligation were well expressed during the Dodge Shareholder lawsuit and were original in thinking, even if they had no basis in law. He frustrated his engineering department in that he did not want anything changed. If someone happened to patent something, the patent was in Henry Ford's name with the real inventor listed as "et al." Ford refused to have an organization chart so people could know what they were responsible for. He dismissed the whole subject as a waste of time. This company was the largest industrial firm in the world.

As a manager or businessman, Henry Ford was incompetent. Those are the only words to describe a manager that lost a total of $59 million in the decade from 1927 to 1937. This was the largest or second largest industrial firm in the world and at a time when Chevrolet made $582 million in the same market. This comparison is based on the only material that is available to a modern researcher. It supports the Tex Thornton report that Ford Motor Company did not make money for over 20 years. There was nothing positive about Ford's management methods, particularly during the last decades of his life.

Economics and Accounting

Henry Ford's views were that of the populist Midwestern farmer and they did not change throughout his life. Money earned by hard work was somehow more noble than money made from money. In 1902 the investors in the Detroit Automobile Company or in the Henry Ford Company were greedy in wanting a return on their money, in Ford's view. The Ford Motor Company Shareholders that wanted to continue their dividends rather than investing it in building a Rouge plant were parasites, in Ford's view. Only the Dodge lawsuit it 1917 forced him to pay dividends to these unworthy people, in his view. When he had total control, he would not borrow from bankers in 1920.

His thinking from 1911 to 1913 on factory wages was original. It was a new concept that his workers would be shareholders so they could receive dividends from the company as a justified reward for their work. That thinking made the $5.00 a day wage decision of 1914 a logical conclusion for him.

Ford's biggest blunder was in accounting—in not knowing and not managing costs. If Henry Ford had known the true state of his finances, he would have cut costs or raised prices to be sure that his was a viable firm. A part of the problem was that he had a cash system for accounting. The flood of money that the company generated was so huge compared to the understanding of a single person, or in fact for the family, that it seemed limitless. In fact, it was nowhere near what a billion dollar operation needed to sustain itself.

If his goal was to run his company for the benefit of the employees and public, as he testified at the Dodge lawsuit trial, then he succeeded, but only for the short term. Before his strokes in the late 1930s, he may have realized that his method of running his company would not have allowed maintain-

THE CELEBRATION OF LIGHT—One of the high points of Henry Ford's life was the Celebration of Light, 50 years after Thomas Edison invented the light bulb. Ford had the entire Menlo Park Edison Laboratory moved from New Jersey and rebuilt at Greenfield Village in Dearborn, Michigan. On October 21, 1929, almost 300 of the most prominent government and industrial leaders in America joined Thomas Edison as he re-enacted his light bulb success of 1879. This event was recorded in a large oil painting with the faces of these prominent people. This is a photograph of the small section that shows Henry Ford with President Herbert Hoover at the left. This painting is on permanent display at the Henry Ford Museum and Greenfield Village in Dearborn, Michigan.

ing reserves. These were required to replace the capital base of the company so that it could survive in the long term for the benefit of the employees. The public could always buy from other car companies and that they did as Ford slipped into third place in sales. He left a firm that did not have the funds for the difficult task of modernizing itself. Henry Ford II found that out in the late 1940s and spent most of the rest of his life in correcting this legacy from his grandfather.

2

William Durant (1861–1946)

William Durant, like Walter Chrysler, grew up in small town America. He was born two years prior to Henry Ford. He developed a vision of an automobile market that had no bounds.

While at Buick he had a certainty of the future of car sales, and founded G.M. in 1908. He again was certain of the future and expanded the company until he needed major bank loans. He was forced out of management, but the market of the early teen years proved him correct. In 1920 he again was certain of the future and bought huge amounts of G.M. stock as it crashed in price, and again he was forced out of management. The boom market of the '20s again proved him correct. Without William Durant, capitalism's favorite child would not have found a business organization method to achieve the riches of the automotive market.

Salesmanship: A Great Listener

William Durant was the grandson of one of the most prominent men in Flint. Henry H. Crapo was a Lumber Baron who had made a fortune in lumbering off the stands of trees in the Flint area of mid–Michigan. During the American Civil War he used his prominence to serve the people of Michigan as Governor of the State. The family fortune was reduced across the two generations, but William grew up with a middle class background and a sense of loyalty to his neighbors of Flint. Crapo was William Durant's middle name.

If there is any one thing that marked his life it was salesmanship, or more accurately, the optimism of a salesman that anything is possible. As a young man he sold cigars, parent medicine, real estate, and insurance. His sales method was interesting and very successful. He would ask the customer what he wanted and just let him talk. He would make just a few comments about the features of what he was selling and was an intense listener. Before long the customer had convinced himself that he needed whatever Durant was selling.

When traveling around Michigan, he saw a very useful wagon or road cart with a patented seat design and found that it could be made for $15.00.

WILLIAM DURANT—This photograph was taken around 1908, about the time William Durant made his first million. He was head of Durant and Dort Carriage Company, the largest selling wagon maker in America. He had also taken control of Buick Motor Company and was about to use it to form General Motors, the basis of his second million. This photograph is from the Archives of The Alfred P. Sloan Museum, Flint, Michigan.

He believed that he could sell it for $30.00 and proceeded to borrow $2,000 and buy the patent and move the entire company to Flint. Then he sold half the company to a hardware clerk, Dallas Dort, for $1,000 and incorporated the Durant and Dort Carriage Company in 1886. Before long Durant and Dort were selling 50,000 wagons per year. By 1904, Durant and Dort were selling 150,000 wagons per year and their company was the largest wagon maker in the world. Both William Durant and Dallas Dort were millionaires.

The Durant and Dort company had many characteristics of the later General Motors Corporation. They dominated their field, they were vertically integrated in Flint, they had several (in this case 14) assembly plants, and Durant spent his time in New York playing the stock market (successfully) while Dallas Dort ran the company in Flint. Durant, in his early 40s, had risen to a position of prominence and wealth in his hometown and there was no reason that he should risk his success and his wife and son's future. His opinion of automobiles was that they were dirty, smelly and unreliable and they had no future market potential.[1]

Buick: The Foundation

David Dunbar Buick was a very successful President of Buick and Sherwood Plumbing Company. He had invented and patented a method of applying porcelain to stamped steel or cast iron. The same basic method is still used today for sinks and bathtubs. He was a member of the Detroit Yacht Club and was interested in gasoline engine power for his boat. At the time, steam was the only power choice, but steam had an open fire, which tended to be a major problem. A gasoline engine would be a great deal safer. In the late 1890s he started to tinker with gasoline engines for boats. In 1899, he sold his plumbing company for $100,000 and started to spend full time on his engine interests.

During these years, he employed Walter Marr and Eugene Richards as engineers and between them they invented an overhead valve engine. There was an ongoing dispute as to which of them actually did the inventing, but Buick was the only constant member of the group of three. The design was a good idea because the usual side valve engine would have only 60 percent actually open when the valve opened because the rest was blocked by the side wall of the combustion chamber. The overhead valve could be located anywhere over the piston and as much as 85 percent of the valve area would be free breathing as the valve opened, because it could be placed away from the combustion chamber side wall. The benefit increases with engine speed, but even with the slow speeds of the engines of that time, there was more power with overhead rather than side valves.

In the fall of 1902, Buick ran out of money, but the two Briscoe brothers, Benjamin and Frank, expressed an interest in the Buick car project and invested money. In May 1903, the Buick Motor Company was formed with Briscoe money, but by mid-summer they did not have a production design and Benjamin Briscoe wanted out. He asked Jonathan Maxwell to evaluate the Buick car. His evaluation was that the Buick was not a commercial product.

The Durant and Dort Carriage Company was the largest wagon maker in Flint. There was, however, a smaller company run by James Whiting and he was certain the new automobile would make wagons obsolete. When Benjamin Briscoe found out about Whiting's interest, he sold the Buick Company to Whiting and the whole operation was moved to Flint by September of 1903. Benjamin Briscoe joined with Maxwell to create the Maxwell-Briscoe Corporation that later became just Maxwell and the basis of Chrysler Corporation.

The Buick Company in Flint floundered with somewhere between 6 and 15 cars being made in late 1903. In 1904, Buick joined ALAM and paid their Selden Patent fees, but with only 37 cars built, it was obvious to Whiting that Buick was doomed. His plan for salvation was to interest Billy Durant, a fellow wagon maker and most successful man in Flint, in the Buick car, and so he loaned Durant a Buick car. Durant, however, did not believe that there was a future in automobiles. As usual, he took the car to local stores and to some of his friends and listened to their comments in a way not unlike his very successful sales methods. Before long he realized that not only was he wrong in his evaluation of the automobile market, but automobiles would replace wagons and his comfortable life in the wagon business in Flint was at risk.

Durant underwent an almost religious conversion. James Whiting had exhausted his funds with the Buick Model B and Durant had to come up with new money to restart the Buick Motor Car Company. The problems of the Buick Model B had to be solved and a new Model C introduced for 1905. There is no record of the funds that Durant expended, but we know that the original FMC investors used $28,000 and that Dodge Brothers spent $70,000 in addition to start the Ford Motor Company in 1903. There is reason to believe that a similar amount of money must have been used by Durant to restart the Buick Motor Company in 1904. Durant had come from being a doubter of the future of the automobile market to becoming a serious investor in the Buick Motor Company.

Durant did not do things by halves. On November 1, 1904, Buick Motor Company was formed with $75,000 in capital stock, it was increased to $300,000 and then to $500,000. In less than a year it was $1.5 million, of which Durant had sold $500,000 in stock to his Flint neighbors. This was a salesman. David Buick was stunned by the speed that Durant moved and was glad to settle for $100,000 and leave the company. He went to California and lost it all on an oil speculation.

Durant had run a successful wagon business and knew exactly how to make Buick a spectacular success. In 1906, it made $400,000 on $2 million in sales, $1.1 million on $4.2 million in sales in 1907 and $1.7 million on $7.5 million in sales in 1908, a year of a nationwide slowdown in the economy. This would be called outstanding growth and earnings even by the standards of today's stock market. Under Durant's leadership, the business was a major growth company and by 1908 Buick was the second largest selling brand in America, behind only Ford.[2]

Make or Buy

Durant organized Buick the same way that he had organized Durant and Dort. Every part of the car that could be made as a practical matter was made by Buick and locally in Flint, Michigan. Unlike Henry Ford, who later made everything including the commodity items of iron, steel and glass, Durant did not tie up Buick capital on these items. Most businessmen would feel that Henry Ford was making a mistake to manufacture "commodities." If Ford had done a cost analysis, he would have found that he could buy all the iron, steel or glass at a price that was very close to the cost of the same material made at the Ford plants. The difference would be so low that it would be very difficult for the Ford facility to pay for itself. Ford's only motive could be that, like owning all the stock of the company, he would have complete control of the manufacture of Ford cars.

Except for commodities, Durant made as much of the Buick or G.M. cars that he could. There was a major reason that this was desirable. Then, like today, a car company agreed to buy the material that it needed three months into the future and raw material for the fourth month into the future. The production schedule was written for what was expected to be built for the first month, 10 percent less for the second month and 20 percent less for the third month. Raw material commitments are for 30 percent less than expected. A new schedule was written as each month passed, and the needs were increased by 10 percent so that the company did not buy excess material. This resulted in an ongoing commitment that represented about 25 percent of the annual sales of the company.

The automobile business is highly cyclical, both then and today, and a drop of over 10 percent in sales results in a huge inventory buildup and a drain on cash. If a company controls most of the manufacturing as Buick or G.M. did, then these severe reductions can be managed within the company. General Motors buys only about 30 percent of the material that it needs from outside vendors. If most of the material is purchased from outside businesses, then there are valid purchase contracts with a supplier that expects to be paid, even if the material is not needed. For a company that had only assembly plants, this purchasing commitment might be several times the invested capital that the company had. When Ford Motor Company was founded in 1903, it had $28,000 in cash and was committed to buy 650 running cars from Dodge Brothers at almost $170,000. This was about six times the capital that it had. It is easy to see why an automobile company would be bankrupt in even a slight market downturn.

This is not a problem from the distant past, but is today's headlines. The ratios of the automobile business are as valid today as they were a century ago. The Chrysler part of DaimlerChrysler buys about 70 percent of the material that it needs. In most business situations this is a very desirable way of controlling costs and is a direct legacy from Walter Chrysler. In a sudden market drop, this problem is hard to manage. In the year 2000, the market had been running at an annual rate of about 17 million units through the first half of the year. In June, Chrysler wrote their production schedule for the balance of the model year and knew that there were new cars to be built and the old material must be used to make cars by the end of the model year. It could not carry over to the new model. The market then dropped to a 14.5 million unit annual rate (-15 percent) and Chrysler owned material to make more cars than could be sold at the lower sales rate. The problem was compounded by a union contract that required Chrysler to pay 95 percent of the wages if plant workers were employed or not. The result was that Chrysler could pay the material and labor costs of cars that were not to be built and therefore would have no profit. These would be costs on the profit and loss statement and on the balance sheet. The other choice was to build the cars and even if they had to be rebated to be sold, they still would have some profit. The financial press was highly critical of Chrysler's actions which resulted in an increase in car inventory and chose not to understand the facts of how the automobile industry has always worked. It is small wonder that the production schedule that was written each month, or more frequently if the market was moving rapidly, was called a "bet your company" document within Chrysler Corporation.

General Motors: A Business Model

The automobile business of the first two decades of the last century was like the Internet of a few years ago. Everyone knew that automobiles would be "the next big thing," but the question was how to make an investment play in the automobile business. Samuel Smith enjoyed early success with the Curved Dash Oldsmobile, but he decided to go upscale with the Oldsmobile brand. That started an argument with Ransom Olds that resulted in Olds leaving the company that had his name in 1904. Olds started a new company with the name of his initials, REO. The REO was a low priced car and enjoyed good success for Ransom Olds. The Oldsmobile was turned into a huge car with little in sales and by 1909 the company was almost bankrupt under the direction of Samuel Smith.

William Whitney tried the electric car route; however, he died in 1904, and Anthony Brady, another financier, continued the quest. By 1907, the Electric Vehicle Corporation that William Whitney founded was bankrupt. Only two years later, with the success of the Selden patent lawsuit, it appeared that this patent control route succeeded with a monopoly lock on the entire industry. Two years after that, 1911, the Court narrowed the scope of the Selden patent and there was no longer a lock on the industry.

Any town of size would have a local tinkerer that would make a car of some type and the local bank or town leaders would raise money for the hometown project. They would quickly fail and in some cases they were out and out swindles. There were between 30 and 50 new companies formed each year, but an equal number were also going bankrupt each year. In all, 2,000 automobile companies were formed, but at the end of World War II, only 8 had survived. In another decade, that would be cut in half.

J.P. Morgan, an investment banker, made a small investment in the automobile business by loaning $360,000 to Benjamin Briscoe for working capital to start the Maxwell Briscoe Company in 1904. In 1908, Morgan made another attempt on the automobile industry by being part of a bold plan to combine the four largest selling companies into one. It would be a virtual monopoly with the largest selling company outside the combination selling fewer than 5,000 units per year. The largest selling companies were Buick (Durant), Ford (Henry Ford), REO (Ransom Olds), and Maxwell-Briscoe (Benjamin Briscoe). Combined, they had 65 percent of the market and a meeting was scheduled by J.P. Morgan in New York to discuss the details. Henry Ford may not have had Billy Durant's understanding of how these mergers are made, but he did know that cash was never a part of the deal, it was all done with stock transfers. The Ford Motor Company was valued at about $7.5 million but Henry Ford demanded $3.0 million in cash and the balance in stock of the new company. Ransom Olds demanded the same $3.0 million in cash and the balance in stock. All this cash was not the way investment bankers worked and the Morgan interests withdrew.

The Morgan concept still made sense to Durant, and in 1908 he used Buick as the basis of forming General Motors. General Motors started on September 16, 1908, in New Jersey with an initial capitalization of $2,000. The press was so used to the formation of "fly by night automobile companies" that there was not any press coverage of the event. Twelve days later, on September 28, 1908, Durant raised the capitalization to $12,500,000. The next day he had G.M. buy Buick for G.M. stock and $1,500 in cash. A month later, Durant bought Oldsmobile for $3,023,574 in G.M. stock and $17,279 in cash.

Samuel Smith's Oldsmobile Company was an empty shell. The only useful assets were that of the "Merry Oldsmobile" song that applied to the Curved Dash Oldsmobile that they no longer made, a series of roadside signs and a company with no future products planned. Durant solved the last problem in a typically direct manner. He had the body of a Buick Model 10 shipped from Flint to Lansing, where the Oldsmobile plant was located. The Oldsmobile was higher priced than the Buick. He had the Buick body cut in quarters (it was wood) and had them mounted on the floor. He had the pieces moved apart sideways and lengthwise until he liked the proportionality and size, and then said, "That is the new Oldsmobile."

Durant then moved to have the same kind of vertical manufacturing integration that he had with Durant and Dort. Cars were more complex than wagons, but the idea was the same. He bought Weston Mott Company, a maker of axles, moved it to Flint to be part of G.M., and Albert Champion, a maker of spark plugs, was also bought and moved to Flint.

In 1909, he bought Cadillac and Oakland (later Pontiac) with the same kind of G.M. stock trade that he used with Oldsmobile. He tried to buy Ford Motor Company but the price was now $8.0 million in cash. No one, then or in today's stock market, uses cash to make these kinds of mergers and the deal for Ford fell through.

Durant also bought Cartercar, Elmore, Marquette, Randolph, Ewing and Welch cars. Most survived only a few years. He bought Rapid and Reliance trucks, then combined them into GMC trucks. In all, he bought 20 companies, but only Buick and Cadillac were money makers. The Durant combination did not have the 65 percent market control of the failed Morgan proposal, but it did have about 25 percent of the market.

Financiers and investment bankers had failed to create a business model for a successful automotive play, but Billy Durant of little Flint, Michigan, had. His approach with different brands was different than the other successful automobile company at the time in that Ford had several models (K, N, R, S and T) at different prices under the Ford brand. Later in 1910, Ford canceled all models except the Model T to improve manufacturing efficiency and to create a clear brand position for Ford. Most observers at the time felt that Ford was making a business mistake by only selling his lowest priced and lowest profit model. How wrong they were. The Durant business model had several brands with each selling several models. In this way Durant could create a separate market role for each brand without the confusion that had existed in 1909 with a Ford brand, for example, ranging from a $600 Model N to a $2,000 Model K. A Cadillac was clearly different from a Buick or an Oakland.[3]

Banker Usury: Maybe Henry Ford was Right About Bankers

This is when the market approach of Ford and Buick parted direction. Both the Model T and the Buick Model 10 were introduced in 1909 at the same price of $950. In 1910 the Ford Model T was the only car available from Ford Motor Company and the price was dropped to $780 while Durant raised the Buick Model 10 price to $1,000 to try to solve some of his cash flow problems. In addition, the Model 10 was the lowest priced in a range of cars up to $2,500. When the bankers took over in late 1910, they saw no reason to ever follow Ford in lowering prices.

Durant ran into difficulties and bankers took over G.M. from 1910 to 1915, but all they did was prune some of the failed companies that Durant had bought. The Durant concept was unchanged by the bankers and it would be a powerhouse. By 1910, Durant's expansion had been so rapid that Buick and Cadillac revenue could not keep up with expenditures. There was no working capital left. G.M. had used up $6.0 million and needed about the same amount in new working capital to continue operations. For all the interest by bankers and financiers in getting into the automobile business, only two investment bankers recognized the future success possibilities of General

BUICK MODEL 10—The Buick Model 10 was introduced in 1909 at $950, the same price as a Ford Model A. As William Durant's financial problems mounted, he had no choice but to raise prices for 1910. This did not solve the problem and he lost control of General Motors to a group of bankers at the end of 1910. This picture is of a Buick Model 10 on display at the Alfred P. Sloan Museum, Flint, Michigan. A 1909 Buick Model 10 is on permanent display at the Henry Ford Museum in Dearborn, Michigan.

Motors. Those firms were Seligman of New York and Lee & Higginman of Boston. Only they would make the needed $12,750,000 loan. Their demands, however, could only be called usury. They wanted 6 percent interest. They wanted a $2,250,000 commission. In addition, they wanted Durant, the creator of what would be the future success, out of the management of the company. On November 11, 1910 it was done and Durant was out of the management of the company he created. He did retain a seat on the Board of Directors because of his large stock holding.[4]

In the first year of operation by G.M. in 1909, 29 million dollars was made and a 150 percent dividend was declared to the stockholders. For 1910, the G.M. volume increased but not the earnings because of the rapid expansion. The divisions did not control their inventories and working capital became inventory and the reason for the need of cash. Durant had to give up his position in management to the conservative bankers, but he was correct about the unbounded growth potential of the automobile business. The market grew from 125,000 in 1909 to 182,000 in 1910, to 200,000 in 1911 and to 300,000 in 1912. From 1914 to 1916, G.M. doubled profits each year.

During the five years that the bankers controlled G.M., they did not grant any stock dividends despite very good earnings. Sales had tripled from 30,000 to 102,000—but no dividends for the stockholders. To use a modern term, there was shareholder value that needed to be unlocked and Durant knew how to do it. Worse, the banker control from the east coast interfered with the practical men who ran the company. A statistical report was required to have banker Strouss understand that moving cargo from shore to ship to shore again for a Great Lakes shipment would cost more than a direct railroad haul from one factory siding to another.[5]

General Motors Division of Chevrolet: The Minnow Swallowed the Whale

The G.M. board did not pay a great deal of attention to Durant's activities and they should have. In 1910 and 1911 he started three car companies, but they did not have much success. One of them was named for a famous race driver of the day, Chevrolet.

This was also the period that Ford started the Model T at the Highland Park Plant and Ford sales exploded by going from 19,050 in 1910 to an unbelievable 308,162 in 1915. The Ford price drops that followed each year proved that there was a huge market for cars priced at less than $500. Durant saw the future and started to develop a new car, the Chevrolet 490, for introduction in 1914. Everyone in America knew that the model name was the $490 price of the Ford Model T. The Chevrolet was an immediate success in spite of the fact that Ford had dropped their 1914 Model T price from $490 to $440 by the start of 1915. Ford was going to kill the competition while it was still in the nest.

The 490 continued to be successful in spite of Ford's actions. The Chevrolet stock climbed in value. The Chevrolet stock also paid dividends, which the banker-dominated G.M. board refused to do for G.M. stock. Durant learned another very important lesson in that it was not necessary to match Ford dollar for dollar, but to be near in price with more features such as an overhead valve engine and a three speed transmission in place of the L head engine and two speed planetary transmission used by Ford. The Ford also had become so popular that there was a value in owning a low priced car that was not a Ford.

The Durant concept for G.M. was correct for 1910, but the changes that Ford had made to the market in the teen years required a new concept. The success of Ford had forced all other competitors, including G.M., into a small share of the market. The G.M. share had dropped to 9 percent by 1915. A successful G.M. of the future must have a low priced car, but the bankers that ran G.M. would never agree to what appeared to lose money. In the summer of 1915, Durant even proposed that G.M. buy his Chevrolet Company, but he was turned down flat by his fellow Board members. They should have listened.

Durant was not without resources. He owned a large block of G.M. stock. Each of his mergers to build G.M. had resulted in his making a personal friend in the management of the company that was acquired. This was typical of Durant's power to make lasting friends and this resulted in more stock that would vote with Durant. Durant then offered five shares of Chevrolet stock for one share of G.M. stock. G.M. stock had not had a dividend for five years, not since the bankers took over. In today's language, it was time to increase shareholder value and that is what Durant's friends did. They traded G.M. stock for Chevrolet stock and the nights of mid–September of 1915 were spent by Durant and friends counting the G.M. stock that he controlled.

The September 16, 1915, meeting of the Board of Directors of General Motors could only have been scripted in Hollywood. The first subject on the agenda was to renew the five year old financial arrangement that G.M. had with their banks. Of course, the bankers on the Board wanted to continue the very attractive arrangement. Billy Durant was small in stature and always spoke in a quiet way. That was part of his success as a salesman. He quietly said he had control of the G.M. stock and he voted against the proposal. The Board was stunned. It took several months to sort things out, but Durant did have the shares and G.M. was owned by Chevrolet. Of 825,489 G.M. shares that were outstanding, Chevrolet (Durant) controlled 450,000.[6]

One of the things that Durant did for Chevrolet was to have the car designed for a three speed transmission, an improvement over the Model T's two speed planetary transmission. While Durant may not have had a technical background, he did know that selling points were very important. As with the patented wagon that he used to start Durant and Dort, he knew the improvement was significant to customers. The Model T was correct to use a two speed planetary unit because in 1909 when the car was designed, the customers were buying their first car. The planetary unit was easy to drive in that a pedal was pressed down to go forward in low gear and released as speed increased to be in high gear. A three speed transmission had to be double clutched at each shift. Double clutch meant that the clutch was pressed to go to neutral, released to spin the transmission gears and depressed again to ease the shift lever to the next gear. It was called a "crash" transmission because that was what usually happened. By the teen years, customers learned how to shift gears and that the advantage of the three speeds was worth the effort. A two speed Ford Model T had 20 hp and applied power to accelerating the car only twice. The Chevrolet had 26 hp but applied engine power to accelerating the car three times. The result was that a Chevrolet had more performance than a Model T. In the 1920s that became a critical issue. The public started to demand closed car bodies, but the two speed, 20 hp Model T was hopelessly burdened under the weight of the glass and steel. By the mid-'20s there was a market for the three speed 26 hp Chevrolet but not for the Model T, no matter how low the Ford price was.

A New General Motors: An Operating Company

Durant completed his invention of the General Motors Company with the acquisition of several other companies. Delco Electric Company, New Departure Bearing Company and Hyatt Bearing Company became part of a United Motors, a parts division of General Motors. He also made a major investment in Fisher Body Company, and bought Sampson, a tractor company, and Frigidaire. His vision of G.M. was complete and he then addressed the problem of management control.

General Motors was a holding company, meaning that G.M. held the stock of the operating companies and so each company was free to do much as it pleased. On October 13, 1916, a new General Motors was incorporated as an operating company in Delaware.[7]

Durant had the vision to create the G.M. business model, but he did it in an unknown way. Alfred Sloan said, "My experience had convinced me that facts are a precious things, but Mr. Durant would proceed on a course of action guided solely by some intuitive flash of brilliance." Durant's ability to create was not matched by an ability to manage.[8]

Alfred Sloan knew him best as a business man at this time and later as Sloan worked for him during the 1920 debacle. Sloan admired his feel for the automobile business, human qualities, integrity and imagination. He alone had created G.M., but Sloan felt that he was too casual as an administrator. Everything was reported to him and he would make assignments to whoever was near him when a question came up. Walter Chrysler was head of Buick and a Corporate Vice President and after Durant overrode Chrysler's decisions several times, he asked Durant to stick to the decisions that they had agreed on. Durant responded they he would change policy as often as the office door opened or closed. They were good personal friends; in fact Chrysler said that Durant could coax a bird out of a tree. Later in life, Durant started to write an autobiography and he dedicated it to "my best friend, Walter Chrysler." Unfortunately, Durant only wrote the introduction and never finished the book.

Walter Chrysler had started a purchasing agreement with A. O. Smith and Company to supply automotive frames to Buick. He had discussed all the details with Durant, had his agreement, and was about to sign the contract. There was a luncheon meeting with some Flint civic leaders, and Dallas Dort, Durant's former partner, held a telegram he had just received from Durant announcing that Buick would build a new frame plant in Flint and employ hundreds of workers. Walter Chrysler was on the dais and was to be a speaker. When Chrysler learned of the new frame plant, he was livid and did not make a speech. Later events resulted in Chrysler quitting General Motors.[9]

Durant's management style was to assume that everything could be changed and he did. Chrysler and other managers worked with the idea that most things were fixed and they should concentrate on the few changes needed to solve a problem.[10]

DURANT THE STOCK INVESTOR

As at Durant and Dort, Durant's real love was Wall Street. Durant still had a large position in G.M. stock as a result of his Chevrolet takeover in 1915 and continued to be very active on Wall Street.

The same market downturn that hindered Ford as he was trying to raise the money to buy out the Ford shareholders also hurt Durant. G.M. sales

THE G. M. BUILDING—One of the financial problems in 1919 and 1920 was the expansion that William Durant wanted. A major item in this problem was $20 million for a new headquarters building in Detroit. As seen here, the building was huge. When it opened in 1920, it was the second largest building in the world at over 1.1 million square feet of space. The building is now used by the State of Michigan for office space. This picture was taken on Grand Boulevard in Detroit.

were 47,000 units in June of 1920, but sales dropped to below 13,000 units in November. The G.M. Divisions had a huge plant inventory and inventory of finished cars. Wall Street could read the numbers and G.M. stock that was near $40 fell off a cliff to $12. Durant was ever loyal to his company and tried to make a market and steady the stock price at $30, then $20, and then $15. When it was all over at $12, Durant was more than $30 million in debt and would have to declare bankruptcy. Durant's G.M. holdings were so great that if sold on the open market, it would ruin the $12 value of the G.M. stock. E. I. du Pont and J. P. Morgan formed a holding company to buy Durant's stock at $4.50 below market price. Durant was allowed to have 40 percent of the holding company but without any vote in its decisions. Durant also had to leave G.M. for the second time.

Durant never wavered in believing in the market potential of the automobile industry. A share of G.M. stock that was selling at $25 in 1919 was earning an 18 percent net income on sales before taxes. Durant was so sure of the future that he invested a major part of the company's assets in increasing

THE DURANT CREST—The G.M. building was to be known as the Durant Office Building. William Durant was out of the affairs of G.M. for the second time in November 1920. The name was changed to the General Motors Building, but this "D" crest was retained over the entrance as a memorial to the man with the vision to create the company.

manufacturing capacity and particularly Chevrolet, from a G.M. total of 223,000 units in 1918 to a G.M. total of 750,000 units that could be made by 1922. The 1922 sales were nowhere near that high, but Durant was sure that production at that level would soon be needed. He would be right. In late 1920, the stock dropped to $12 per share, but he knew of the future production that was in place and was sure that a fortune could be made. General Motors sales were only 215,000 units for 1921 but jumped to 457,000 for 1922 and 800,000 for 1923. Durant was no longer involved with management in 1923, but Alfred Sloan, the new president of General Motors, had to invest only $60 million for added production capacity beyond what Durant had put in place in 1920 to be able to make the 800,000 units of 1923.[11]

Durant After G.M.: An Assembled Car

Durant was out of G.M. for the second time at 60 years old and, he said, would retire. That lasted six weeks. Just after Christmas of 1920, he wrote 67 of his friends about re-entering the automobile business. His friends came up with more money than he had asked for and Durant was on top of the world again. He formed Durant Motors.

Durant sold Durant Motors stock to the public in a unique time payment plan. The stock opened with sales to insiders at $10 and then to the public, where it was bid up to $70 per share. At that time, this was a company that did not have a car, any tooling or a plant. This is not unlike the Internet craze of the late 1990s. At that time he was confronted by a financial writer and asked if he had any qualms about selling stock and taking the life savings of families with his time payment plan. He responded that this plan was one of the most important campaigns ever undertaken in getting people to save money, bit by bit, and to invest it in the stock market.[12]

In 141 days he sold enough stock in "Durant Motors" that it was the most widely held stock in America except for the telephone company. He was a salesman. He had bought plants in Long Island, Indiana and Flint, and outbid his friend Walter Chrysler for a plant at Elizabeth, New Jersey. He had signed contracts for $13 million for material to make 31,000 cars. Durant Motors would sell a low priced Star and a mid-priced Flint, and Durant bought the Locomobile Company to provide a high priced entry. By 1923 he had 10 plants that could make over 600,000 cars, with 4,000 dealers. The stock price rose to just short of $85 but then sank to about $10 in 1925.

The cars themselves were assembled cars and the advertising said that the Durant Company was proud of the fact that they were assembled. They were made from the best parts available anywhere in the industry. Durant, and any other car maker, could buy all of the parts to make a complete car and needed only an assembly plant. Engines could be bought from Continental, transmissions from Borg Warner, electrical parts from Autolight, axles from Timken, springs from Eaton, and body stampings and complete bodies from Budd or Briggs. Durant, himself, could not have believed that suppliers were superior because he had organized Durant and Dort, Buick and G.M. as companies that made everything. Buick advertising, during Durant's tenure, said that they made everything from the hub caps to the ignition wires. The truth was that Durant did not have anywhere near the capital to buy any more of the automobile business than assembly plants. His vision for G.M. had been an automobile business that needed financing as a sideline. Durant Motors was a financing business that happened to make cars.[13]

The King of the Bulls

Durant went back to his first love. In the mid–'20s, Durant was back at Wall Street. He had a rack of over 20 telephones to various brokers, spent each day when the market was open trading stock and was handling $1 billion in his accounts. His favorite ploy was to find a stock with only a limited number of shares in the market and form a "pool." Walter Chrysler was part of some of these pools. He would use some of his brokers to quietly buy the stock to further reduce the supply. If he did this correctly, the price would not move upward. He would then make "a technical corner" on the stock by placing a sizable buy order with his other brokers. The new demands in a market with only a few shares available would drive the price up sharply, and as others bought in at the higher price, he would quietly sell at a sizable profit. He reportedly made $2.5 million in cast iron, and in the mid–'20s he was making $5 million per year.

He was known on Wall Street as "The King of the Bulls," one of the "Prosperity Boys." In mid–1929, he noticed that everyone seemed to be in the stock market and he felt that it was time for him to get out. During the summer of 1929 he had quietly turned his accounts to cash. October 1929 proved that he was correct as the market plunged. In 1930, the public hated him and the rest of "The Prosperity Boys" that had cashed out in mid–1929 while the public suffered huge losses at the end of 1929. The "King of the Bulls" thought that the drop in stock prices would only last a year, as had all the earlier drops in stock prices, and by the end of 1930 he was back in the market again. He was wrong. He rode the market down to 1932 when he had to declare Durant Motors in bankruptcy. In 1936, he had to declare personal bankruptcy with debts of $914,231 and assets of $250—the clothes on his back. It would be easy to say that Durant was at his peak with the creation of General Motors. The reality was that the stock market was his real love and during the late 1920s, he was at his career peak.[14]

He suffered a stroke in 1942 that made him wheelchair bound. Alfred Sloan and other G.M. officials used their own money and saw to it that Durant's wife received $2,500 every three months for his care. The man with the vision to found G.M. died at 85 in 1946.

Summary of a Life: What a Life!

He had a fortune at Durant and Dort, a fortune at Buick, and a fortune at General Motors, but the biggest of all was as a tycoon on Wall Street. He lost them all.

He was perhaps the only person with the Wall Street smarts to know how to put together the vision of a fully integrated automobile company and the financial methods to achieve it. The industry will be forever in his debt of that invention.

His impact is best summarized by a very knowledgeable contemporary, Alfred Sloan. Sloan said Durant's business life had three patterns. The first was to form a company with a variety of cars for customers with different tastes and economic levels. This is very different from the other success in the market, Henry Ford. The second is diversification as to engineering features that may be important in the future of the automotive market. The most notable is the Cartercar with a friction drive transmission. It has been used as an example of one of Durant's failures, but at the time of the investment it was far from certain the friction transmission was a failed idea. There was a car with a two cycle engine and a mix of truck companies. The former was a failure but the latter became GMC truck and an outstanding success. The third pattern was carried over from Durant and Dort. The Buick was a fully integrated manufacturer in that component companies such as Weston Mott, an axle maker, or AC Spark Plug were acquired by Buick and Buick made all the parts of the car. The last concept was later adapted by Henry Ford on a huge scale as he built the Rouge complex. Ford went further into the low profit areas of making commodities such as iron, steel and glass.

While Durant could create all the parts, including the financial controls, he could not manage. When he bought the Hyatt Roller Bearing Company he acquired a most vital asset for General Motors, the services of Alfred Sloan. He was a man who could manage a complex company and thereby put the capstone on Durant's invention. Henry Ford also created a fully integrated company. The Ford concept, however, did not have any financial controls and was unmanageable.

The later years with the Durant car contributed no more to the automotive industry than any of the other hundreds of other "assembled" cars did. Also, it should be pointed out that many of Durant's Wall Street methods are now illegal.

3

Alfred Sloan (1875–1966)

Alfred Sloan had a big city background unlike the other giants, who had rural or small town backgrounds and was the only one with a college degree. Alfred Sloan did not have a background of running an automobile company as the other automotive giants did. He was a successful businessman when he came to G.M., but he started at the top of the company as president to add his management skills as his contribution to the industry.

The Early Career: A Business Family

Alfred Sloan, Jr., was the son of the partner of a successful tea, coffee and cigar business, Bennett, Sloan and Company, in New York City. The senior Alfred Sloan saw to it that his son received an excellent education as an electrical engineer at Massachusetts Institute of Technology. After graduation, Alfred Sloan, Sr., used his connections in the business community to get a letter of recommendation for his son for a job opening at the Hyatt Roller Bearing Company.

The Hyatt Company was a tiny, money losing operation that appeared to have no future. The founder was John Wesley Hyatt, who had invented celluloid, the first plastic. He went on to invent the roller bearing and patented it. The only market for the product was as a low friction replacement for the plain bearings used on the long line shafts that powered machines by leather belts in a manufacturing plant. Hyatt roller bearings would save fuel and pay for themselves, but it was a difficult selling job. When Sloan started in 1897, he made his first sale to his father's wholesale business that used overhead line shafts and belts to power coffee grinding machines.

The Hyatt Company faced reorganization and Alfred Sloan's father and another man came up with $2,500 each to keep the bankrupt company going. With a good friend as sales manager and Sloan as technical engineer and general manager, they had only six months to make a profit. They did—$12,000—and Alfred Sloan would never forget the accomplishment. Sloan made slow progress and in five years the profit grew to $60,000.

The market was for low friction applications like a ball bearing, but a ball bearing has all of the working load on the small point of pressure on a

ALFRED SLOAN—This picture is of Alfred Sloan in the early 1960's. The other giants of the automobile industry had died by 1948. Alfred Sloan not only lived into the 1950s and '60s but was Chairman of the Board or Honorary Chairman of the Board with full control of the largest industrial firm in the world during those years. This photograph shows him with a G.M. idea car of that time. Photograph courtesy of the Alfred P. Sloan Museum, Flint, Michigan.

ball. A roller bearing has the load on the line of the roller and therefore a roller bearing could operate with much higher loads than a ball bearing. The company got a letter from Elwood Hayes, an automotive pioneer, about using their roller bearing in an automobile he was building. This woke up Sloan to the fact that a perfect application for his roller bearings would be in automobile axles and gear sets.

A Professional Manager: The Engineer in Charge

Both Sloan and his sales manager traveled to every car company and the superior performance of roller bearings closed the sale. At Cadillac, Sloan

LINE SHAFTS—The Hyatt Roller Bearing Company had only one market and that was to sell their bearings as a replacement for plain bearings for line shafts at industrial plants. They were more efficient and could save fuel for the steam plants that powered the plant. This picture is of a model of a line shaft system. A complete plant system can be complex and the small improvement of Hyatt roller bearings efficiency at each location resulted in a sizable savings in fuel. This model is on permanent display at the Henry Ford Museum in Dearborn, Michigan.

was taught an essential lesson by Henry Leland. "Mr. Sloan, Cadillacs are made to run, not just sell, you must grind your bearings. Even though you make thousands, the first and the last must be precisely alike."[1] Alfred Sloan did as Leland wished and was in the position of making interchangeable parts. His next big customer was Henry Ford because these interchangeable bearings were essential to the new production methods that Ford was adapting. Before long, Hyatt was supplying between 4 and 16 bearings in each car made in America. Ford was half their business, G.M. one third and other car companies as the rest. Hyatt was shipping almost 60,000 bearings each day.

HEAT TREATMENT

Alfred Sloan was right in the middle of one of the important changes in manufacturing process. The steels that were being used at the turn of the last century were the cause of major problems. They did not have the strength for use as bearings in an automotive application such as gear teeth, where they would break. The Hyatt patented design managed some success with the turn of the 20th century steels because the rollers were tubular and had a spring action as they worked around the weak and poorly sized bearing races.

Alfred Sloan was well acquainted with Henry Ford and his quest for vanadium steel. When Ford went to vanadium steel, so did Hyatt. The basic problem was that machined steel parts could be made to size as interchangeable parts, but when they were heat treated for the required strength, they would warp in an uncontrolled way and they were no longer interchangeable. The steel industry and the machine tool industry were soon in a major effort to develop steel alloys, heat treatment methods and grinding machines that would result in interchangeable parts that were tough and strong. As other alloys were available, Hyatt used them. They also developed heat treatments and grinding machines for their bearings and were on the forefront of this critical new manufacturing development. The automobile industry, aircraft industry, in fact all American manufacturing, is indebted to development of hardened alloy steels and the grinding tools that could make durable, interchangeable parts.

Alfred Sloan was in a position to know all the pioneers of the automobile industry with his monthly visits to their plants. He called on Henry Ford and C. H. Wills, the Ford chief engineer, as the Hyatt bearings were used on all Ford cars. In Flint, he called on C. S. Mott, who made the axles for Buick and later for all of General Motors cars and trucks, Charles Nash, the head of Buick, and William Durant, the G.M. head. He met Walter Chrysler, the head of Buick production, and they became friends for life. They later lived in New York and shared family vacations, and since they both had yachts, they shared many boating experiences.

In 1916, Alfred Sloan and his father owned 60 percent of the Hyatt Bearing Company with 4,000 employees. In about 20 years, Sloan had singlehandedly built it from almost nothing. It was a career goal.

There was a problem that Sloan had to solve. The company had three divisions—one for machinery, one for tractors and farm machinery, and one for automotive. Just two companies, Ford and G.M., made up about threefourths of the total sales. The Hyatt patents expired in 1916 and either big customer might decide to make their own bearings.

In 1916, William Durant was back as president of G.M. and had a concept for an automotive parts division for G.M. He approached Alfred Sloan about G.M. buying Hyatt Roller Bearing Company and making it part of a new parts division, to be called United Motors. Sloan was to be the president of that new division.

Besides Alfred and his father with 60 percent of the stock, there were only two other stockholders. After some discussion, the four agreed on a price of $13.5 million for Hyatt Roller Bearing Company and Durant bought the company for General Motors. Both Sloans were wealthy men.

United Motors Corporation: Learning Management Methods

Alfred Sloan's background with Hyatt prepared him to manage the AC Spark Plug Company and the New Departure Bearing divisions of the new United Motors Corporation. These divisions made products that were high cost, small in size, used several per car and did not change from year to year. Remy Electric, a maker of starters and ignitions; Delco, a maker of electrical items similar to Remy; and Perlman Rim Company, a maker of road wheels; were also part of United Motors. Sloan was a successful business manager but his was a highly centralized company. His new challenge was that centralization would not work with such a diverse group of companies. Sloan made the problem more difficult by adding Harrison Radiator Company, a maker of automotive radiators, and Klaxon Company, a maker of automotive horns, to the United Motors Corporation. The combined group had sales of $34 million in the first year. Sloan's background had not prepared him to manage a group of companies in so many different fields.

Before he could think about a solution, United Motors stock was bought by G.M. in 1918, and as head of the Parts Division, Sloan was elected to the G.M. Board of Directors. What he saw there was each division head trying to gain Durant's favor to advance requests for their division with no thought of the needs of General Motors. In his own operations, the system used when he became a part of G.M. did not allow him to determine which part of United Motors had the better return on investment. For the corporation as a whole, it was impossible to tell which part of the Corporation had the better return on investment. Even for day to day operations, some divisions had excess cash and others had to borrow at bank rates. This was a cost to the corporation that was a waste because there was little coordination of cash management at the corporate level.

1920s Crisis

The end of 1920 had a recession that revealed the flaws of the G.M. management at the Board level. There were the recent expenditures for various companies that Durant had made. There were new expenditures for a $20 million G.M. building in Detroit, the purchase of New Departure Bearing Company at $7.0 million, the purchase of the remainder of Fisher Body Company, and $10.3 million in projects requested by the operating divisions. There was no system for the Board to evaluate the requests, but there was a feeling that G.M. did not have the cash for them all. On November 5, 1919, the Board and its Finance Committee approved all of the expenditure requests and directed that $100 million in debenture stock be sold to cover the costs. By spring of 1920, the debenture stock offering failed with only $11 million raised of the $85 million that would have entered G.M. as new cash. This was a wake-up call that the realities of Wall Street were not consistent with the finances at General Motors.

Walter Chrysler was on the G.M. Board and, seeing the situation coming, quit the company and cashed his G.M. stock and options for $10 million in cash at the end of 1919. Chrysler was right in the short term and picked a good time to sell since the G.M. after-tax earnings had been about 13 percent, but in 1920 they dropped to 6.65 percent and were a 12.7 percent loss in 1921.

The du Pont interest in G.M. started with a personal investment by Pierre du Pont in 1915 to support Durant in the Chevrolet takeover of General Motors. The du Pont company was making an incredible amount of money as a supplier of explosives during World War I and was looking for an investment with good peacetime earnings. The automotive industry was an obvious choice and since Ford was not available, then G.M. was the stock to buy. Du Pont started with 23.8 percent of G.M. on December 21, 1917, by the end of 1918 had 26.4 percent and at the end of 1919 had 28.7 percent of the company and complete control. Du Pont preferred a passive role because he knew little of the automobile industry. That was to change in 1920.

The failure of the debenture stock issue in early 1920 placed a severe constraint on the company cash needs. In May of 1920 the Board Executive Committee set a limit of $150 million for plant inventories for the whole corporation. Inventories for the corporation were at $137 million, but had grown to $168 million in April and then to $185 million in June of 1920 rather than dropping to the $150 million limit. In September the bottom dropped out of the market and all G.M. plants were closed except Buick and Cadillac, and even they began short work weeks. By October, G.M. inventories grew to $206 million. The divisions had the company out of control and G.M. no longer had the cash to pay vendor bills or meet payroll. G.M. had to borrow $83 million in short term bank loans. Any other company probably would not have been able to borrow $83 million in short term loans because that amount of money represented one sixth of the total assets of the company. G.M. would have been bankrupt. Over a quarter of G.M. was owned by the very profitable du Pont Company, however, and the short term bank loans were made.

The next crisis was in November 1920 with Durant's support of G.M. stock as it dropped in value. That situation was saved with a bailout by du Pont and J. P. Morgan. Alfred Sloan was on the Board and knew the real situation at G.M. and referred to this time as one of "ruin." Durant had a clear vision of the future needs of G.M. in an ever expanding automobile market and the stock at $12 or $15 was a sure way to share in that success. Durant was the president of the company and had no reason to share his thoughts of the future with either Sloan or Walter Chrysler. Sloan was right to call it "ruin" for it was, in the short term. Chrysler left the company over the issue and there was a short term problem to be addressed. Durant, with a sure vision, was right in that after a short downturn, G.M. would need all the production capacity that Durant was putting in place.

Reconstruction: A New G.M.

The du Pont stock holdings had given them control since 1917 and they used the Board of Directors Executive and Finance committees to exercise their control. The events of 1920 with the bailout of Durant resulted in du Pont adding Durant's shares to the du Pont holdings. A total of 36 percent of G.M. was owned by du Pont. There was no choice but for Pierre du Pont to step in as president of G.M. in December of 1920.

The first order of business in 1921 was to get the cash of the divisions under central control. The Treasurer's Office started a procedure in which all divisional deposits and expenses for the corporation were cleared each day at one bank. Later there was a monthly cash budget for each day of the month, and short term bank loans or short term U.S. Treasury deposits were used to balance daily cash needs with interest earned on daily cash surpluses. These actions turned a serious problem into a way to make money for General Motors.

The Board did not have an objective method of evaluating expenditure requests and in 1920 had approved of them all with a financing plan that did not work. Alfred Sloan did not have an objective way to evaluate the several divisions that reported to him at United Motors. In the middle of 1920 Sloan developed a long report on how to evaluate divisions of a corporation. Durant approved of Sloan's ideas, but the events of 1920 overwhelmed him. In 1921, Pierre du Pont placed Sloan on a study committee to determine how expenditures should be approved.

One of the du Pont managers transferred to G.M. in 1921 was Donaldson Brown. Early in his career at du Pont he had the task of developing a rational method of pricing the various products that du Pont made. He based his concept on return on investment but recognized that the number of times the investment is turned over was important. In other words, a 3 percent return that has a turnover of 4 times per year is better than a 5 percent return twice a year. He developed a way of stating relationships in a standard format that made facts visible. The system worked well at du Pont and it was exactly what Sloan had been talking about for G.M. It was implemented as quickly as possible.

This unique return on investment system became not just how expenditures were compared but also how operating divisions were compared to see the profit contribution of each part of the company. This was the bedrock of the new General Motors.

Failure to forecast the slowdown in the economy at the end of 1920 was a major part of the G.M. crisis. In order to manufacture the material to support automotive production it is necessary to make a purchasing commitment three months in advance and for raw material, four months. The drop in sales and car production at the end of 1920 caused the brush with bankruptcy. Sloan added a new function of analysis of the economy so that economic events and car production would match. At first it was crude, but in time it has improved and the process gives an independent basis for production control. It is still used today by all car companies.

Sloan also instituted a system in which dealers reported new and used car sales and inventory to the G.M. staffs. He also put in place a report of all car registrations for the country which could be used by all manufacturers, and both systems are still used today.

Inventory buildup was a result of incorrect production schedules, as the 1920 events proved at General Motors. Getting control of inventories was a must in 1921. All purchases were stopped, inventories were analyzed and an agreed upon purchasing plan was put in place at each division. Inventories that had reached a peak of $215 million and two inventory turns per year in September 1920 were under control at $94 million and four turns per year by June of 1922.

Sloan introduced the concept of "standard costs." The automobile industry was then, and is today, highly cyclical and a sales volume was agreed on by all parts of the company. Production was planned for 120 percent of that volume, but financial plans and budgets were planned on 80 percent of this "standard volume." This concept has become a General Motors cornerstone that is used by all manufacturers today.

THE COPPER COOLED ENGINE

The copper cooled engine program illustrates how a management without technical support almost made a major blunder. Charles Kettering was a much respected scientist for his development of the self-starter and the related electrical system that revolutionized the American automobile industry. His company, Delco Research Laboratory, was just bought by G.M. This was part of Durant's concept of how a complete automobile company should be organized. A research project at Delco Labs was an air cooled engine, which was called "copper cooled." Air cooled engines were not new in the industry. One car, Franklin, was only available with an air cooled engine. The advantages of an air cooled engine are that it is light in weight and will not freeze in the winter. The problems are the difficulty of brazing the copper fins on the cast iron cylinders and heads and achieving good, cool air flow over the fins.

Kettering took the development of the copper cooled engine personally and wanted to prove that his research could develop a major new product for General Motors. The engine was developed for Oakland and Oldsmobile brands as a six cylinder and later for Chevrolet as a four. Chevrolet required an overhead valve engine, which they had been using since the first Chevrolet. The six cylinder versions were dropped, but the top G.M. management thought the copper cooled engine would be the correct engine for Chevrolet to use to compete with Henry Ford.

Development was going badly. The copper fins could not cool the engine, particularly around the overhead valves, rocker shafts and springs. William Knudsen, the former head of all production at Ford, was hired for the same job at Chevrolet. On March 22, 1922, Knudsen was made head of Chevrolet. Knudsen reviewed the copper cooled engine and wanted a backup to avoid committing the brand to an unproven concept. In May of 1922, he had the engine redesigned to fit the carryover chassis that also fit a conventional water cooled engine. This simple example of good judgment would, as future events occurred, prove to be a very important decision. The car was introduced at the January 1923 New York Automobile Show and it was a sensation. It was priced $200 over the water cooled model.

In early 1923 two things happened. First, the market demand for cars exploded and Chevrolet could sell all the cars it could make, regardless of engine. Second, the copper cooled engine ran into cooling problems and production came to a halt. In May of 1923 a group of G.M. engineers made the following report about the copper cooled engine:

> The engine pre-ignites badly after driving at moderate speeds in air temperatures of sixty to seventy degrees. It shows a serious loss of compression and power when hot, though the power is satisfactory when the engine is warming up from a cold condition."[2]

Kettering's engine was not ready for production, but Kettering felt that it was a simple matter of more development and that Chevrolet Division was damaging his program. It was too late, and Sloan, with a technical background, overruled everyone and cancelled the program in the summer of 1923. Chevrolet had built 759 copper cooled engines but 239 were scrapped at the production plant. About 500 were delivered to the sales force, of which 300 were in dealers' hands and 100 were retail sales. All were recalled in June of 1923.

Kettering was ready to quit the company and it was almost a year before he came to the viewpoint that his copper cooled engine that could not be made in quantity would have put Chevrolet and maybe G.M. out of business. The lesson Sloan took from the copper cooled engine program was that the Divisions should not be forced to accept a program they opposed.

ORGANIZATION

The basis of all financial decisions was the G.M. unique return on investment concept, but there were more issues to be addressed. How should the operating divisions be managed? With Durant, they had a great deal of freedom and were trying to get Durant's attention to support their financial requests. That freedom almost bankrupted the corporation during 1920. Sloan proposed the following:

1. The responsibility attached to each chief executive of each operating division shall in no way be limited. Each such organization headed by its chief executive shall be complete in every necessary function and enabled to exercise its full initiative and logical development.
2. Certain organization functions are absolutely essential to the logical development and proper control of the Corporation's activities.[3]

Sloan recognized that the first statement "shall no way be limited" was in conflict with the second "control of Corporation's activities." He was to spend the rest of his life as the head of G.M. trying to find the balance in this conflict. One way he established a general balance was having the Divisions estimate their next quarter's operating budget and the central finance staff report on progress. All capital items were approved only at the G.M. Board level and evaluated on a return on assets basis. Each division had product control with engineering, car production, sales and marketing reporting to the division head. Each division head had responsibility for success in the marketplace. That system had been used at G.M. and it was what Walter Chrysler was familiar with when he headed Buick Division.

Fisher Body and Styling

Neither Fisher Body nor Styling followed Sloan's strict logic. Fisher Body joined General Motors on a piece by piece basis as G.M. bought increasing shares. During the wood body era, Fisher Body had a unique asset base with major forest holdings, wood sawing and curing plants, and woodworking and finishing plants. A separate division made some sense.

Steel bodies and inner and outer panel body construction methods (see Walter Chrysler, Chapter 4) changed body construction at its core. In 1937, Fisher Body was the last manufacturer in the industry to change to steel bodies because of their huge wood products investment. They went to the inner and outer panel method of steel body construction with the advantage that piece cost is measured in dollars, but the disadvantage that tooling cost for the same part is measured in the millions of dollars. This was a good decision for General Motors since they had the highest volume in the industry, but even G.M. must be careful about body panel interchangeability. The detail parts of the car could be interchangeable with very little notice by the customer of the several G.M. brands. Body engineering and production was done by Fisher Body to achieve interchangeability for economic reasons. Later, Sloan would insist that the same engineers from Chevrolet also design

WOOD AND STEEL BODIES—Wood bodies were more related to furniture making than mass production. The 1925 Ford wood body pictured here would have steel panels of a simple form tacked to this wood frame to give the appearance of a steel car. The result was a very weak body assembly that added no structural strength to the total car. Steel bodied cars in the American market started with the all-steel Dodge open cars of 1914, the all-steel Dodge closed sedans of 1923 and the Dodge cars of inner and outer panel steel construction of 1928. This is a permanent display at the Henry Ford Museum and Greenfield in Dearborn, Michigan.

the new 1926 Pontiac to ensure that the two cars were truly interchangeable. The same idea applied to Fisher Body, where body panel interchangeability is essential for economic reasons. This kind of Fisher Body organization continued during the wood body era and into the steel body era.

Styling was a central staff function—then and now. While it was desirable to share body panels for tooling cost reasons, it was also important to maintain separate appearances for each brand so that each car would appeal to different customers. A great deal of creativity was needed by Styling to meet these opposing goals. These styling themes became important marketing tools. Pontiac had a Silver Streak, or more recently the Wide Track look. The Oldsmobile rocket, Buick portholes or Cadillac fins were brand statements by Styling that could be designed on bodies with a great deal of interchangeability at Fisher Body. Styling was always a separate central function

WOOD AND STEEL DOORS—The wood framed doors were painted in the body color, as on this 1917 Willys. Closer inspection shows that the outer steel panel is folded over the wood frame and the door lock is mounted in wood with wood screws. This car is on display at the Walter P. Chrysler Museum in Auburn Hills, Michigan.

to invent these brand themes that could be made as a common body by Fisher Body, also a central function.

THE TURNAROUND

As the du Pont team took over, they retained outside consultants to advise them on future actions. They recommended that the Chevrolet brand be dropped because they felt it was futile to compete with Henry Ford. Alfred Sloan was not of an automotive background but he saw what the automotive experts did not see. The market role of the Model T as basic transportation was changing. The entry in the car market was not to a basic transportation car like a Model T, but was moving to a used G.M. car because it had size, features and was a technically superior car at the same price as a new Model T. Sloan made a very strong case to du Pont that the consultant's recommendation was in error. Chevrolet should be retained and was important in providing the volume base that was so vital in the automobile business. Sloan won the argument and Chevrolet was retained in the new G.M. lineup.

In just two short years, the short term debt was paid off and $90 million in inventory adjustment, extraordinary write-off, and liquidation losses were taken against earnings. This was an amount equal to one sixth of the G.M. assets. Pierre du Pont became Chairman of the Board and the man who did the most to develop the new methods of control was made president—Alfred Sloan.

Du Pont and Sloan had the good fortune to have a strong automobile market after the 1920–21 recession, with Chevrolet moving into a leadership position. The success against the Ford Model T was exactly as Sloan had predicted in 1921 when he argued to keep the Chevrolet brand.

Table 7. G.M. Sales—1921–1923

	1921	1922	1923
Chevrolet	62,000	208,000	415,000
Oakland	12,000	20,000	36,000
Oldsmobile	19,000	22,000	35,000
Buick	83,000	123,000	201,000
Cadillac	11,000	22,000	22,000
	187,000	395,000	709,000

Sloan said, "To Pierre du Pont must go the credit for the very survival of General Motors and for laying the foundation of its future progress."[4] It is also true that Sloan and his leadership had put in place a system:

- to control cash,
- to have an objective measure of expenditure requests and divisional performance, and
- to have a national economic and current sales input into the production control and inventory control procedure.

He also knew how to use Chevrolet to wear down the Model T market and turn it into a Chevrolet market. He deserves much of the credit he gave to Pierre du Pont.

Marketing and Product: The Market Revolution of the 1920s

Sloan devised a way that Chevrolet could compete with Ford in the basic transportation market and showed that Chevrolet should be retained by General Motors. Alfred Sloan was getting regular reports of car registrations from around the country and saw that used car sales were leading new car sales by an increasing margin. He and his advisors were the first to see that used car sales were displacing the Ford Model T as the customer choice for a basic transportation product. Durant had shown that a Chevrolet could sell very well against a Model T and now Sloan had the reason why. A low mileage, two year old Chevrolet was a better buy for the customer than a new Model T. Sloan now had to exploit that trend that the marketplace had started.

A 1921 Chevrolet had a 103 inch wheelbase rather than the 100 inch wheelbase of the Model T. It had 26 hp overhead valve engine rather than 20 hp, a 3 rather than 2 speed transmission, and was a much newer looking car than a 1923 Model T. They would sell at the same price and the used Chevrolet was the customer choice. GMAC changed the terms of sale—an older car could be the down payment and the cost of the 1921 Chevrolet was a monthly payment, not the whole price of the car, as in the case of the new 1923 Ford. Ford Motor Company was the last to have a new credit system, although GMAC was such a competitive advantage that many Ford dealers had financing arrangements with a local bank.

Sloan played this same market plan over and over again against the Ford products. The new Model A was introduced in 1928 but was not a volume product until late 1929. A used 1928 Chevrolet had a 35 hp overhead valve four that was smaller than the 40 hp Model A four, but it was on a 107 inch wheelbase rather than the 103.5 inch of the Model A and was a bigger car in all measurements. Chevrolet changed all the rules in 1929 by using a 46 hp overhead valve six. The used Chevrolet cars were a better value than any new Model A and sold at similar or lower prices.

A used 1936 Chevrolet had a 109 inch wheelbase and a 79 hp overhead valve six and would be a poorer value than the new 1938 V8 Ford with 85 hp and a 112 inch wheelbase. The used 1936 Chevrolet was the choice, however, because it had hydraulic brakes standard rather than the poorly operating mechanical brakes of the new 1938 Ford. Throughout the entire Ford V8 era, a two year old Chevrolet was a better value compared to a new V8 Ford. In addition, the new Chevrolet was priced about $20 under the new Ford. It does not appear that an aging Henry Ford ever understood what Alfred Sloan was doing to the Ford Motor Company in the marketplace. Walter Chrysler understood very well and always had his Plymouth priced with the V8 Ford, but with hydraulic brakes standard and an unbeatable reputation for Plymouth durability.

DUCO PAINT

The involvement of the du Pont Company in the affairs of G.M. led to the development of Duco paint to reduce one of the bottlenecks in automotive production. Early car bodies, and the buggies before them, were painted with multiple coats of varnish (12 or more) with sanding or polishing between. The result looked good when new, but would crack or craze and would last only about a year or two. The multiple coats would require 3 to 8 weeks to dry and a volume producer such as a Ford could have 20,000 car bodies in various stages of drying. Ford went to only black varnish in 1914 and to black baked enamel in the late teen years. He summed this up with his famous "any color you want as long as it is black." Black baked enamel would normally be baked at 450 degrees and all Dodge cars had all steel bodies that were painted in a day. Ford had wood bodies that would burn at that temperature and Ford had to use six thin coats at 165 degrees. It took three days to paint a Ford and about 4,000 bodies in inventory to maintain Ford production.

The cost savings of black enamel vs. the multiple coats of black varnish for Ford was sizable. A 1923 study in the archives of the DaimlerChrysler Historical Collection, done at Maxwell, showed that the cost of a varnish paint job was $53.25 and enamel was $22.63, a $30.71 per car saving under the cost of the multi-coat, multi-sanded varnish painting method. For Maxwell, with 34,000 club sedans (the cars in the report) to be produced, this was over a million dollars per year in savings. If Ford had similar savings from going from varnish to enamel in the late teens, their volume of 700,000 units would be a 20 million dollar cost improvement for Ford Motor Company. In addition to the cost savings, the time car bodies spent in the plant float (drying paint) was reduced from 14 to 4 days.

The solution to the problem came from du Pont in the form of Duco paint. It was called a lacquer but it was a liquid celluloid. Unlike varnish, it would not crack, craze, turn yellow or chalk with time. It came in all the colors of varnish and would dry in 30 minutes. It required the same priming or "rough stuff" preparation as any other paint. It did not require sanding between coats as varnish or enamel did. It did, however, require final polishing that the others did not. The final advantage that outshone all others was that the Duco system was slightly less costly than baked enamel. The $30.00 savings noted in the Maxwell study by going from varnish to baked enamel also applied to Duco, which is at the baked enamel cost level. The industry savings from Duco paint was monumental (20 percent of the cost of a car body or 5 percent of the total cost of a car).

The industry talked about the durability and colors that were available, but the cost savings was the real story. The paint was introduced on Oakland (Pontiac) in 1924 and in some colors on Chevrolet the following year. In 1926 it was used on all Chevrolet cars and the difference in appearance from the all-black Model T Fords was a real competitive plus. The cost savings was, no doubt, a reason that the 1925 Chevrolet went from being priced $155 over a Ford to only $130 in 1926, the year Chevrolet went to Duco as standard.

The Market of the 1920s

Alfred Sloan was not an "automobile man" like Henry Ford, Billy Durant or Walter Chrysler since he never had responsibility for a car company until he started at the top as president of General Motors. He did talk to dealers, and his new systems of reporting dealer sales, dealer inventories and car registration gave him a current knowledge of what was selling. He was the first to see that a new market was developing beyond the entry level of the Ford Model T. During the 1920s he expanded his ideas about how to use Chevrolet to defeat the Model T in the marketplace. Sloan saw the new market forces as installment selling, used car trade-in, the closed car body and the annual model change. He saw to it that G.M. and Chevrolet took the lead in all four areas during the 1920s.

Installment selling. Bankers across the country took the very conservative view that automobiles were the plaything of the rich or of other irresponsible people who were not credit worthy. In 1915, the automotive business was the largest business in America in terms of sales but the industry did not have a retail credit structure. That was in part due to the success of the Model T and Henry Ford's belief that consumer credit was unethical. The industry had to develop the credit system because bankers felt it was risky. GMAC was formed in 1919, but it was in the turnaround years of 1921 to 1923 that it became a force on the market. Installment selling started to set the terms of retail sales, not as the whole price of the car as a Model T, but as the monthly payment after a down payment. Bankers were wrong—car owners were solid citizens who used their cars for personal transportation, and cars had become a basic part of their lives. GMAC knew this and knew that an automobile was unlike other consumer credit items. Other credit systems usually involved an appliance or furniture that was in a home and required a court order to enter a home to repossess. A car was usually parked on the street, where it could be repossessed easily. The retail loss ratio on installment paper was 0.3 percent from 1919 to 1929. In 1931, in the Depression when there were valid reasons to default a loan, the loss ratio rose to only 0.6 percent. Bankers had missed a real opportunity in the car loan business.

Used car trade-ins. The first payment of an installment loan was usually a trade-in car, and as used cars they became the basic transportation cars to replace the market role of a Model T. This was the shift in the market in the 1920s that Henry Ford did not recognize. It was the reason that the Model T could no longer be sold and the reason the new Model A would have only a four year life. A low mileage G.M. used car had more features or size at the same or lower price than a new Model T or Model A. The Model T basic transportation market was gone.

Closed car bodies. Open cars were 90 percent of the market in 1919 but only 10 percent in 1929. The open touring cars could not be used in winter months in the northern part of the country. A closed sedan added 3 months of useful service to car ownership. The Model T had too small an engine for the heavy closed bodies. Closed cars were usually expensive custom bodies, but in 1923 the Hudson Essex sedan was priced at $100 more than a touring car and the revolution started. Closed cars were the only kind that the public wanted and the Model T market vanished. In 1926, 580,000 of the 1.13 million Model T's were closed cars. The same year, Chevrolet sold 410,000 closed cars of 480,000 total cars. In 1927, only 230,000 Model T's were closed cars of the 390,000 well behind Chevrolet at 550,000 closed cars of 650,000 total sales.

Annual model change. The annual model change did not start as a product policy at G.M. It grew from the idea that cars would be improved as engineering developments were made. It soon made sense that the changes be made at the same time so dealers and customers would be aware of the new features. The next step was to make an appearance change in the car that had the new features. Styling was started as a G.M. corporate function with the impact of the 1927 LaSalle, a lower cost Cadillac, and that success has set policy to current time.

These forces were understood by Sloan, but it does not appear that Henry Ford could grasp what the marketplace was doing to the new Model A Ford. The new Ford had a 40 hp engine that was barely enough for the closed bodies that the public was demanding. The old Chevrolet four had 35 hp in 1928 but it was raised to 46 hp as a smooth six cylinder in 1929. The Model A was a small 103.5 inch wheelbase while the Chevrolet sat on a 107 inch wheelbase. There was no plan to restyle the Model A, but the car was restyled at the cowl area in 1930 because the first Model A looked old fashioned compared to the 1928 Chevrolet. The Chevrolet was only the second styling project by the new G.M. Styling Studio, and the hood was integrated into a horizontal shape at the cowl. Chevrolet led Ford in sales in 1927, 1928, and 1931 to 1934. The market was forever changed to the advantage of G.M.

Product Lineup

Durant developed the concept of offering a variety of products, but it was Sloan who refined the idea. The Durant product lineup had some holes in it that Sloan addressed.

The first was the market space between Oakland and Chevrolet. Durant had shown that a Chevrolet did not have to match a Model T in price to be successful. Sloan went further and said that Chevrolet would be a better value than a Model T. It had the advantages of size (103 vs. 100 inch wheelbase), a 26 vs. a 20 hp engine with overhead valves, three speed vs. two speed planetary transmission and better trim and color availability. The Chevrolet had enough engine size to be used with closed bodies and a three speed transmission to apply that engine power.

Chevrolet needed to move down, not up, in the market. The space above

Chevrolet was large and the Oakland six was a weak product with only 40,000 units per year. The six cylinder was the right engine to power the closed bodies and Sloan developed the concept of a new car with a six. To meet the objective of the lowest priced six, the new car would use Chevrolet components. The head of Oakland Division agreed there was a place for the new product, but insisted that Oakland would develop the new car. Sloan's response was interesting in that he insisted that Chevrolet develop the new car. Sloan said that "the only chance for success is to have it developed at Chevrolet Division. There will be no chance for an engineer to inject his own personality in the picture."[5]

In other words, Sloan directed that the new car be a Chevrolet by part number with only a longer wheelbase to make room for the new six cylinder engine. The new car was introduced as a 1927 Pontiac and was an immediate success. Oakland sales with Pontiac jumped from 40,000 to 140,000 and Chevrolet sales also increased by 100,000 units, greatly increasing the volume base for Chevrolet tooling. It was a brilliant market and product plan that closed a market gap. It also allowed Chevrolet tooling to be amortized on more units, thereby lowering the Chevrolet cost and price to be nearer that of a Ford. The Chevrolet Coach was $155 over the Tudoor Model T in 1925, $130 more in 1926 and only $100 higher in 1927 when the Model T went out of production. Pontiac Division replaced Oakland Division in 1932.

The second product problem was the price space between Buick and Cadillac. Both cars were successful, but there was a market for expensive cars with more style and flair than a Cadillac. Changing the Cadillac would alienate the more sedate Cadillac customers. The problem is not unlike the one Cadillac and Lincoln have in today's marketplace in trying to appeal to a younger customer who buys a Lexus or BMW.

The west coast movie stars were having their cars customized and one of the more popular designers was Harley Earl. Sloan invited him to Detroit, was impressed with his work and hired him to form a color (later styling) studio. The first production assignment was to create a lower priced Cadillac with a youthful appeal. The result was the 1927 LaSalle. It was stunning in styling and was a market success. The 1928 Chevrolet was the next styling success and styling impacted all G.M. cars from that day forward.

These product actions by Sloan were best summarized by him in his famous phrase, "A car for every purse and purpose." The well known lineup from Chevrolet, Pontiac, Oldsmobile, Buick and Cadillac dominated the industry for the next 80 years.

Sloan as Head of G.M.: 33 years as the Boss

When Durant bought Hyatt Roller Bearing he had the concept of a division of G.M. that would supply parts to G.M. He formed United Motors

PONTIAC—Alfred Sloan wanted a car to fill the market gap between a Chevrolet and the next higher priced car, an Oakland. The new car would have a six cylinder engine but to achieve the price targets, Sloan directed that the new car, called Pontiac, would be engineered by Chevrolet engineers. The new car was the same as a Chevrolet, by part number, except for the engine. The price target was achieved and the car was a success when introduced in 1926. By 1932, the name of the G.M. Division was changed to Pontiac. Here is a 1928 model which was on display at the 2002 Old Car Festival at Greenfield Village, Dearborn, Michigan.

with Sloan as the head and a member of the G.M. Board of Directors. Sloan could see, first as an observer and then as the most active member of the Board, how the Board operated. He identified the following periods of his pre-war time at the Board level.

Early expansion period—1918 to 1920. Durant saw the post–WWI period as one of opportunity to expand the manufacturing base of G.M. to be ready for a future boom in automotive demand. G.M. assets in 1918 were $135 million and at the end of 1920 they were a staggering $575 million. Not all of Durant's ideas were a success—Sampson Tractor, for example—but the production base grew from 200,000 units in 1918 to 393,000 in 1920 and was

1927 LaSalle—Harley Earl was hired by Alfred Sloan to add some style and grace to General Motors cars. The Cadillac appearance was too sedate, but if it was changed it would not sell to the older customers that liked the Cadillac as it was. A new car, LaSalle, was designed by Harley Earl and it was a sales success. Harley Earl started on a program to make G.M. cars "longer, lower and wider." For this LaSalle, he raised and widened the hood so that it made a long form from the radiator to the rear bumper. This photograph of a 1927 LaSalle was taken at the 2002 Concours d'Elegance at Meadow Brook in Rochester, Michigan. There is a 1927 LaSalle on permanent display at the Henry Ford Museum and Greenfield Village in Dearborn, Michigan.

ready for the 750,000 units of the 1922 market. Durant saw a future that Sloan, Walter Chrysler and bankers on Wall Street did not. But that vision did not help him survive the 1920 stock crisis.

Contraction and firming up—1921 to 1925. The level of expenditure could not be financed out of earnings and a $100 million debenture was to be sold. It failed as Wall Street did not share Durant's view of the future. Durant was out and Sloan, with a clear idea of how to manage the complex company, became president. Sloan's ideas touched every part of the company. Fortunately the production expansion that cost Durant the presidency of G.M. in 1920 now allowed Sloan to sell 750,000 cars in 1922. That grew to 836,000 in 1925.

Alfred Sloan was able to accomplish this 1925 production rate with only $60 million more invested in production capacity than had been put in place by Durant.

New expansion—1925 to 1929. The roaring 20s demanded a new level of production expansion. The 1926 sales totaled 1,235,000 units and that grew to 1.9 million in 1929. Assets increased from $700 million in 1926 to $1.3 billion in 1929. G.M. was making about 21 percent as a return on sales during this period. It was the Microsoft of that era.

Depression and recovery—1930s. The financial controls that Sloan put in place worked very well during the Depression. The fact that G.M. did not lose money was proof of the system. He did do some things that were not the best from the management viewpoint. He had to combine the Buick, Oldsmobile and Pontiac sales forces, which would not help the long term prospects of any of the brands, but the middle priced market had shrunk to the point that there was no choice. He was forced to use the same engines in different brands, an Oldsmobile engine in a LaSalle, for example.

He did not see the Depression coming any more than anyone else did. He said the only advantage he had was that his system reacted quicker, and that was due to the requirement of reporting registrations (sales) directly to the central G.M. staff that he set up in 1921. Sales declined from $1.5 billion in 1929 to $432 million in 1932. Net income dropped from $250 million in 1929 to $165,000 in 1932, which showed the remarkable budget control that Sloan had developed.

Chevrolet became a powerhouse with sales over 1 million in 1935, 1936 and 1937 and $60 million had to be invested in plant expansion in the middle of the Depression. After 1935, Chevrolet was well ahead of Ford in sales. Over the decade of the '30s, G. M spent $346 million in new plants and equipment.

World War II—1940 to 1945. G.M., like the rest of the automobile industry, converted the entire company to war material. It was the largest producer in the world, the backbone of the "Arsenal of Democracy." The company did about $4 billion in sales of war material each year but it was on a 'cost plus' basis that assured that G.M. earnings were kept at about 5 percent of sales. The company's cash position and working capital doubled during the war years and there was the capital for the re-conversion back to automotive production.

Greatness: The Postwar Era, 1946 to 1956

A new era dawned for G.M. after World War II. Ford Motor Company floundered with the short-lived Model A and the mistake of the V8 decision. G.M. outsold Ford every year after 1932. By 1936 the difference was at least double the Ford volume. It was General Motors, not Ford, that was the largest

1941 CADILLAC 60 SPECIAL—By the end of the 1930s, Harley Earl had achieved his styling goals of "longer, lower and wider." The hood flowed with the body, the fenders flowed into the body, the trunk was within the body, headlamps and taillights were within the fenders, the grille was a horizontal form and the Cadillac 60 Specials were so low that they did not need running boards. This photograph of a 1941 Cadillac 60 Special was taken at the 2002 Concours d'Elegance at Meadow Brook in Rochester, Michigan. The 1938 Cadillac 60 Special, the first of this series, is on permanent display at the Henry Ford Museum and Greenfield in Dearborn, Michigan.

industrial firm in the world. It was Alfred Sloan who masterminded the market shift and an aging Henry Ford who failed to understand what was happening.

In the post-war period, G.M. moved to a new level of operation that had never been reached before by any firm. It was similar to an Alice in Wonderland passing through the "looking glass." Chevrolet volume exceeded 2 million units and the G.M. total went over 4 million units. A body stamping production line has a total volume of a little over 2 million units before the dies are worn to the point that they must be scrapped. A Chevrolet body stamping line would not only run full time for a year but at the end of the year the tools would be completely worn and would have to be replaced for the new model year. New tools for Chevrolet were required every year and every other year for the rest of the G.M. cars. Restyling the G.M. line of cars had to be done every year or every other year and this set the entire industry on a model year change cycle treadmill that some companies could not maintain. Studebaker and Packard merged and were out of business by 1956. Hudson and Nash merged in 1955, but the two historic brands were dropped by the new American Motors in 1957.

The biggest problem that G.M. had during this period was the fear of an anti-trust action by the U. S. government to break up G.M. into separate companies. At the beginning of this period, 1946, a 71 year old Sloan reduced his commitment as G.M. Chief Executive Officer. He retained his position as Chairman of the Board and was still in full control of the company. His policy reaction to the possibility of a government mandated split was to make "more car per car." If G.M. dollar volume was limited to a maximum number of units, then G.M. would make more of each car that was sold. This would increase the assets that the company had and return on assets, the basis for G.M. financial analysis, would be lower because components are priced at a lower margin than car sales. This was the plan that Sloan adopted and sales grew from $2 to $10 billion during the period, with the net income on sales at the $2 billion range and moving back to the pre-war level of about 20 percent of sales.

A major change in the market started in 1955 when the three low priced cars had overhead valve V8 engines and good performance was no longer an exclusive of the medium priced cars. The Ford, Chevrolet and Plymouth cars had the engine power for automatic transmissions, air conditioning, power steering and power brakes. The features of the middle priced car were available to everyone. The second breakdown of the middle priced market came in 1957 when Chrysler Corporation built the entire line of cars, from Plymouth to Chrysler, on one large body shell. Chevrolet followed in 1959 with one body from Chevrolet to Cadillac. Ford followed in 1960 with a large body shared with Mercury. There was now no difference in size nor in features between the low priced three and the cars of the medium priced market. It would be several years before the market caught up to what was happening, but there was no longer much of a reason to buy a medium priced car. This was the market that the ill fated Edsel was introduced into in 1958 and by 1960 the medium priced market was so small that DeSoto could no longer survive. These market changes were not all resulting from the leadership of General Motors, but Alfred Sloan's company fared better than any of the other of the big three in this changing market situation.

In 1956, an eighty year old Alfred Sloan became Honorary Chairman of the Board. He did not release much of his control of the company because he retained his position on the Finance Committee and on the Bonus and Salary Committee. Alfred Sloan had reached the peak of his abilities as the very active Honorary Chairman of the General Motors Board. His was the only voice that mattered at G.M. until his death in 1966.

THORNS

In the early '50s, Eiji Toyoda, of the Japanese Toyota Company, studied Ford and G.M. operations. He found entire press lines that made Chevrolet parts every day for an entire year, and stocks of parts at the stamping plants, rail cars, and at the assembly plants around the country. These stocks greatly exceeded the normal three month supply that was the usual practice. Local managers had a "just in case" feeling about inventory and they could see no reason why parts would ever change once production started. If a quality problem should occur, the dealers were more than able to handle the repair and fix the cars. This reliance on dealers was a vestige of the Ford Model T era in which Henry Ford required his dealers to make many of the final assembly operations at the dealership in order to save shipping costs. Later, it was usual and, in fact, "a rite of passage," for a new car owner to make long lists of things that he wanted the dealer to fix.

Toyota had a different problem. They were selling cars halfway around the world and dealing with dealers and customers who did not understand their language. Repairing cars in the field, at that distance, was out of the question. The only policy for Toyota was the seemingly impossible goal of making the cars as perfect as possible so they did not need repair, anywhere in the world. If quality improvements demanded a change, the G.M. system was unacceptable for Toyota and they must create their own solution. G.M. could have as much as a half year of parts in inventory before a quality change was effective. Toyota adopted a policy of as small an inventory as possible so quality driven changes would be effective as quickly as possible in the plant. This "just in time" inventory approach demanded excellence at all levels of the Toyota manufacturing and supplier base. There was no inventory to use to continue production while a problem was solved and implemented in production. Everything stopped. It took years, but Toyota made it work, and while U. S. manufacturers (they all used the G.M. system) might have 400 to 500 problems with each 100 cars, Toyota and the Japanese would have only 100 problems with each 100 cars built. The reputation of Japanese cars being almost perfect would cause a major shift in the American marketplace and that change is still going on today.[6]

Summary of a Life: A Professional

From 1923 to 1946, Alfred Sloan was the chief operating or chief executive officer of G.M. After that, at age 71, he was Honorary Chairman of the Board until 1956. His duties as Honorary Chairman kept him in direct involvement on the Finance and Bonus committees. This was 43 years at the top of the largest industrial firm in the world.

Balancing central control of a huge corporation with autonomy in its operating divisions has been the subject of countless business studies. Sloan's writings and those of others such as Peter Drucker have formed a body of knowledge that is arguably the basis of the business administration academic field.

Alfred Sloan built G.M. as the first conglomerate. In the late '20s G.M. had earnings of 21 percent. It was the Intel or Microsoft of that time. The financial control system he put in place adapted to the needs of the Depression of the '30s and G.M. did not lose money, unlike most companies.

G.M. expanded car and truck production around the world, and expanded into fields such as aviation with stockholdings in North American Aviation and Bendix Corporation in the 1930s, and Allison Engine Division, which developed the first American 1000 hp fighter engine in the late '30s. G.M. research developed a new two-cycle diesel engine and revolutionized the railroad industry with the very economical diesel electric locomotives that dominated American railroading. That same engine in a smaller size dominated over-the-road trucking. It moved into the appliance market with Frigidaire air conditioning and appliances.

The size and success of G.M. presented an objective for other American companies. Car and truck sales passed 1 million in 1926, 2 million in 1940, 3 million in 1950, and 4 million in 1955. G.M. made $100 million in pre tax earnings in 1925, $250 million in 1927, $500 million in 1947 and $1 billion in 1949. One thousand shares of G.M. stock in 1922, just before Sloan became president, would have cost $13,000. Twenty-five years later, in 1947, the stock would be worth $112,000 and would have paid $117,000 in dividends. This was a total of $229,000 for a $13,000 investment. This was a public company and wealth for everyone, not just for the handful, as was the case of those who invested in 1903 in the Ford Motor Company.

4

Walter Chrysler (1875–1940)

Walter Chrysler was a small town boy who grew up in the barely settled Kansas frontier. He was an exact contemporary of Alfred Sloan and although their backgrounds were drastically different, they became lifelong friends when they both lived in New York. Chrysler was a high school graduate and a Master Machinist. Most importantly, he had developed an uncanny skill in judging other men. He had a lifelong interest in learning, read widely, and took every kind of extension course he could find during the railroad years. In the later years, as head of Chrysler Corporation, he had a curiosity about almost everything.

His contribution to the automotive industry was to take the unreliable automobiles of Henry Ford and the G.M. cars of the early '20s and engineer them into the modern automobile. He recognized that the customer would accept the ease of repair of a Ford Model T or Model A, but what they really wanted was a durable car that did not need repair. The company he founded was based on detail engineering to achieve this goal.

The Railroad Years: "The Old Man"

Walter Chrysler, age 18, started as a railroad sweeper and wiper at 5 cents per hour, a total of $135 per year, "bring your own tools." His father wanted to send him to college but he was determined to work at the same railroad shop where his father worked as a locomotive engineer. In three more years he was an apprentice mechanic at 15 cents an hour ($405 a year). He then went to the Santa Fe railroad as a journeyman mechanic at 27 cents per hour ($729 a year).

It was there that he learned an important lesson that would influence the rest of his life. A master mechanic took him under his wing and taught him how to set the valves of a steam locomotive. This was the most difficult job at a locomotive repair shop and done only by the master mechanic. The engine had a marking for the top dead center (TDC) position of the steam piston and it was made by the locomotive manufacturer, but sometimes it was not made correctly. The correct location was essential to the correct setting of the engine and as the engine had increasing wear, the actual TDC would move but the mark would not. The master mechanic told Chrysler to make his own TDC mark to be sure that the job was done correctly. "Only trust yourself" was the lesson. Later in life, Chrysler could lie in bed late at night and tell by listening to the sounds of a locomotive in the distance if the valves were correctly set.

Several years later he worked his way to master mechanic on the Colorado and Southern Railroad at $115 per month ($1,380 a year). At 30 years of age, he was a foreman, "the old man," at $140 per month ($1,680 a year). A symbol of his position as master mechanic was his tool chest. The kind of tools that he had and the fact that he made many of them were the symbols of the kind of workman that he was. The precision of his tools was a measure of the quality of work that he could do for his employer. He had them

Railroad Roundhouse—Walter Chrysler worked at this kind of railroad roundhouse at several railroads in the start of his career. He changed jobs to increasing levels of skill and became the "old man," the foreman. The size and weight of locomotive repair parts, locomotive tools and machine tools required an unusual amount of physical strength. The early pictures of Walter Chrysler show a very well built young man. This roundhouse was in Marshall, Michigan. Its turn of the 20th century design is identical to many that were used by the railroads throughout the mid–American states where Walter Chrysler worked. This building now stands at Greenfield Village in Dearborn, Michigan.

WALTER CHRYSLER—This picture is of an oil painting of Walter Chrysler at the peak of his life. His company was not only one of the "Big Three" but Chrysler Corporation was in second place in sales. His cars were sold around the world and he has built the Chrysler Building in New York. The painting is interesting in that his big, square hands are prominent—a reminder of his career that started as a railroad sweeper and grew as he became one of the richest men in America. This picture is from the archives of the DaimlerChrysler Historical Collection, Detroit, Michigan.

on display at the Chrysler Building in New York during his lifetime. His tool box still exists and is now on display at the DaimlerChrysler Technical Center in Auburn Hills, Michigan.

At another railroad and a year later he was making $160 per month ($1,920 a year). Another year and another railroad, the Chicago and Great Western, he was making $200 per month ($2,400 a year). He was then promoted to Superintendent of Motive Power for the entire railroad at $350 per month ($4,200 a year). He had developed an essential ability to be an excellent judge of men and their ability to do an assigned job for him.

A Love Affair

What happened when, during his travels for the railroad, he went to the 1908 Auto Show in Chicago can only be called a love affair. It was big, it was white with a red interior—it was an automobile. In 1926, he was quoted as recalling that moment as a vision of the future. As Walter Chrysler visualized the automobile's possibilities, a car far outran railway development, which in a sense had reached its zenith, because the automobile provided flexible, economical, individual transportation which could be utilized for either business or pleasure. It knew no limits except a right-of-way. An automobile was bounded by no greater restrictions than individual effort and will. To Chrysler, it was the transportation of the future, and as such he wanted to be part of it. That was where Chrysler saw opportunity.

That the above opinion was his complete thought in 1908 might be in question, but what he actually did indicates that, for whatever reason, he was moved to exceptional action. He took his life savings ($700) and went into debt for more than his annual salary to buy the car, a Locomobile. He had it shipped to his home in Kansas because he had no idea how to drive. He then spent his nights and his weekend free time taking the car apart and understanding every detail of how it worked. He must have been motivated by some view of the future, because he later said that it almost broke up his marriage.

During the three years he owned the car, he took it apart forty times. He also had dealings with some of the college trained engineers who worked with him while he was head of motive power at the railroad. "I had been pounding away at my correspondence courses for six or seven years, until there was no word or term of mechanical engineering used by those college men which lacked meaning when they spoke to me. ... I had inside of me the essence of their knowledge, and something more—I could get out on the floor of any shop, walk into any roundhouse and do any man's job, with calipers or a hammer or with any turret lathe. I had not been handicapped by the overalled route that I had followed. I felt, when I tackled a tough job, that there was nothing that I could not accomplish if I wanted to."[1]

He realized that he was at the top of his field. The railroad industry was a mature industry with a structured organization of line and staff departments. There has never been a case of someone like himself, as head of the Motive Power Division, being promoted to the head of the railroad. He must redirect his career. His many correspondence courses also gave him an excellent background in accounting, finance and cost control.

He decided to be part of the manufacturing side of railroading, where he could use his ability to judge men, his well developed management skills, and his skill in finance. He quit his job and joined American Locomotive Company in Pittsburgh, Pennsylvania, with a pay cut to $275 per month ($3,300 a year). Within two years he was the boss as Works Manager (V.P. Manufacturing) at $6,000 a year and he had turned the operation around to be consistently profitable. In 1911 his pay was raised to $8,000 per year. This was a career goal and he was a respected business leader in a major city, Pittsburgh, Pennsylvania. But he still wanted to be part of the future and that was the automobile industry.

The Buick Years: Cost Control

Chrysler was offered a job as Works Manager at Buick in Flint, Michigan. This was the chance to join the automobile business that he had dreamed of. He was offered $12,000 to stay at American Locomotive but refused and started at Buick for $6,000 per year, a $2,000 cut from his current pay, and he had to move his family to the small town of Flint.

Walter Chrysler started at Buick in 1911. What he found was unbelievable to him. American Locomotive was in a mature industry and cost control was essential; in fact, that was how he turned the company to be profitable. A locomotive might cost $40,000 but at American Locomotive, Chrysler knew the costs to point and in such detail that he could successfully make low bids to win contracts and still make a good profit. Walter Chrysler used the well developed cost control system of the railroad industry and it was one reason he was particularly successful as Works Manager.

The automobile business at that time was totally different. It was wide open, bordering on being out of control. Cars were shown at automobile shows in January and the plant would be in a crisis to build the orders until late summer, when the last orders were filled. They would then close the plant until the next burst of orders arrived in January. Buick at Flint was even more out of control than most and a real "wild west" operation in the automobile business.

When Chrysler came to Buick he asked for cost information, but no one knew what he was talking about. He showed them what he wanted and soon started to receive cost information and to get the plant under control.

When he started at Buick, new cars were taken out of the plant to be road tested. Within the first day he noted that more cars were sent out to be road tested than were being returned. He started a sign out system and had saved enough money in the first week to pay his annual salary.

There was a capital request for Buick to build a new sheet metal plant. He analyzed the problem and discovered that much of the existing floor space was taken by stacked material during the work day. He had the parts trackers come to work one hour later than the main work force. They would work through lunch and clean up the plant and bring new material for the afternoon shift. At night they would again work late and do the same so the plant was ready to start production in the morning when the main force came to work. This simple change freed so much floor space that the planned plant expansion was not necessary.

He developed a cost control system for Buick. He had budgets developed for every department. When waste was found, he was ruthless in stopping it immediately. He was quoted as saying, "I will stop waste the moment I discover it." In six months he had increased production from 45 cars per day to 75 cars per day with essentially the same manpower and plant space.

One of the items of waste was that the Buick frame was painted and sanded for several coats and then polished. Most of the Buick work force had worked at Durant and Dort Wagon Company and that was the way the wood frames for wood wagons were made. On a car, the frame was steel, not wood, was almost completely hidden and would be covered with mud in the first mile of driving. He stopped the painting of frames by such a complex process.[2]

Later in life he was asked how he evaluated manufacturing companies for cost savings. He said, "I have the floor space measured and estimate the amount of its productive capacity and then check to see whether it is overcrowded or is running under its capacity, also whether the plant is overmanned."[3] While he did not use the exact words, in his method he is very aware of earnings per square foot of plant space, machine output, manpower utilization and inventory turns. This is the language of a financial analyst, not that of just a Works Manager.

He went on to say that if there was an extra machine in a department, then he wanted it removed to storage. He did not want the men in the department to think that if something happened to break, a replacement was available. Each man was to be responsible for his machine. He felt the same about extra manpower. The ideal department, in his view, had only the exact number of machines and the exact manpower to make the required production schedule. Every worker could see the machines and manpower that his team could utilize to make the production goal and how essential his work and machine was to the total department.

There may have been other ways that a cost control structure was transferred to the automobile industry, but Walter Chrysler, with his rapid promotions at Buick and at G.M., was one of the main contributors to the development of cost control in the automobile industry.

In 1914, he was still making $6,000 and went into his boss's office and demanded a raise to $25,000 per year. His boss was Charles Nash, who later started the Nash Motor Car Company. Nash reviewed Chrysler's performance and agreed with the $25,000 wage. Walter Chrysler responded that next year he wanted $50,000. The following year, that is what he was paid.[4]

His decisions on other subjects were as quick as his decisions to eliminate waste. There was a problem with ignition wiring that would short out and stop the engine. Chrysler assigned an engineer to the problem. He discovered that the clutch linkage would rub the wiring and cause the problem. The solution was to cover the wiring with a "slip on" piece of loom and the engineer discovered that the plant supply room had an adequate stock on hand. Chrysler met the engineer in the plant, approved of the addition of the loom, wrote down the serial number of the car that the change started with, and told the plant manager to repair all cars that were still in the plant. When he returned to his office he directed the Service Department to repair all cars in the field. Such a change, in less than an hour, would have taken weeks at most automobile plants.

Among the personal items that Walter Chrysler left in his estate was a cost notebook dated 1912. The book was small enough to fit in a coat pocket and had fold-out pages with detail costs that were kept up-to-date by the accounting department. Such cost information would be essential to making responsible decisions to solve problems on the plant floor.[5] The archives of the DaimlerChrysler Historical Collection has two such notebooks. One is from Maxwell Corporation for 1922 and was something that Chrysler had a direct involvement with, since he was the head of the company at that time. The other one is from Dodge Brothers in 1924, a time that Dodge was a separate company from Chrysler Corporation. Walter Chrysler's influence on having the head of manufacturing keep detailed costs at his fingertips must have spread throughout the industry. Of course, Ford Motor Company was an exception.[6]

The chassis assembly building at Buick was typical of all buildings built prior to the Albert Kahn revolution. The building design did not accommodate what the building was to be used for. This building was one story but had posts every 20 feet. It was impossible to move a car chassis in any direction without hitting a post. Chrysler had the building rebuilt with a clear span in the middle. He then had the frame assembled with axles and wheels, lifted on a pair of wooden tracts and pushed by hand along in the open space of the plant. Parts were added until the car was complete. Walter Chrysler claimed that this was final assembly in advance of that of Henry Ford. It was no doubt true, because Ford started with the Flywheel Line in early 1913 and did not have a moving final line until the end of that year. Chrysler started with the final assembly line and worked backward to the detail parts. The result was the same, in that the speed of the assembly line caused problems with a shortage of the component parts. As those problems were solved, they caused more shortage problems to solve until, just as at Ford, the entire plant was running smoothly. Walter Chrysler described this period as a new invention every day. Walter Chrysler had the final assembly line ahead of Ford, but Ford had the entire plant running smoothly as an assembly system ahead of Walter Chrysler.

In 1914, Buick was to launch a new car, but instead of developing the cost of the new car as over or under the old car, as would be usual practice, Chrysler had the cost developed from base cost for all the parts. He was very familiar with all the costs and was sure he had them under control. He went to the Board of Directors with his cost studies. The costs were so low that they did not believe that a Buick could be made at this cost level. He offered to take the difference between the actual cost and his estimates as salary if he was wrong. The Board did not take him up on the offer. If they had, he would have made a fortune because his cost numbers were correct. This impressed the banker-dominated Board of Directors.

THE HEAD OF BUICK

At the beginning of 1915, Charles Nash became the president of G.M. and Chrysler ran the Buick Motor Company. At the famous September 16, 1915, G.M. Board meeting, Billy Durant took control of G.M. with his Chevrolet Company in a most dramatic way.

It took several more months to sort out the details, during which time Durant, who had always been a supporter of Charles Nash, learned that Nash was now supporting the banker faction of the G.M. Board. Such lack of loyalty was unacceptable to Durant and Nash was forced to resign on June 1, 1916. Within another month, Durant offered the job of President of Buick Motor Car Company to Walter Chrysler for $500,000 per year in combined salary and stock options. He was to be paid $10,000 per month as cash and he chose the rest of his salary in stock options, which would be valued at the 1916 price. The G.M. stock rose in price but Walter Chrysler's options were set at the 1916 price.

Buick prospered under Chrysler. The new Buick six of 1914 was a success and the 21,000 sales of 1914 grew to 42,000 in 1915. In 1916, the figure was an unbelievable 122,000 cars and it stayed at about that level until Chrysler quit the company at the end of 1919.

But before he left, his reputation in manufacturing and cost control resulted in him taking on the added responsibilities of all G.M. manufacturing. In 1919, he was promoted to First Vice President of G.M. in charge of all manufacturing and he retained the job as President of Buick Motor Car Division. His salary was increased to $600,000 per year.

The final break came in 1919 when Chrysler was about to sign a contract with a vendor, A. O. Smith Co., to supply Buick frames. Durant had agreed and knew all the details. There was a civic group luncheon in Flint with Dallas Dort, Durant's former partner, as the main speaker. In the middle of the meeting, Dallas Dort was handed a telegram from Durant that Buick would spend $6.0 million to build a new frame plant in Flint and employ hundreds of workers. Walter Chrysler was at the head table and was to give a later speech. He was livid at being overruled on something that he and Durant had agreed on and gave no speech. The facts were that A. O. Smith would supply frames with no capital cost and at a lower price than Buick could make them. In addition, Flint was a "boom town" with the success of Buick and housing for workers was already critical without adding hundreds of new workers for a frame plant.

Chrysler confronted Durant with the financially bad decision that Durant had made, and the fact that Durant had overruled him on something they had agreed on. Chrysler was so angry that he discussed it at the next G.M. Board meeting. The Board formed a fact-finding group and Chrysler was proven correct. The Flint frame plant was not built. As head of G.M. manufacturing, Chrysler then signed a contract with A. O. Smith to make frames for all G.M. cars at a savings of $1.75 million in the first year alone. The challenge to Durant at the Board level destroyed Chrysler's relationship with Durant, and as a practical matter Chrysler would have no choice but to quit.

The actual event that caused Chrysler to quit came later in 1919 when a major capital expansion was discussed at a G.M. Board meeting. They talked about new plants and the purchase of companies such as Sloan's Hyatt Roller Bearing Company, a major part of Fisher Body Company, a $20 million office building in Detroit and a farm tractor business. Chrysler and Durant agreed on many items, but Chrysler was opposed to the tractor addition. Chrysler felt that expansions were going faster than the economy and G.M. earnings could support. Their voices became louder and louder until Chrysler said, "What am I roaring about? I'm roaring as a stockholder, if you really want to know. Everything I have in the world is tied up in this Company and I don't want to lose it." After a smart remark by Durant, Chrysler said "I quit."[7]

When Chrysler left G.M. at the end of 1919, he was 45 and had $10 million cash from selling his G.M. stock and stock options, which were valued at a 1916 price. He was right about the future economy. Late 1920 proved to have a recession that caused Henry Ford a financial crisis, Leland to fail with his new Lincoln car and Durant to be bankrupt with his buying support of G.M. stock as it dropped from $40 to $12 per share. Walter Chrysler had sold all of his stock near the high in 1919.

The Company Doctor: Willys

Retirement lasted two months and his wife started to complain about his cigar smoking friends that were always around the house. She also knew that he was bored.

Although retired, Walter Chrysler, as former head of Buick and of all production at General Motors, was one of the most respected production and cost control men in the industry. In February of 1920, Walter Chrysler was retained by a group of investment bankers to keep the Willys Corporation from going bankrupt. It was a two year contract for $1 million for each of the two years.

John Willys, like many other automobile men, had expanded during WWI and his was the first car company to feel the impact of the slowdown in 1920. It owed bankers $46 million with little prospect of repayment. In the late teen years Willys Overland was second to Ford in sales with a four cylinder car. John Willys planned to follow that success with a new six and bought a huge assembly plant in Elizabeth, New Jersey, for making the new six. The cost of the plant was one of several items that caused the huge banker debt.

Walter Chrysler's first action as he took over the Willys Company was to meet with John Willys in his office and tell him that his $150,000 per year salary would be cut to $75,000 per year. John Willys paused for a moment, laughed and said "I guess we've put our problems in the right man's hands."[8]

As usual for Chrysler, he reviewed costs and discovered that Willys had agreed to some very high costs in the late teen years when the economy was going strong. Walter Chrysler knew the suppliers from his Buick days and renegotiated the contracts to improve Willys' profitability. John Willys, freed of day to day operations, did what he did best. He was a born salesman and a great leader of his dealers. Before long, and in a down market, he had the Willys car selling again. In a few months the work of both men had cut the debt to the bankers to $18 million. This was a major achievement and a reason that Walter Chrysler was worth $1 million per year.

He and John Willys agreed that the new six would be sold by Chrysler Motors Company, a Division of Willys Corporation, and the new company was incorporated in Delaware in June of 1920 with assets of $50,000. It was announced that the six would be in production in the spring of 1921. This is a remarkable action by a bankrupt company.[9]

Walter Chrysler went to the Elizabeth, N.J., plant and reviewed a new six cylinder car that Willys was planning to introduce. The car was almost tooled and the Willys engineers were sure of success. The head of Willys Testing was more forthcoming with the report that the new car was junk. Putting the Chrysler name on a failure was unacceptable and Walter Chrysler asked people that he knew about a good engineering team.

ZSB: Zeder, Skelton and Breer

Fred Zeder was the Chief Engineer at Studebaker and they were in the middle of never ending maintenance and durability problems. Zeder got the Studebaker Board to approve of hiring some graduate engineers to solve their problems. Zeder hired Owen Skelton and Carl Breer, both graduate engineers, and added staff to Studebaker Engineering. The result was a very successful and durable 1918 Studebaker. Studebaker management did not acknowledge the major contribution that their revitalized engineering department had made.

News of the distress of the Studebaker engineers reached Walter Chrysler and he asked to meet with them. The first proposal was for the three, Fred Zeder, Owen Skelton and Carl Breer, to come to New Jersey with their fields of knowledge to evaluate the Willys six. They agreed with the earlier evaluation that the car was not a commercial product and on July 14, 1920 they were hired at Chrysler's direction, along with 23 other engineers from Studebaker, to be Willys employees and to fix the car.[10]

They were the beginning of modern engineering in the automobile industry. An automotive engineer had a background as a mechanic and approached a problem with a trial and error method much like Henry Ford, but without his skill. The team of college graduates could analyze a problem and study alternative design solutions with paper studies, and the first parts that were made from this study would be close to a correct design to solve a problem.

Carl Breer summed up the problem of the Willys six design: it had copied the chassis used on the Willys four. Leaf springs were used at the axles but they were unusual in that the spring eyes were attached to the axles and the multi leaves of the leaf spring were u-bolted to the frame. The result was that while there was a 100 inch wheelbase, the rear springs would lengthen the wheelbase as the car was loaded. This was an advertising claim for a better ride but in actuality had no advantage. This design worked on the four but when applied to the heavier and more powerful six, it was a failure. There was a problem of springs breaking. Zeder, Skelton and Breer, who became known as ZSB, tried stiffer springs that would not break, but then the frame would break. If they stiffened the frame so it would not break, the car ride was awful. There was no solution but to start over. ZSB worked through the summer of 1921 and made remarkable progress on all parts of the car design, particularly on the design of the engine.[11]

The First Chrysler: A Breakthrough

A way to increase power is to run the engine faster. Power is "the time rate of doing work" and the faster an engine runs, the more power it has. The obstacle to this approach is "engine knock" from the poor fuels at the time and lack of detail engineering development work. Increasing the compression ratio has the direct effect of causing "knock" by compressing the gasoline to the point that it will self-ignite, in the same way a diesel engine works. The archives of the DaimlerChrysler Historical Collection has several of the ZSB engine studies. The first combustion chamber design, dated December 1920, was at a 4.2 compression ratio. It was conventional and was tested at 3,000 rpm. It used 7 main bearings on the crankshaft to safely run at these high speeds.[12]

Walter Chrysler was involved in every decision about the new car, and it was to be called a Chrysler. Development was going well. A study on April 9, 1921, showed that it would take $8.2 million to tool the new car and that the Willys Elizabeth, N.J., plant was worth $5.0 million.

The new car was developed to the point that a detailed cost study could be done. A copy still exists and these 95 single spaced pages constituted the detailed engineering parts list, which was estimated to four decimal places. Just as Walter Chrysler's personal success was based on good cost control, so his new car would rest on the bedrock of complete cost control. The total cost of the new Chrysler was estimated to be $605. The list price was $945, less 25 percent for the dealer mark up, which gave a wholesale price of $709 or a $104 profit on each car, a 15 percent margin.[13]

The first Chrysler was moving toward production at the Elizabeth plant when the Willys Company was thrown into bankruptcy on November 30, 1921, and the ZSB staff was out of work.

Later, in an interview in *Forbes* magazine in January 1929, Walter Chrysler said: "I maintained out of my own pocket, a plant—a sort of experimental plant—in Jersey, for three years, employed as many as thirty five engineers before one car was exhibited publicly. I actually spent three million of my own money in designing, creating and perfecting the Chrysler in this Jersey plant."

With the ZSB team out of work, the leaders approached Chrysler about forming an engineering company. In Carl Breer's notes it appears that Chrysler agreed but did not realize that they meant the whole team of 25 engineers. He agreed and then directed that ZSB start a new design that would be superior to the one they had been working on. In December 1921 the new firm of Zeder, Skelton and Breer Engineering Company, 24–26 Mechanics Street, Newark, New Jersey, was formed as a New Jersey corporation. They had only one project, to design a better car for Walter Chrysler than their first one for Chrysler Division of Willys Corporation.

The Company Doctor: Maxwell

The Maxwell debt to the bankers was only $26 million but the company was far worse off than Willys. There were 26,000 unsold cars of which 16,000 were at rail sidings around the country, unwanted by the dealers. The car had serious engine durability problems, a fuel tank mounting that would break and drop the tank to the ground, and a rear axle that would also break and drop to the ground. The number of dealers that sold the car had dropped to 50 for the whole country. The plant had purchased a large inventory in the boom times of the late teens and now could only assemble these expensive parts into very costly cars. Why Chrysler took this added challenge on top of the Willys salvage task is unknown, but he did in August of 1920. His pay for this task was $100,000 in cash per year with Maxwell stock options that would bring his total pay to $800,000 per year.

Walter Chrysler's first action was a reorganization of the Maxwell Motor and Chalmers Motor companies dated September 20, 1920, with Chrysler as chairman. That reorganization merged both Maxwell and Chalmers companies into a new Maxwell Corporation with $15.0 million in new capital. He next asked Fred Zeder to recommend an engineer to correct Maxwell product problems. Zeder recommended Harry Woolson, who was part of the ZSB team that came from Studebaker. Woolson created the field fixes for the cars and sent teams around the country to repair the cars that had been built.

As he did at Willys, Chrysler renegotiated costs with suppliers to get the Maxwell cost of production under control. The Maxwell Board was in shock when he priced the cars that were repaired in the field at only a $5.00 profit, but the cars sold and some of the former dealers took a Maxwell franchise again. The lower cost of the production allowed new cars that were built to be sold at a profit. In a remarkable piece of engineering, Harry Woolson managed to not only find a way to put a third, center crankshaft bearing in the weak Maxwell engine, but he also installed pressure oil lubrication. The resulting car was introduced as the 1922 "Good Maxwell."

The reorganization plan attracted stockholder lawsuits from former Chalmers stockholders that their future earnings were lost. One way to settle the suits was for Maxwell to pay cash for a settlement (what the plaintiffs wanted). A harder way is to bankrupt the company and thereby prove there was no value to the future earnings of Chalmers stock. In April 1921, the assets of the Maxwell and Chalmers companies were sold at a public auction. The active bidders were John Willys, William Durant, the White Family from Cleveland, Ohio, Studebaker and several brokerage houses from New York. One of the assets that the bidders hoped to gain was the ZSB engineering team. ZSB was a separate company and not part of the bid. The high bidder was Walter Chrysler at $10,915,100, representing the Maxwell Reorganization Committee.

The new company, Maxwell Corporation, was formed with a clean slate. In the first six months, it depleted its capital by $4.2 million to retool for the "Good Maxwell" and repair cars. It also reduced inventory by $5.0 million. In 1922 Maxwell made $2.0 million but Chalmers lost $1.1 million. In 1923, Maxwell made almost $4.0 million but Chalmers lost $878,000. This could not continue; the Chalmers cars had to be replaced and Walter Chrysler knew exactly what to do.

The Elizabeth, N.J., Plant: Opportunity Lost

The bankruptcy sale of the Willys Elizabeth, N.J., plant was set for June 9, 1922. The receivers expected a quiet auction and about a $3.0 million price. It was high drama. The Maxwell Board had voted to allow Walter Chrysler to bid as high as $6.0 million for a plant that cost $12.0 million to build. An earlier study of April 9, 1921, showed that the plant was worth $5.0 million.[14]

William Durant was at the sale and bid aggressively. Studebaker was represented, as was Walter Chrysler (Maxwell). The bidding topped out at $5.5 million and then Durant outbid Chrysler by $25,000 at $5,525,000. Not only did Durant get the plant for his new Flint car, but he also got the first ZSB Chrysler car that was to be introduced as a Chrysler from Willys Corporation.

In later years Walter Chrysler made much of being outbid by Durant by $25,000. That does not explain why he did not go to the $6.0 million limit that the Maxwell Board had authorized. An explanation may be that he remembered the plant was worth only $5.0 million or that he knew ZSB was developing a better car for him to call a Chrysler.

Durant did not understand the kind of breakthrough that the ZSB car represented and had the engine enlarged and the wheelbase lengthened so the new car that he called "Flint" was a Buick competitor. The added weight made it a good car but not exceptional. The new car did not have the performance of the ZSB Chrysler prototype and Durant gave a contract to ZSB to do development work on the engine for $150,000. This gave ZSB access to the Elizabeth plant laboratories to not only develop the engine for the Flint car, but also the new engine that they were designing for Walter Chrysler.

1926 FLINT—The engineering team of Zeder, Skelton and Breer designed an excellent car to be a Chrysler made by Chrysler Motors Division of Willys Corporation in 1922. The Willys Corporation went bankrupt and the Elizabeth, N.J., plant and the Chrysler car were bought by William Durant. He made the car larger and sold it as a "Flint" made by Durant Motors. This car is on display at the Alfred P. Sloan Museum, Flint, Michigan.

The New Chrysler Car: Final Design Hurdles

During the summer of 1922, ZSB had approached all parts of the engine development problem. They started with the 3,000 rpm and seven main bearing designs that they had used on their first concept.[15]

Exhaust Valve Cooling. A major problem in engine design is how to keep the exhaust valve cool. If it is too hot, it will pre-ignite the fuel, causing a "knock" which limits engine power. The exhaust valve is in the direct heat of the combustion gases and is cooled only when that heat can be conducted away while on the valve seat. The faster the engine runs, the less time per cycle that the exhaust valve has to cool from the hot combustion temperature. It will run hot and pre-ignite the fuel. The hot valve also results in a loss of valve or valve seat shape and seal, which was a major problem for engine durability, as evidenced by contemporary engines of the 1920s that required frequent valve reseatings. The engineering challenge faced by ZSB was that of careful design of the water passages around the exhaust valves to obtain excellent cooling. The new Chrysler engine had full water jackets around each valve and cylinder. It also used a cylinder block mounted water pump to assure that the coolest water was distributed to all cylinders and valve seats rather than shortcutting across the front of the engine.

Manifolding. Another problem faced by ZSB was even fuel mixture distribution. At the time, the updraft carburetor used by the industry tended to be rich at the middle cylinders and lean at the end cylinders. A December 27, 1923, story in *Automotive Industries* reports that during the earliest development of the Chrysler engine, gas samples were taken from each cylinder. This was done to be sure that the manifolds provided each cylinder with an even fuel mixture and even, low exhaust gas pressure. Even and full power with all cylinders working was the result, and therefore this was a very smooth and powerful engine.

Combustion Chamber Shape. During 1921, there were several design studies of combustion chambers, including an interesting chamber that was partially machined. A major design change in late 1921 incorporated the combustion chamber concepts of Sir Harry Ricardo. At the time, events dealing with the seemingly instant events of flame front travel were beyond the level of practical engineering study. At 2,000 rpm, the speed of contemporary engines, the top dead center events (within 18 degrees of crankshaft rotation) occur every 0.0015 second. At 3,000 rpm, the speed of the new Chrysler engine, the time scale is 0.001 second and flame front travel time is very much in scale with the top dead center events.

Sir Harry Ricardo, a British engineer, concluded that the advancing flame front, as the cylinder fired, would squeeze the remaining fuel mixture at the edge of the chamber, causing it to pre-fire and "knock." The solution that he proposed was to have a thin "squish" area over the piston that would have an exceptionally large area for cooling the last of the fuel mixture to prevent pre-fire and knock.

The exact date of the new combustion chamber design cannot be determined because the drawing is undated in a series of other dated drawings of late 1921. An added benefit of this design was that the fuel mixture was turbulent as the piston moved, thereby increasing mixing for faster flame front travel, and more complete burning and power. The ZSB drawing clearly shows the Ricardo design feature, and the compression ratio shown on the drawing was raised to 4.4. The chamber also had a dome over the valves to improve breathing around the valves. This feature was later called "Silver Dome" in Chrysler advertising.

Engine Design Details. The later machine tools for the new engine were designed so that the final boring of each cylinder was made by the same tool to reduce size variation between cylinders. This engine, like the first ZSB design, also used seven main bearings to assure engine life at the higher than usual 3,000 rpm of the new engine. The later production design had the squish area made thinner, from ¼ inch to 0.05 inch thickness to the top of the piston. This is the same design that is used today on engines that have a squish area. The compression ratio was then raised to 4.7, and still, 50 octane fuel (regular gasoline) could be used without knocking. This was a major engineering accomplishment. This was a full featured engine with aluminum pistons, full pressure engine oiling, oil filter, air filter, and an engine temperature gauge on the instrument panel.

Final design. The result of excellent exhaust valve cooling and seven main bearings was to allow a high speed engine with durability. A carefully worked-out manifold system and modern combustion chamber resulted in full power from each cylinder. The new Chrysler engine developed 68 horsepower at 3,000 rpm from only 201 cubic inches of engine displacement. This was a new industry standard of 0.34 horsepower per cubic inch of engine displacement. Table 8 shows the engineering practices of 1924.

Table 8. Engine Output—1924

Name	Size—CID	Power	HP/CID	RPM	C.R.
Six Cylinder Cars					
Chrysler	201	68	0.34	3,000	4.7
Hudson	288	75	0.26	2,400	4.7
Flint	268	69	0.25	2,600	4.2
Buick	255	65	0.25	2,600	3.5
Stutz	268	66	0.24	3,000	4.5
Packard	268	54	0.20	2,600	4.5
Four Cylinder Cars					
Dodge	212	35	0.16	2,000	4.0
Chevrolet	171	26	0.15	2,000	4.0
Ford	176	20	0.11	1,600	4.0

The first ZSB design that was used on the Flint car obviously was a competitive design. The second ZSB design that was done at Walter Chrysler's expense can only be called brilliant.

On November 11, 1922, Walter Chrysler saw the remarkable results that the Ricardo type cylinder head had on engine performance. He expanded his development contract to have ZSB build a prototype car, a very costly step for Walter Chrysler.

In April of 1923, he was pleased that the prototype was a breakthrough car and ordered that a production design be started, but it must be done quickly because Walter Chrysler wanted to introduce the new Chrysler Car at the January 1924 New York Automobile Show. Five cars must be made by ZSB by September of 1923, five months away.

Ownership

Walter Chrysler now had a problem. He owned the new car design but could not use Maxwell company funds to develop and tool a car that Maxwell did not own. His problem was compounded with a Board of Directors that were finance men and were interested in getting out of debt, and not buying unproved car designs.

In March of 1922, an unusual event happened in that Fred Zeder went to Cleveland, Ohio, to meet with the White Brothers (later famous as White Truck) about using the empty Cleveland Traction Plant to make a new "Zeder" car. The nameplate for the car was already designed and it featured lightning flashes to symbolize the Zeder name. The event was covered in the automotive press, but within a month the deal fell through. We know that Fred Zeder did not own the design for the Zeder car, Walter Chrysler did, and a deal could never have been be made. The Maxwell Board no doubt read of the Cleveland discussion and thought maybe the new car design that Walter Chrysler had did have value. We will never know the reason for the events in Cleveland, but they may have been part of Walter Chrysler's effort to have the Maxwell Board allow him to offer a $6.0 million bid for the Elizabeth, N.J., plant in June of that year. That purchase of a plant and the first Zeder design failed, but a year later, in the spring of 1923, this same board could buy an even better version of the Zeder car that Walter Chrysler would sell for $100,000 so that it could enter production. What Walter Chrysler was offering was a fully developed replacement for the failed Chalmers car line. He also had a running prototype of the car with the remarkable new engine installed for all board members to evaluate. Maxwell may have been a troubled company, but it still had a greater ability to borrow money than Walter Chrysler did as a private citizen.

The art work for the Zeder car still exists and is in the archives of the DaimlerChrysler Historical Collection. The "Lightning Bolts" that represented Fred Zeder were placed in the field of the seal design that was

CHRYSLER SEAL—This seal design was used on the first Chrysler car. It features lightning bolts that are a representation of the importance of Fred Zeder. The engineering firm of Zeder, Skelton and Breer was responsible for the very successful design of the first Chrysler car in 1924. The seal design would have importance to the more agricultural population of the mid-'20s since a prized crop or animal would receive such a prized seal at state fairs. The same design is used on all Chrysler cars of today. This is the grill emblem of a 2002 Chrysler.

used on the first Chrysler car in 1924. It is still used and that same 1924 seal with the Zeder lightning bolts is on every Chrysler brand car that is built today.

In May of 1923 the Maxwell Board signed a new employment contract with Walter Chrysler. Section Eight of that contract said that Walter Chrysler exclusively controls designs of a new car and agrees to sell and the Corporation agrees to buy all rights for a sum of $100,000. Walter Chrysler, of all people, knew how little money that Maxwell had and he agreed to accept $50,000 in 1923 and one third of the balance in each of the years of 1924, 1925 and 1926. He sold the design to Maxwell at a bargain price because Maxwell would start to spend money on the new car, but must own the design for the expenditure to be lawful.[16]

In June of 1923, ZSB moved their company from New Jersey and occupied Maxwell company space at the Chalmers plant in Detroit. They would start to build the five prototypes required by September 1, 1923.[17]

What they found at Maxwell explains a great deal about Maxwell and the state of the automobile industry in the 1920s. It was the practice at both Maxwell plants for a workman who found an assembly task or another task difficult to find the workman in the plant who made the parts and have him change the machining, so the first workman's task was easier. This had gone on for years and the car that was made had no relationship to the engineering concept. Finished cars were always being repaired at great cost and they were still not good cars for the customer.

ZSB had seen the same practice at Studebaker and stopped it at Maxwell on the spot. The part had to match the blueprint and if it did not, either the part or the blueprint must be changed. This requirement, along with the fact that a moving assembly line requires detail structure to run smoothly, lifted the new Chrysler car to a higher level of quality and manufacturing efficiency. Both were subjects in which Walter Chrysler was an expert.

Disaster

Nicholas and James Brady had been major investors in the Maxwell Company and had been through some major financial problems. In the fall of 1923, Nicholas Brady informed Walter Chrysler that the Bradys would like to sell their Maxwell interests. Studebaker was interested in either buying the Brady stock or in a direct merger with Maxwell. This was a disaster for Walter Chrysler. The first "Chrysler car" was a Flint and now the second "Chrysler car" would be a Studebaker. Worse than that, if Studebaker had either the Brady stock on the Board or there was a joining of the two companies, there would be no room for Albert Erskine, the Studebaker President, and Walter Chrysler in the same company.

Some historians feel that Walter Chrysler went along with the Brady plan too easily, but that is not the nature of what the man had done in the past. He had talked John Willys into spending $50,000 of the funds of a company near bankruptcy to create Chrysler Motors, a Division of Willys. He hired the best engineering team to fix the defective Willys car that would have had the Chrysler brand in the future. He directed that a second car be designed by ZSB, at his own expense, and had sold that design to Maxwell so it could enter production. Now Maxwell was to resell it to Studebaker.

Chrysler had to create a plan where he appeared to do the wishes of his Board and of the Brady family and at the same time kill the Studebaker plan. The only thing of value that Maxwell had was the ownership of the new car. He had to show that the new car and ZSB would not be part of a Maxwell merger and still appear to support the Board and the Brady interests. This was a very tricky bit of politics.

He called a meeting with Fred Zeder, told him that they were all set, and would be wealthy men because Studebaker would buy them out and make then rich. The meeting was widely reported in that Zeder said that all Studebaker wanted was the car and not Zeder or Chrysler. Chrysler appeared to be an active supporter of the proposal, as he had the prototype car shown to Studebaker officials and earlier had offered to the Board to step aside and let the merger go ahead. At the same time, he was so sure that he could stop the Studebaker proposal that he had advertising themes for the new Chrysler car introduction developed by an advertising agency.

The showdown came on November 29, 1923, on Wall Street in New York. All parties were present, including Fred Zeder, since ZSB was a part of Maxwell at the time and their continued service was an essential part of the purchase by Studebaker. As the meeting started, Fred Zeder said he was opposed to the deal and if it continued, he would call Carl Breer in Detroit and have the drawings of the new car destroyed. The drawings belonged to Maxwell and destruction would be illegal, but this set a dramatic tone to the meeting. The Studebaker faction offered $26.0 million for Maxwell. Maxwell was worth only $10.9 million at the bankruptcy sale in April of 1921 and the only new asset of the company was the new car design and the services of ZSB. It was now obvious to everyone at the meeting that ZSB would not be part of the deal and the Studebaker price that had been prepared in advance would be withdrawn. Walter Chrysler did not even try to reach a deal because he made a counter offer that was even higher than the Studebaker offer. Later the same day, Walter Chrysler told the advertising agency to place ads for the announcement of the new Chrysler car.

The engineering drawings were not destroyed and in fact still exist. They, along with the ZSB drawings done for Durant Motors, Continental Motors and Chrysler Motors Division of Willys Corporation are currently in the archives of the DaimlerChrysler Historical Collection.

Walter Chrysler had the last bit of financing in place for the new car when in late November two banks, Blair and Company and Chase, withdrew their combined loan of $6.0 million to Maxwell because the company was overextended. There was no doubt that it was overextended by any historical measure of Maxwell Motors, since Walter Chrysler was raising funds to tool the new car.

At the same time, the Show Committee of the New York Auto Show said that due to a lack of floor space, only production cars could be shown at the Auto Show in January of 1924. The new Chrysler car was not a production car and could not be shown.

The auto show was vital because it was a way to sell Maxwell bonds to replace the bonds that the two bankers had just withdrawn, and the money was required to tool the new car. In addition, Walter Chrysler knew every Buick dealer and most G.M. dealers that would be at the show and it would be a great opportunity to have them become dealers for the new Chrysler. Without the show, all was lost.

Walter Chrysler had taken one of the biggest gambles in the world and now it was about to pay off. When he started to fund ZSB in December of

1920, it was at least partly out of loyalty. He had hired ZSB and 23 more engineers and moved them to Elizabeth, N.J., to fix the new six cylinder car that was to be introduced as a Chrysler from Chrysler Division of Willys Corporation. All those who had moved were now out of work. The cost to continue the ZSB engineering might have been $100,000 per year, but that was something that a man of Chrysler's wealth could afford. The ZSB car design turned out to be a true breakthrough, particularly with the new Ricardo cylinder head. Walter Chrysler was at a crossroads. The odds of finishing the design and getting it to production were almost nonexistent. The engineering work would be a very costly set of useless drawings if the car was never produced and Walter Chrysler would have lost several hundred thousand dollars.

Chrysler made a major decision in November of 1922 to continue to spend money—in this case over $100,000 to make the castings, machine them and build a prototype engine. The odds of ever making a production car were still no better and Chrysler's investment loss would now be compounded. He later funded the construction of a prototype car at even more money. This only raised the stakes of his gamble and did not improve the odds. In a 1929 *Forbes* magazine story, he claimed that he spent $3.0 million on the new Chrysler. That may not have been an accurate cost, but it would be a total loss, just scrap, unless the car design could be produced and make the money to repay Chrysler.

THE 1924 NEW YORK AUTOMOBILE SHOW

Walter Chrysler loved to tell the story of how he was denied space at the New York Automobile Show to show his new car.[18] He put the new car on display at the lobby of the Commodore Hotel where all of the dealers from out of town stayed and that "while the car was not in the show, it stole the show." He liked the story so much, he put it in his 1937 autobiography, *Life of an American Workman*.[19]

The story is untrue. To use a more modern expression, he was being "economical with the truth." The impression that it gives, that Chrysler overcame huge odds to bring the new car to the public, is certainly true. He did. It did not involve the 1924 New York Automobile Show, however. The show had always been held at the Grand Central Palace that was next to the Commodore Hotel on 42nd street. The show was becoming very crowded and at one point, the Show Committee may have restricted the cars to only production cars, and the new Chrysler could not be in the show. The Committee moved the location to the Armory, which was in the Bronx. It was a huge space and the new Chrysler would be shown both there and at the Commodore Hotel. There is an oral history in the archives of the DaimlerChrysler Historical Collection that 20 cars were prepared for the New York Show (two Chalmers, six Maxwells and twelve Chryslers). Photographs taken at the 1924

New York show have two cars and one open chassis in the Commodore lobby, and one open chassis at the Bronx show. The picture at the Bronx show is not clear enough to be sure there were eight more Chrysler cars there, but several Chrysler cars can be identified in the picture.

The most important business at the show, since bankers had withdrawn $6.0 million in November, was for Walter Chrysler to secure the minimum amount of cash that he thought he needed, $5.0 million. The first banker that Chrysler cornered was reluctant to buy Maxwell bonds and the best price Walter Chrysler could get was $70 per $100. Chrysler was desperate but this was an insult, and Chrysler let the banker know that with some of the language he used when working in the railroad shops. The next banker he cornered was from Chase Bank. This was one of the banks that had backed out of the deal in November. At that time, they were buying the Maxwell bonds at $92 per $100. The success of the car at the show must have changed some minds because Chrysler negotiated $94 per $100 from Chase Bank for $5.0 million in Maxwell bonds. At last, the new Chrysler was to be a production car and Walter Chrysler had won an impossible gamble.

The 1924 Chrysler: The First Modern Engine

Many have said the 1924 Chrysler was the first modern car, and in many ways, it was. The engine certainly was, in that it could run for hours at highway speeds, as is now expected on our modern expressway system. Cars of that era that did not have full pressure lubrication would slowly have the oil at the top of the cylinder wall and at the top piston ring dry out, and it was necessary to close the throttle to increase the engine vacuum to suck crankcase oil to the top of the cylinder wall. This usually happened anyway due to the driving conditions at that time. The Chrysler engine did not rely on such chance events and could drive all day, as a modern car can.

When Walter Chrysler took the Willys salvage job in 1920, he moved to a hotel room and later moved his family to an apartment on Park Avenue in New York. The Willys Headquarters was located in New York. In February of 1923, he bought a 23 room mansion at Kings Point on Long Island. This was the center of the "Roaring Twenties" culture and Walter Chrysler loved it all.

When the first prototype was finished on September 1, 1923, it was test driven from Detroit to his Long Island home. The test was a success, but when Walter Chrysler asked about the car, he was told that it would be perfect if it had four-wheel hydraulic brakes. It had two-wheel mechanical brakes. Walter Chrysler called Detroit and directed ZSB to put four-wheel hydraulic brakes on the production cars. The first car with the mechanical brakes still exists and is on display at the Walter P. Chrysler Museum in Auburn Hills, Michigan. Hydraulic brakes are currently used on every car and light or medium duty truck made in the world.

1924 CHRYSLER PROTOTYPE—This is the first Chrysler prototype and it was driven from the Chrysler plant in Detroit to Chrysler's home on Long Island, in September 1923. Walter Chrysler was told that his new car would be perfect if it had four-wheel hydraulic brakes. He telephoned Detroit to direct that all production cars have four-wheel hydraulic brakes. This car is on permanent display at the Walter P. Chrysler Museum in Auburn Hills, Michigan.

The 1924 Chrysler had the engine and brakes of a modern car, but other parts of a modern car were not developed until the 1930s. The first modern body, with inner and outer steel stampings which were spot welded together, was first used on the 1928 Dodge before it became part of Chrysler Corporation.

All cars of the '20s had the majority of their weight on the rear wheels and as passengers loaded onto the car, the weight bias moved heavily to the rear. Dynamic handling would be as expected in that when the car was steered, it wanted to go heavy end first, i.e., turn end for end. At highway speeds, this was a most unsafe condition. The first car to solve this problem with roughly equal weight distribution was the 1934 Chrysler Airflow. This car also addressed the problem of engine power waste due to poor aerodynamics.

FRONT WHEEL OF THE CHRYSLER PROTOTYPE—This car was built with rear two wheel mechanical brakes as was usual practice in the mid–twenties. All production Chryslers would have four wheel hydraulic brakes, the front drums of which would be visible in this picture if this were a production car.

Cars with a solid front axle tended to have "shimmy" as the parts developed wear. There was no solution except to slow the car down until the shimmy stopped. The cause was a complex group of forces that self-excited each front wheel with the front axle transmitting the forces between the wheels. An independent front suspension would solve the problem and the 1934 Plymouth through Chrysler Airstream cars had such a system. It was not until the late '30s that Chrysler and G.M. cars had all of above modern car features. They were not on Ford cars until 1949, two years after the death of Henry Ford.

Drivers at the time said that the Chrysler had a flow of engine power and smooth braking. That was what was new about the car, in that the attention to detail that was lavished on the engine was also applied to the whole car. The appeal was to the emotions as well as to the practical matters of the excellent performance. It was the 1924 Chrysler that introduced the engine and brakes of a modern car.

Nineteen twenty-four was a poor time to introduce a new car. The total

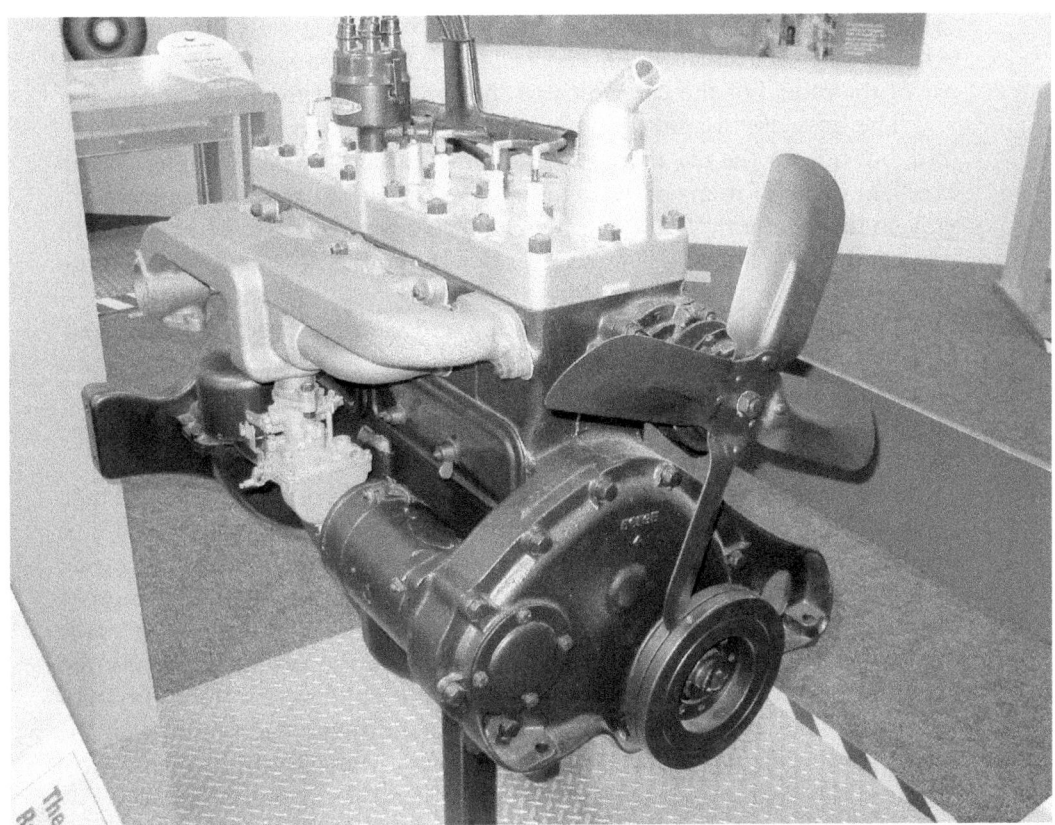

CHRYSLER ENGINE—This is the engine that started a company. The engineering team of Zeder, Skelton and Breer developed a full featured engine with much higher output than any other engine on the market. It had a smooth flow of power and a performance level that was equal to the most expensive cars made in America. Note that the water pump is in the cylinder block, where it could force the coolest water from the radiator to the cylinders and valves and to the ends of the engine. It was fully developed for exceptional durability and could be called the "first modern engine." This engine is on permanent display at the Walter P. Chrysler Museum in Auburn Hills, Michigan.

market was down; Alfred Sloan's General Motors saw sales drop from 798,000 to 587,000 between 1923 and 1924. Maxwell jumped from 49,000 to 66,000 sales on the strength of the new Chrysler. Maxwell profitability rose from $2.67 million in 1923 to $4.89 million in 1924 because of the new Chrysler, and the stage was set to rename the company.[20]

Chrysler Corporation: A Dream Realized

The last Chalmers car was made in 1924, and on June 6, 1925, the new Chrysler Corporation was formed to replace Maxwell Corporation. Nineteen twenty-five was also the last year for the Maxwell. A greatly improved four cylinder Chrysler replaced the Maxwell as the Chrysler Model 58. The number of the model of the car indicated the top speed of the car.

The business organization used by Walter Chrysler was highly centralized, but not for the usual business administration reasons. Chrysler was an excellent judge of men and wanted only the very best people in the top positions in his company. These top people were given complete control of their areas with Walter Chrysler as an overall automotive polymath to assist and coach each expert.

The cornerstone was manufacturing and George Mason was the head. He later went to Kelvinator, then Nash-Kelvinator, and in 1955 was the Chairman of the Board at American Motors. The reason he left Chrysler Corporation was that Walter Chrysler replaced him with K. T. Keller. Keller shared Walter Chrysler's zeal for manufacturing cost control.

The Chrysler business approach was to control costs but then add high value customer features such as hydraulic brakes and still have a total cost that was the same as the competition. This concept marked Chrysler's career since the American Locomotive days. This approach tended to solve problems on the sales side of the company. Walter Chrysler said that they made the cars and would not tell the dealer how to sell the cars if the dealer did not tell him how to make the cars. This way to treat dealers worked throughout his lifetime, because he saw to it that Engineering had features on the cars that were the best in each market segment. Manufacturing cost control balanced the total cost of the cars to be the same as the competition.

Zeder, Skelton and Breer were the best engineers in the industry and had total control of the product. Total control meant that the engineers who worked in the various plants were controlled from Central Engineering and were on the Engineering payroll. This gave the local engineers an advantage in dealing with manufacturing management. It also assured an engineer that his career was always back at Central Engineering. Each Engineering department was responsible for the design of a specific part of the car and the engineers of the department knew not only the plant layout, but also the tool engineers and manufacturing people on a first name basis. The designs from Engineering were a good first step toward the cost control that was so important to Walter Chrysler and later to K. T. Keller.

This approach was different from what Walter Chrysler was familiar with from his Buick experience. As head of Buick, he had total control of the product that he was selling and engineering was decentralized to each division. Walter Chrysler put engineering control in one location in his company.

B. E. Hutchinson was head of Finance and regarded as the most knowledgeable in not just the automobile industry, but also in the finance community. Like Engineering, he had an Auditing Department in each plant that reported on plant operations to his central staff.

Joe Fields was head of Sales and again was at the top of his profession.

Because the Chrysler cars were the best value in their market segments, he developed a series of comparison tables to train salespeople. He also developed salesmanship classes that showed salesmen where to stand and how to point out the features of the cars. Both techniques are still used today and by all manufacturers.[21]

Together these men were known within the company as the "princes" and they, and their leadership of Chrysler, were major reasons for the success of Chrysler Corporation.

Not only was the company strongly centralized in management in Detroit but it was geographically centralized also. All Chrysler, DeSoto, and Dodge cars and trucks for the American market were assembled in the Detroit area. Ninety percent of the Plymouths were assembled in Detroit. A small remainder of Plymouth cars was assembled in Evansville, Indiana. All engines, transmissions, axles, castings, forgings, body stampings and bodies—in short all the parts that Chrysler made—were made in the Detroit area. The only exception was the steering and suspension parts that were made in a New Castle, Indiana, plant. Later in the '30s, a few cars were assembled in California but that did not change the Detroit area dominance.

MAKE OR BUY

Walter Chrysler handled the "make or buy" decision in a different way than either G.M. or Ford. Ford made commodities like gray iron, steel, glass and rubber at the Rouge and neither G.M. nor Chrysler did likewise, for sound economic reasons. G.M. tended to follow the Durant-Buick practice of fabricating as much of the car as possible. This was particularly true under Alfred Sloan in the post–WWII era when the success of G.M. cornered over 50 percent of the car market. There was concern that anti-trust lawsuits would break up G.M. into smaller parts. Since G.M. could not make more cars, the Sloan approach was to "make more car per car." This meant making more of the dollar content of the car, and it rose to over 70 percent of the content of G.M. cars during that time. The Walter Chrysler "make or buy" decision followed his product philosophy. Every part of a Chrysler car was fully engineered with drawings and releases to production or purchasing. "Chryslerness" was the engine, driveline, brakes, steering and suspension, and Chrysler Corporation made most of these components as well as the related castings and forgings.

The body was also important for "Chryslerness," but Walter Chrysler had lived through the change in body construction from wood to steel in the 1920s and 1930s. The change was led by the body suppliers, and Fisher Body, as part of G.M., was last in the industry because of huge capital investments in forests and woodworking shops rather than stamping shops and die makers. Chrysler made about half the bodies needed and bought half to stay current in the latest body manufacturing methods.

For the rest of the car, Walter Chrysler carried over his frame purchasing experience from Buick and felt that vendors were better at specialized manufacturing methods than Chrysler Corporation could ever be. Heavy stampings like frames require special skills. Engine electrical components, starters, generators, radiators, carburetors, shock absorbers and other specialty items were best left to specialty vendors, in his view.

No one in the industry had more firsthand knowledge than Walter Chrysler. He had been Works Manager and head of Buick when they made almost every part of the car. He was on the G.M. board when Durant conceived of the parts division, United Motors, to make the components of G.M. cars. He and Alfred Sloan were personal friends during the formation of United Motors. It is interesting that when it was time to form his own company, Walter Chrysler chose to buy specialty parts.

The difference between Chrysler and G.M. is shown below:

Table 9. Chrysler / G.M. Parts Sources

	Chrysler Vendors	G.M. Divisions
Frames	Midland Steel Co. Budd Co. A. O. Smith Co.	Made by each Division
Transmissions	New Process Gear Co. Borg Warner Co. Majority made at Dodge	Made by each Division
Electrical Parts	Autolight Co.	Delco Remy Division
Radios	Philco	Delco Remy Division
Engine Electrical	Autolight Co.	A. C. Division
Bearings	Timken Bearing Co.	New Departure or Hyatt Division
External Trim	Various Vendors	Ternstead Division
Springs	Eaton Spring	Made by each Division
Electrical Wiring	Various Vendors	Packard Electric Division
Bodies	Briggs—half the volume	Fisher Body Division
Carburetors	Carter Carburetor Co.	Rochester Products Division
Propeller shafts	Universal Products Co.	Saginaw Gear Division
Lamps	Various Vendors	Guide Lamp Division
Radiators	Various Vendors	Harrison Radiator Division

The chart shows a dramatic difference between Chrysler and General Motors. The system that he chose when he headed his own company was completely different from that he had managed earlier as head of Buick manufacturing, Buick Division and G.M. manufacturing. The result was that Chrysler Corporation did not have capital tied up in plants for those components and tended to have a better return on assets than G.M., but G.M. tended to have a better return on sales. There is no way to make a similar comparison at Ford because these were foreign concepts at Ford until the post–WWII era.

INTERCHANGEABILITY

Walter Chrysler once said, "Standardized engineering design is the prime factor in reducing costs."[22] This was in 1926 and it was not only his view, but that of ZSB as they organized Chrysler Engineering. The same year, the new Pontiac was introduced. It was Alfred Sloan who demanded that the Pontiac be a twin of a Chevrolet, except for the engine, and that it be engineered by Chevrolet engineers. This demonstrated that the increase in usage of Chevrolet parts because of their inclusion in the Pontiac caused the Chevrolet parts to be lower in cost. There are two elements to cost. The total cost is the sum of what it can be made or bought for and the per part share of the tooling cost. Walter Chrysler and ZSB used the Chevrolet-Pontiac Engineering example to see to it that the same engineers designed similar parts and that they were as interchangeable as possible across cars and across years. A part on a Plymouth might be more costly than need be because it was also used on a heavier Chrysler, but when the tooling cost was spread on the added volume, the total cost might be less. Only a cost study could determine the correct answer. The tooling cost for a part that was used on all Chrysler cars, and across years, would result in a total cost for Chrysler Corporation that was the same as or sometimes lower than the Chevrolet cost.

In 1928, a new engineering center was opened at Chrysler Corporation and Fred Zeder said at the dedication that the new Engineering Division would be organized like a hospital. A hospital has specialists for the heart, bones, lungs, etc., and Chrysler Engineering would have specialists for every part of the car. The result was staffs for engine, transmission, axle, body, steering and suspension, and designs were similar in concept across all cars and across years because they were engineered by the same people. The Chrysler Engineering blueprint system used sequential part numbers. The first cars of the 1920s had 4 digit numbers; 5 and 6 digit numbers were used in the 1930s and 7 digit numbers were used in the 1940s and '50s. In the 1950s it was not unusual to find that drawings for a current production car had some low part numbers, sometimes in the six digit or five digit series of the 1930s. These low numbered parts were used with little change for years or maybe decades. In addition, the title box would show the car line usage. It was not unusual for parts, particularly for chassis parts, to be common on all cars. This meant that Chrysler parts were used on Plymouth cars. Plymouth cars were known for exceptional durability in taxi service and severe customer use. Much of it was due to the over designed parts from a Chrysler car that were used on a Plymouth.

The corporation grew in 1926 and 1927, but it was at the limit of car production that the two assembly plants could make. Sales were 130,000 in 1926 and 154,000 in 1927. Chrysler also had a dealer problem—all the easy-to-attract dealers had been signed and now the company must develop them one at a time.

In 1927, the unbelievable happened. The Ford Model T went out of production and the low priced market was wide open. To make a low priced car, basic parts such as castings and forgings could not be bought at market prices. These parts must be made in-house to control cost. There were only two choices: build the plants, at a then-estimated $70.0 million in cash, or buy another car company.

The Dodge Purchase: A Successful Plan

The 1928 purchase of Dodge Brothers by Chrysler Corporation stunned the industry; a "minnow swallowing a whale" was the view of the press. The material in the archives of the DaimlerChrysler Historical Collection reveals both a careful plan by Walter Chrysler and major engineering and business mistakes by Dodge management. These combined to make this purchase possible in mid–1928.

From his office in Highland Park, Michigan, Walter Chrysler could see the solution to his problem across the skyline at the huge, eight story Dodge Plant. How could he buy a company with facilities that were worth 3 times the value of the facilities of his corporation?

The Dodge brothers had died in 1920 and their widows had sold the ownership to the investment banking firm of Dillon and Reed in 1925. Walter Chrysler was a friend of Clarence Dillon and in 1926 approached him about buying Dodge. Chrysler did not have the resources to make a serious offer. It was a wish more than an offer, and the matter was dropped.

In 1926, the low priced Pontiac 6, "a six at the price of a four," was introduced. It revitalized Oakland Division of General Motors and eventually replaced the Oakland brand in the G.M. lineup. Alfred Sloan's idea to have the Chevrolet and Pontiac be identical except for engine was not lost on Walter Chrysler. The Chevrolet parts that were shared with Pontiac had greater total volume and therefore were lower in cost to Chevrolet.

At that time, Chrysler started the development of a low priced six that was later introduced as a DeSoto. Chrysler's plan was to introduce the new, fully engineered, full featured DeSoto six with hydraulic brakes at a price below a Dodge and literally take the market away from Dodge. If Dodge were smaller, he could then buy it. It would be a bluff, because Chrysler Corporation did not have any added production capacity to profit from a future DeSoto success.

Dillon and Reed were not well suited to manage an automobile company. The manufacturing facilities and dealers were excellent but the four cylinder product was old and some decision had to be made about introducing new Dodge cars.[23]

The success of the Pontiac indicated that a new six was required. Rather than follow the Pontiac example of a "six at the price of a four," the Dodge banker-dominated management chose to go up market with their six cylinder product from the $800–$900 range of the Dodge 4s to $1,595 for the new Dodge 6. Taking a brand to a higher price in the market is difficult at best, and Dodge sales dropped from 219,000 in 1926 to 125,000 in 1927.

INNER AND OUTER STEEL BODY PANELS

The first Dodge car introduced in 1914 had a steel body developed by Budd Company and it was an industry first. In 1923, Dodge and Budd developed a closed car steel body, another industry first.

At that time, steel bodies were made simply and had reinforcements, stiffeners, and local struts to give them strength where it was required. These additions involved a great deal of hand work and cost. Budd Company pioneered the concept of a body with both an outer and an inner panel stamping to make the complete front, sides and rear of the car body. The combined inner and outer panels were welded and would be strong enough so that very few added reinforcements, usually only at the hinge or lock areas, would be required. Dodge was an industry leader in steel body engineering and should have recognized that the new body construction method could have unlimited development problems and the potential for huge tooling bills. The new inner and outer method would have little positive benefit to Dodge, which already used steel bodies. Dodge, however, was a company of declining volume and big tooling bills would be a business disaster. It is not known how this body construction method was approved by Dodge management for the 1928 car line, but it was a very bad business decision.[24]

At that time, steel companies could not make the 5 foot by 9 foot sheet steel blanks that were needed for these big stampings. Budd, therefore, developed a way to weld two pieces of sheet steel together at their edges, hammer down the seam and grind it smooth to make the wide pieces of steel needed to stamp an entire body side in one piece. More development problems followed and Dodge had to pay Budd at least $10 million for tooling and to solve the problems of this new body construction method. This was a crushing blow to a company with declining volume.

This method was another industry first and is the way modern cars are made. The attraction was a very low piece cost, and in fact it was only slightly more than the cost of the rolled steel that the stamping was made from.

THE FRUITS OF THE CHRYSLER PLAN

The 1928 Dodge six cylinder cars were introduced in May of 1927 at $1,595 for the 4 door sedan. In January 1928, a lower priced six cylinder Dodge was introduced at $1,095 and all Dodge four cylinders were dropped. The Dodge entry sedan price position moved from a 1927 four at $895 to $1,095 for the 1928 six. Dodge dealers were in trouble.

In late 1927, Walter Chrysler hired the National Sales Manager from Dodge and he knew all the Dodge dealers in the country. His task was to add Chrysler's new DeSoto brand to sell with the Dodge brand at Dodge dealers. K. T. Keller, the first head of Dodge Division after the mid–1928 purchase, remembered that he sent the former Dodge sales manager to "unsell Dodge dealers on Dodge and then after the purchase we had to go out and sell them on Dodge again."[25]

In April of 1928, Walter Chrysler announced the new DeSoto Division of Chrysler Corporation. Its product was to be a new 6 with hydraulic brakes. The four door sedan would sell for $885, or $10 less than the former Dodge 4. It was a "six at the price of a four." This was a repeat of what his good

The 1929 DeSoto—Walter Chrysler developed this car as a twin of the later-to-be introduced Plymouth. This car had a six cylinder engine and the Plymouth had a four cylinder. The DeSoto was developed to take the market away from the failing Dodge Brothers Company. Dodge had the manufacturing plants and dealers that Walter Chrysler needed to grow in the market. The success of the DeSoto allowed Walter Chrysler to buy the Dodge Brothers Company. This car is on permanent display at the Walter P. Chrysler Museum in Auburn Hills, Michigan.

friend, Alfred Sloan, had done with Pontiac. By May, there were 500 dealers, 60 percent of them Dodge dealers, now signed as DeSoto dealers. That total grew to 1,500 by end of 1928.

To respond to the Chrysler attack with DeSoto, a new 140 Model Dodge 6 was introduced in April 27, 1928, at a price only $10 over the DeSoto, but the 140 Model was still without hydraulic brakes. The Dodge action was too little and too late.

At the end of 1926, Dodge had $21.5 million in cash and $15.8 in earned surplus. At the end of 1927, cash had dropped to $14.0 million and earned surplus had dropped to $3.7 million. Just four short months later, in April 1928, when the Dodge books were audited for the Chrysler purchase, cash had dropped $6.5 million more, to $8.5 million. Earned surplus had dropped $0.3 million to $3.5 million. In these four months, the balance sheet had dropped from $132 million to $127 million. Dodge was spinning out of control.[26]

Walter Chrysler's company had a balance sheet of $115 million and was almost the size of the rapidly failing Dodge. His plan succeeded beyond his dreams. The Dodge purchase that was impossible two years earlier was now "low hanging fruit." Walter Chrysler then reversed the nature of the Dodge purchase discussions. In his autobiography, *Life of an American Workman*, Chrysler told Clarence Dillon of Dillon and Reed that since he was bringing the offer to Walter Chrysler, he should "make it your best offer." Negotiations started in early May 1928. Within that month, the Dodge situation was exposed to everyone, as they were at risk of not having the cash to meet the Dodge payroll.

Chrysler bought Dodge for $170 million by assuming the Dodge debt and issuing new Chrysler stock. No cash. The experience with the Chalmers stockholder suit caused Chrysler to demand that 90 percent of all classes of Dodge stockholders must approve of the purchase. The Chalmers suit was a diversion by clever lawyers to make the companies in a merger (Maxwell) pay for a settlement. This had nothing to do with stockholder fairness because the lawyers would get most of the money. In the Chalmers case, it was difficult, but the future value of Chalmers stock could be proven as worthless because if it had value as the suing lawyers claimed, they and other bidders could bid at the bankruptcy sale to determine the future value of Chalmers earnings.

The Dodge situation was different. Dodge assets did have value, and future earnings of value and a stockholder suit could not be defended with a bankruptcy sale because it might result in a higher price or better terms than Walter Chrysler was paying for Dodge. If 90 percent of all classes of the Dodge stockholders agreed to the sale, then their interests must have been represented in the price and terms of the Dodge sale that Walter Chrysler was paying. The deadline for the approval of all classes of stock was July 1, 1928, and the entire deal was held up in trying to contact a stockholder in Paris. Finally, the 90 percent requirement was met and at the last second, the deal went through.

Wall Street had made several fortunes with Walter Chrysler. In 1920, he had taken the Willys Corporation from a $56 million debt to a new course that would lead to a $25 million profit in 1925. In late 1920, he took Maxwell Motors from a $26 million debt to a profit by 1922. The Maxwell stock went from $3 to $15 by 1925. The new Chrysler Corporation of 1925 showed a constant profit. The Maxwell stock that was converted to Chrysler stock at $15 in 1925 was split 4 ways by the late 1920s and was then worth $75 for each share. The new Chrysler Corporation stock issue to buy Dodge in 1928 was eagerly bought by Wall Street. The Walter Chrysler name was magic. On August 23, Chrysler Corporation issued 30,000 new shares at an asking price of $57.50. It was promptly sold out and by October 11, Chrysler was selling for $132.00. It was a very good deal for the former Dodge stockholders and for Dillon and Reed.

It was also a good deal for Chrysler Corporation, which acquired a forge, a foundry, stamping plant, a huge machine shop, and an assembly plant that could make 300,000 cars a year. The combined facilities of the new company were valued at $93 million, four times the $23 million of the prior Chrysler Corporation. In addition, there was the excellent Dodge sales force with 2,000 of the best dealers in the country. Chrysler Corporation was now one of the "Big Three."

Chrysler could not have introduced Plymouth without the added production capacity of Dodge. Even more important, a low priced car requires that parts be made "in house" to control costs and Dodge manufacturing provided that ability.

The Budd inner and outer panel construction was a watershed event that changed the economics of the industry. The steel bodies of that day were made at moderate tooling cost with simple panels and with hand applied local reinforcements at moderate piece cost. The new method used complete die lines and automatic welding to make a finished part as much as 600 parts per hour.

A high tooling bill of, say $10 million, was only $10 each if 1 million parts were made. The problem was that if only 100,000 were made, then the parts were $100 each. The moderate volume makers had a serious disadvantage relative to the high volume makers, and this was made much worse as volume dropped during the Depression.

By 1931, Chrysler adapted the new body methods with an innovative way of interchanging parts to support four brands with many parts used across the whole line of cars. Since Chrysler was in second place in sales for most of the 1930s, this was a good volume base on which to spread tooling cost. Ford adapted the new method in 1934 and G.M., because of Fisher Body's holdings in wood manufacturing, was last in 1937.

The independent makers that did not adopt the new methods had very high piece costs and cars they could not sell at a profit with the dropping prices of the '30s. The makers that did adopt the new methods also saw their volume drop and a very high tooling cost for each car, and again, little or no profit. Either way, the independent car makers had little chance to survive the price and volume drops of the Depression. Chrysler would no doubt have been among them without the Dodge purchase and the volume of the Plymouth cars. Chrysler Corporation not only survived the Depression, but prospered during it.

Plymouth: The Possible Dream

There was an industry get-together with Henry Ford and Walter Chrysler having a discussion in which Ford advised Chrysler, "Walter, you'll go broke trying to get into the low priced market. We and Chevrolet have the market sewed up, and as sure as you step in, we'll stop you." The date of this event is believed to be 1926 or 1927. Walter Chrysler had been head of Buick, head of all General Motors manufacturing, was running his own successful company, and knew as much as anyone about costs, profits and the importance of a volume car which would spread tooling and overhead costs. Fortunately, he kept his own counsel about Henry Ford's advice.

In 1926, Ford sales dropped to 1.1 million cars. This was a company that had sold 2 million cars each year in the recent past. The 20 hp Model T was no match for the heavy, closed car bodies that the pubic was demanding in the 1920s. In 1927, sales dropped to just under 400,000 and then, on May 25, 1927, Model T production stopped. The world was stunned. The car that everyone had grown to love was gone, and Ford did not have a replacement car planned. What an opportunity for a man like Walter Chrysler.

Like the Chevrolet-Pontiac, the DeSoto-Plymouth cars were identical by part number except for the engine. The two cars were made on the same assembly line, except that the DeSoto was a 1929 Model 6 sold by DeSoto and former Dodge dealers and the Plymouth was a 1928 Model 4 sold by the Chrysler dealers.

In one of the great public relations events in automotive history, the new Model A Ford was introduced on December 2, 1927. The car had not been properly developed, however, and had monumental production problems. Only 633,000 cars were made for the entire year, or less than one third of normal Ford production. The opportunity was there for Walter Chrysler to introduce a low priced car, but the Dodge purchase would not be finalized until July 30, 1928.

Walter Chrysler "seized the moment" and introduced the former Chrysler 52 as the new low priced "Chrysler Plymouth" on July 7, 1928, even though the Dodge purchase was not finalized. He did hedge the bet by pricing the 1928 Chrysler Plymouth at $725 for the 4 door sedan, or $5 over the $720 of the former Chrysler 52. The rest of the Chrysler line, without the Chrysler 52, had been introduced in June 1928. First year sales were

The First Plymouth—The Plymouth was a twin of the DeSoto except for engine, and both were made on the same assembly line. The DeSoto was a 1929 model and the Plymouth was a 1928 model sold by different dealers. The first Plymouth was called a Chrysler Plymouth and filled the market role of the 1927 Chrysler four cylinder car. The car was a promise of the future and was lowered in price each year until it was one of the "Low Priced Three." This car is on permanent display at the Walter P. Chrysler Museum in Auburn Hills, Michigan.

29,000 units. As shown below, Plymouth had many features that Chevrolet and Ford adapted later to their cars.

Table 10. Low Priced Car Comparison

	Plymouth 4	*Chevrolet 4*	*Ford 4*
Body	All Steel in 1930	All Steel in 1937	All Steel in 1932
Brake	Hydraulic in 1928	Hydraulic in 1936	Hydraulic in 1939
Axle	Hotchkiss in 1928	Hotchkiss in 1955	Hotchkiss in 1949
Piston	Aluminum in 1928	Iron until 1953	Aluminum in 1928
Engine Oil	Pressure 1928	Pressure 1935	Pressure 1932

The first year was a promise of what was to come. The Plymouth sedan price was not near the $585 of a Model A Ford sedan, but now that Dodge manufacturing could make parts, a new assembly plant was built for Plymouth. The 1929 Plymouth prices were dropped $30 to $695 for the four door sedan and the Chrysler part of the Chrysler Plymouth name was also dropped. The sedan prices for 1930 were dropped again by $70 to $625 and sales were in the 100,000 range. The 1930 Chevrolet was at the same price but the engine was a six. The 1930 Ford Model A sedan was $590. Neither car had hydraulic brakes. This price and the above mentioned features were close enough for Plymouth to be part of the low priced three market. This was a point that Walter Chrysler made in his famous "look at all three" advertisements of that time.

Chevrolet had gone to a six cylinder engine in 1929 and Plymouth responded in 1931 with "Floating Power." It was called the smoothness of an eight with the economy of a four. It was a stopgap measure until a new Plymouth six could be tooled and it started production on November 6, 1932. Plymouth was now firmly in third place in industry sales and grew from 250,000 units per year in 1933 to 458,000 units in 1936. The Plymouth success pushed Chrysler Corporation to second place in sales in 1933 and again in 1936. This second place position in the industry continued until 1950.

Dodge introduced its new inner and outer panel method of steel body construction in 1928. It was low in piece cost but had high tooling bills. To be successful, the tooling cost had to be shared by as many cars as possible. Chrysler Corporation developed an innovative way to use major body parts across all four brands. The details varied each year, but typically, all two-door bodies were the same and used across Plymouth through Chrysler. Four-door bodies were sometimes used across all brands, or sometimes only the front half of the body was shared and rear doors, roof, and rear quarters were different on the senior cars. Front end sheet metal was unique to each brand because of wheelbase differences. Grille openings, grilles, tail lamps, instrument panels and interiors were unique to each brand. In any case, well over half the body stampings were used across all the car lines and this spread the tooling cost on about 900,000 units each year. This was more volume than Ford because Chrysler was in second place in sales.

Walter Chrysler's concept of balancing customer features with production cost savings had reached a peak of success. The Plymouth plant in Detroit was the focus of production efficiency. Most car plants at that time had a production line speed of 55 to 60 cars per hour. Both Chevrolet and Ford used several assembly plants, with a single assembly line running at 60 cars per hour, at different locations around the country to build the volume of cars that they needed. Plymouth based production at the plant in Detroit, but it had two assembly lines at a speed of 90 cars per hour. Three cars per minute was the Plymouth assembly rate. This might seem like a breakneck speed, but the number of operations to assemble a car is the

THE PLYMOUTH ASSEMBLY PLANT—The purchase of Dodge Brothers Company in 1928 provided the manufacturing base for making Plymouth brand a true low-priced competitor. In 1929, this huge new plant was built near the Dodge plant to make Plymouth cars. Other low priced cars were made in assembly plants around the country at about 60 cars per hour. Walter Chrysler used his production experience to have cars made at 90 cars per hour on two assembly lines. Three cars per minute would be completed at this plant at the corner of Mt. Elliot Avenue and Lynch Road in Detroit. The building is no longer in use as an assembly plant and the huge space is divided among several companies. This photograph was taken facing south along Mt. Elliot Avenue.

same and if the car is moving at half again the speed at each work station, then half again as many work stations are needed. The assembly line is half again as long. The Plymouth final line was over a half mile long. The direct labor to assemble a Plymouth was about the same as that of any other car, but there were major savings in production support and overhead costs. The two assembly line, 90 cars per hour, Plymouth system continued until 1959, when cars became so complex that to continue to lengthen the assembly line was no longer practical.

As far as profitability is concerned, Plymouth was at an industry high. In a December 1940 *Fortune* article, "Of Arms and Automobiles," the following profits were reported:

Table 11. Plymouth-Chevrolet Profit Comparison

		Price	Units/Year	Unit Profit
Plymouth	1934	$491	315,000	$23
	1935	453	385,000	46
	1936	456	459.000	66
	1937	503	458,000	49
Chevrolet	1934	469	607,000	26
	1935	459	795,000	36
	1936	464	995,000	38
	1937	502	905,000	29

For these four years, Plymouth made an average of $46 profit per car compared to Chevrolet at $32.[27] Both Chrysler Corporation and General Motors were public corporations with "generally accepted accounting practices." Ford was not; it was a private company wholly owned by Henry Ford.

The *Fortune* article shows that there is more than one way to run an automobile company, and Walter Chrysler was very successful with his method based on manufacturing cost control. Clearly, Henry Ford's advice to Walter Chrysler in the 1920s underestimated Walter Chrysler's ability.

In 1940, the last year of Walter Chrysler's life, Chrysler Corporation was marked as the fulfillment of his philosophy, in that manufacturing cost reductions should offset the cost of customer features. The "Amazing Plymouth" was the advertising campaign for the car that led Chrysler Corporation out of the Depression. The 1940 Plymouth and the 1940 Chevrolet are compared below.

- Engine—Plymouth had an aluminum pistoned, full oil pressured, high speed engine that was a favorite of taxi drivers. Chevrolet did not adopt these features until 1953.
- Body—In 1940, both Chevrolet and Plymouth had all steel bodies. Plymouth had had them since 1928; Chevrolet did not follow until 1937.
- Brakes—Plymouth was introduced with hydraulic brakes in 1928. Chevrolet followed in 1936.
- Suspension—Plymouth introduced an independent suspension in 1933. Chevrolet introduced it on only the most expensive models in 1935 and that was still true in 1940.
- Frame—Plymouth had an all-welded box frame. Chevrolet had an open channel riveted frame.
- Rear axle—Plymouth had a floating Hotchkiss type in 1928. Chevrolet did not adopt this feature until 1955.

This was the Walter Chrysler product approach of giving the customer features as standard equipment at an $805 price for the Plymouth Deluxe 4 door sedan. This was compared to the features of the Chevrolet four door Sport Sedan at $802. Both models were the high volume four door sedans of 1940. The profitability of the Plymouth was as good as or better than that of the Chevrolet.

The Depression: A Test of Walter Chrysler's Company

The Depression hit hard at every part of American society. Unemployment was at 25 percent as the official number, but everyday experience revealed that it was much higher. Economic output dropped to 25 percent of the 1929 level. The stock market dropped at the end of 1929, continued falling in 1930, and dropped 42 percent in 1931–32. This was followed by a further drop of 8 percent in 1933. There was no end.

It is difficult to understand the emotion of the Depression, but if for some reason a customer delayed buying a suit or furniture, he would discover that in a month the price would drop. Another month and the price would drop further. Unlike today when you buy now before the price goes up, during the Depression, you waited for the price to go down, and it did. This seemingly prudent family money management practice was called "underconsumption" by economists. The "think tanks" of the day felt that the very success of the free enterprise system was called into question. If customers could wait and demand lower prices, perhaps under cost, then these same people as wage earners could not earn the wages to pay for what they needed to live on.

A solution to the wage side of the problem could be a massive government employment program. That method works but soon leads to inflation and the loss of the value of money and is a long term economic disaster. A second way to employ large numbers of workers is in major projects funded by revenue bonds. Major examples were such projects as the Hoover Dam, funded by future revenue from the sale of electricity. Another example would be parkways and limited access toll roads to be funded by future toll revenues.[28]

Walter Chrysler lived on Long Island and was in the middle of the Hutchinson Parkway, Long Island Parkway, Merritt Parkway and the Pennsylvania Turnpike discussions while they were in the very early development stages. The Chrysler car was already developed for continuous driving and had suitable brakes, but the handling was no better than other cars of the day. In a March 11, 1928, newspaper interview, Chrysler talked of roads as tunnels under New York so that constant high speed driving could take the driver directly to his office in the center of the city. He went on to describe express highways between major cities. The car of the future had to be designed for these kinds of new roads.[29]

A second part of the solution to under-consumption was the change in product design called streamlining. It started in the '20s when "tried and true" was replaced by "up to date." Packages were replaced by those that were streamlined, advertising was streamlined and appliances were covered by a new exterior and streamlined. Raymond Loewy streamlined the Sears refrigerator and sales jumped from 15,000 to 275,000 in five years. The idea developed that the public had to be shaken out of the mode of "under-consumption" and start to spend money to restart the economy. Streamlining was a way to do it.[30]

The first impact of the Depression on the automobile industry was that the medium priced car market dropped. Buick went from 190,000 units in 1929 to 121,000 in 1930, Oldsmobile from 101,000 to 50,000, and Pontiac from 211,000 to 86,000. DeSoto dropped from 60,000 in 1929 to 35,000 in 1930, Dodge dealers dropped from 150,000 to 115,000 in 1930, and Chrysler dealers that did not have a Plymouth to sell saw the same market drop. Walter Chrysler moved quickly on March 7, 1930 with direct action and had all dealers add the Plymouth brand. There were now 10,000 dealers with the Plymouth brand to sell.

Even with the expanded Plymouth dealers, Chrysler Corporation sales dropped from 450,000 units in 1929 to 267,000 in 1930. The slide stayed at 272,000 in 1931 and then dropped to 222,000 units in 1932. At this rate of sales loss, the last car would be sold in 1936 and Chrysler Corporation would be out of business.

Net profits dropped from $21.9 million in 1929 to $269,000 in 1930. General and Administrative expense (G & A) was slashed from $35 million in 1929 to $23.7 million in 1930, a 31.4 percent drop, to help retain profitability. Dollar sales were $207 million in 1930 and only $183 million in 1931, but continued cost control (G & A) increased net profit from $269,000 in 1930 to $1.5 million in 1931.

Walter Chrysler had not lost his zeal for cost control. At a meeting with his vice presidents, he announced a new wave of layoffs and wanted their recommendations. The head of sales said that rather than layoffs, he should add salesmen to sell more cars. The head of manufacturing said he should add people to improve quality, which would improve sales. The head of engineering wanted to add engineers to add features to improve sales. The head of finance wanted to add cost control people to improve profitability. They had been through layoffs, budget cuts and pay cuts and Chrysler let them vent their frustration. He then asked for the payroll ledger. It was in alphabetical order and he counted down the pages equivalent to the percentage of the needed layoff goal, ripped them off and dropped them in a waste basket. He then slid the remainder of the book to the middle of the table and said, "My method will work but if there are other ideas, we will meet the following day." There were many ideas about the layoff the next day.

The 1929 Chevrolet set the standard for the low priced market with the six cylinder engine. Plymouth still had a version of the Maxwell 4. The "Floating Power" engine mounting system was added in 1931 but it was only a stop-gap measure until a Plymouth 6 could be introduced in 1932. The tooling for that six caused Chrysler Corporation to show a loss of $11.2 million in 1932. Henry Ford also introduced a new engine in 1932, a V8. The following chart shows the financial impact on both companies. Note that the Ford data has the same problems as discussed earlier.

Table 12. Chrysler-Ford Net Profit Comparison—1932–1937

	Chrysler Corporation	Ford Motor Co. w/Lincoln
1932	($11,254,000)	($80,353,600)
1933	$12,129,000	($12,796,900)
1934	$49,535,000	$17,929,500
1935	$34,976,000	$9,250,600
1936	$62,111,000	$19,689,500
1937	$50,729,000	$2,573,800
Total	$198,226,000	($43,707,100)

The dual dealership arrangement and the new six allowed Plymouth to greatly increase sales and Chrysler Corporation matched the 1929 sales in 1933. It should not be surprising that Walter Chrysler's company, with tight cost control, topped the $22.0 million net profit of 1929 with an unbelievable $49.5 million in net profit in 1934. Alfred Sloan's G.M. did not match the 1929 unit sales until 1936 and the 1929 $248.3 million in net profit until 1947. Henry Ford never matched the 1929 sales of 1.3 million units nor the $84 million in net income during his lifetime.

The Airflow: A Century of Progress in a Decade

There is no doubt that the new parkways and toll roads that were being planned and built during the 1930s would have caused a major redesign of automobiles, but the Chrysler Airflow of 1934 was a complete solution to improving handling and offered aerodynamics in one package.[31] The Airflow program started in 1928 as a study into automotive streamlining and aerodynamics with the construction of a wind tunnel at Chrysler Engineering. In the course of testing several models, one of the conventional models that looked like a current production car of the day was tested in the tunnel going backwards. To everyone's surprise, the aerodynamic drag dropped by 30 percent from that of going forward. One of the engineers, while looking out of the window at the traffic said, "look at all those cars going the wrong way."[32]

THE 1934 AIRFLOW was to be a 10 year celebration of the success of Chrysler Corporation. The car was revolutionary but the appearance was a problem for customers. Production problems were endless and competition soon called it a lemon. The "Century of Progress in a Decade" was soon forgotten in a sea of production, appearance and sales problems. This car is on permanent display at the Walter P. Chrysler Museum in Auburn Hills, Michigan.

The development of the Airflow followed logic regardless of the design direction. Aerodynamic tests showed that the widest part of the car should be just ahead of the middle of the car, and that is where the front seat was placed. This brought the rear seat forward to be ahead of the rear axle. The next step was to move the engine forward to be over the front axle rather than behind it, as was usual practice.[33]

The major parts were fixed on an elevation drawing and an ellipse was drawn over the car from bumper to bumper. The ellipse was notched for a windshield in front of the driver and the shape was arched down to the rear bumper. The result was a small round hood and a large round body. The space behind the rear seat that was vacated when the seat moved forward became a trunk with access from the interior by pivoting the rear seat back.

The next step in this engineering "tour de force" was to make the body construction method that of a semi-unit body. Manufacturing engineers did not know how to assemble the car without a light frame to carry the chassis parts on the assembly line. This light frame was bolted to a full sized body, with an internal channel structure that went from bumper to bumper. The result was a very strong combination.

A prototype was built but not tested in the Detroit area. It was shipped 200 miles away to a rural farm. When the car was tested, the result was astonishing. Moving the engine and weight forward resulted in an unbelievable improvement in handling. Cars of the day had most of their weight on the rear wheels and when the car was steered, the heavy rear tended to swing wide of the front, as the car wanted to turn end for end and travel heavy end first. The new car had almost equal front to rear weight distribution and the car tracked exactly where it was steered. The then-current handling problem of all cars for the toll roads of the future was solved.[34]

The next revelation of the Airflow prototype was the ride. Everyone knew that ride improved with a longer wheelbase. The Airflow, with equal and soft springs both front and rear, did not pitch over a bump but was flat as it bounced straight up. Further development showed that if the front springs were slightly softer than the rear, then at most car speeds the impact from the front axle would be delayed by the softer front springs to reach the car body at the same time as the rear axle bump and the car would rise in a flat motion. Wheelbase was no longer as important in car ride improvement. When the springs were balanced to the new weight distribution, the improvement in ride was spectacular and the modern automobile was born in full form. The car felt comfortable. All cars of the day had a ride frequency of about 120 cycles per minute. The new Airflow with the softer springs and equal weight distribution had a ride frequency of 90 cycles per minute, much closer to a natural gait of a person while walking. The car ride felt "right."

The car was developed during the depths of the Depression and it is to Walter Chrysler's credit that no matter how bad things got, that the Airflow project was still funded. Walter Chrysler did not, to use an old fashioned expression, "eat the seed corn."

Walter Chrysler wanted to introduce the Airflow in 1933 but the car was so different in manufacturing methods, it was not possible. The introduction was moved to 1934 but development problems persisted. That was the tenth anniversary of the first Chrysler car and in 1933, Chrysler had outsold Ford to be in second place in the industry. There was much to celebrate and the Airflow was introduced with the slogan "A Century of Progress in a Decade" to take the theme of the 1934 Chicago Century of Progress Fair. Chrysler Brand continued conventional cars but called them "Airstreams"; however, DeSoto committed the entire 1934 line of cars to be Airflows.

Anyone who drove the car realized that this was the car of the future. The first reaction to the style varied from dislike to not knowing how to react to the car. The car itself was hard to take, but the main problem was the small, round hood. The public had been used to seeing cars with a long hood and this car apparently had no hood at all.

It was shown to the public in January of 1934 and was a sensation. Never ending production problems meant that there were few cars in dealers' hands. Spring turned into summer but still no cars in dealers' hands. It was October before dealers had a reasonable number of cars. Ten months had passed, and the fate of the Airflow was sealed.

SEMI-UNIT BODY

The all-steel bodies of the day were very strong but structurally they just sat as a lump on the heavy steel frame, which provided all the strength of the car. Engineers at the time were experimenting with ways to integrate the body strength with the overall car and the Airflow was an early attempt. Carl Breer, in his notes, said that the Airflow semi-unit body was over one inch lower to the ground and 150 pounds lighter than a frame and body car would have been.

The Airflow structure flowed along the lower body as a frame would have. It also went from the front bumper area where the front springs were attached up to the base of the windshield and then over the roof to the rear bumper where the end of the rear spring was. This resulted in a body that was 16 or 17 feet long. Car bodies up to that time were, from the cowl back to the rear bumper area, only about 10 feet long.

The plants where the car was to be built were designed for another era and had 17 or 18 foot centers on the floor support posts that were 2 and one-half feet in diameter. The space was fine for the 10 foot conventional bodies of the day, but a 17 foot Airflow body could not be built or moved in such a small space. The Airflow body was split—one third was the engine compartment up to the center of the front door and two thirds was the rear half of the front door opening to the rear bumper. This was done in order to have body parts that were small enough be made in the plant. The result was a fixturing nightmare because the front door was always of a fixed size and shape but the opening that it was to fit into varied in size and shape depending on how well the front or rear halves of the body fit together. This is the same problem that has existed in more current times. In 1960, Chrysler Corporation made a major product change to unit body cars, but the plants that were to make the new cars were much the same as the plants that made the Airflow in 1934. The new 1960 unit body cars had to be split with the front length made as a stub frame. The body was of unit construction but the length could only be about 10 feet long and fit into the assembly plants. A front stub frame would carry the front suspension and engine and it was mounted to the body at the cowl to front seat area.

Body fixtures in the automotive industry were designed to pull light sheet metal parts to shape to be welded. The Airflow had medium gauge channel parts (as structure) under the sheet metal and they tended to pull the fixtures to the incorrect shape of the channel parts, not to the desired shape of the body. A new rapid welding method had to be invented to get the parts to the correct shape. At one point there were 2,000 Airflows with serious fit problems at the plant that could not be shipped to dealers. The solution to the fixturing problem was to add body solder to achieve the required shape. The amount of solder needed was so great that the lighter weight of the semi-unit body construction claimed by Carl Breer in his notes proved illusory. The actual car was hundreds of pounds overweight. DeSoto sedans in 1933 and 1937 were about the same size as the Airflow sedans that were used by DeSoto in 1934 to 1936, but the conventional sedans weighed about 3,000 pounds and the Airflows weighed about 3,300 pounds. DeSoto handled the added Airflow weight by increasing the 1933 engine from 217 c.i.d. to 241 c.i.d. with the 1934 Airflow. Chrysler increased the eight cylinder engine from 273 c.i.d. in 1933 to 299 c.i.d. when used on the 1934 Airflow. Larger engines that used more fuel were not what the market was asking for in the middle of the Depression. DeSoto Airflows were about $200 more than the 1933 cars that they replaced. Chrysler Airstreams were about $400 more than the 1933 cars that they replaced. These prices were another sales problem in the middle of the Depression.

Production problems were endless and most involved the new semi-unit body. Even usual items were a problem. The interior had chrome tubing that framed seats, but the supplier could not make the tubing with a good enough surface to be chrome plated.

The appearance of the car may have prevented it from being a success, but the 10 month delay gave the competition an opportunity to label the car a failure and it soon was. The combination of appearance, increased weight and engine size, increased price, and lack of cars for people to buy doomed the car for failure.

The competition said that if the car cannot be made for 10 months, it must be a lemon. The structure went over the engine compartment and a side opening hood could not be used; the hood must be front opening. Competition questioned how adjustments on the side of the engine were made. Chrysler showed how easy it was by taking off the front wheel and removing a panel. This explanation only confirmed to mechanics and future owners that they wanted nothing to do with such a complex process to make a simple engine adjustment. The country had frame straightening experts in almost every community. The semi-unit body required new skills. Chrysler published books of several hundred pages in length to show how to straighten the semi-unit body after an accident. Again, the reaction was that new body construction was a mess to fix and it would be expensive to own.

The car itself was so impressive in handling and ride that it made every other car obsolete. General Motors was caught flat-footed by the Airflow; they had no idea such a car was possible, much less that it could be on the

FRONT DOOR DETAIL—The Airflow was built with a semi-unit method of construction which resulted in a body length of about 17 feet. The plant where the car was built was designed for conventional bodies of about 10 feet in length. To make the Airflow fit the plant where it was made, the car was assembled in a front third and a rear two thirds. The two parts were welded in a fixture above and below the front door and this was the cause of monumental problems. This car is on permanent display at the Walter P. Chrysler Museum in Auburn Hills, Michigan.

road. Their response, however, was limited by the capital investment that Fisher Body had in wood and steel covered composite bodies. They did get the steel companies to roll wide sheet metal so the entire roof of the car could be made as one stamping. This was a major improvement over the way that Dodge edge-welded steel panels together in 1928. In 1935, G.M. called the new roof design "turret top" and boasted of its strength. They did not say that the lower body was still wood and steel composite and very weak. It was not until 1937 that G.M. adopted the Airflow concepts. Ford had the sincerest form of flattery. Henry Ford or the Ford Motor Company noticed something that Walter Chrysler or ZSB should have questioned in 1932 as the Airflow was being developed. The Airflow handling and ride had nothing to do with semi-unit body construction, yet the semi-unit body was to be the cause of most of the problems.

The 1935 Ford was of Airflow concept with a frame and body con-

ROOF SURFACE—The two roof joints over the front doors were a particular problem to make as a smooth surface. The Airflow was always overweight because making the body surface correct at the many body joints required lead body solder. This Airflow car is on permanent display at the Walter P. Chrysler Museum in Auburn Hills, Michigan.

struction. The rear seat was moved forward of the rear axle, the front seat was wide enough for three people, and the V8 engine was moved forward 8.5 inches. The weight distribution was similar to that of the Airflow and the springs were softened, although not to the level of the Airflow. The hood opened to the side for engine adjustments, and there was a frame that could be straightened after an accident. Most important of all, there was a hood that looked like all other cars. The 1935 Ford was so successful that Ford outsold Chevrolet for the year.

Walter Chrysler, Fred Zeder or Owen Skelton did ask some questions at Chrysler Corporation, because the weight distribution of all Chrysler Corporation cars jumped from only 46.5 percent on the front tires to 51 percent between 1934 and 1935. Weight distribution is the key to Airflow handling and ride. There is no written record of these events by the above named principal decision makers. The only written record is Carl Breer's

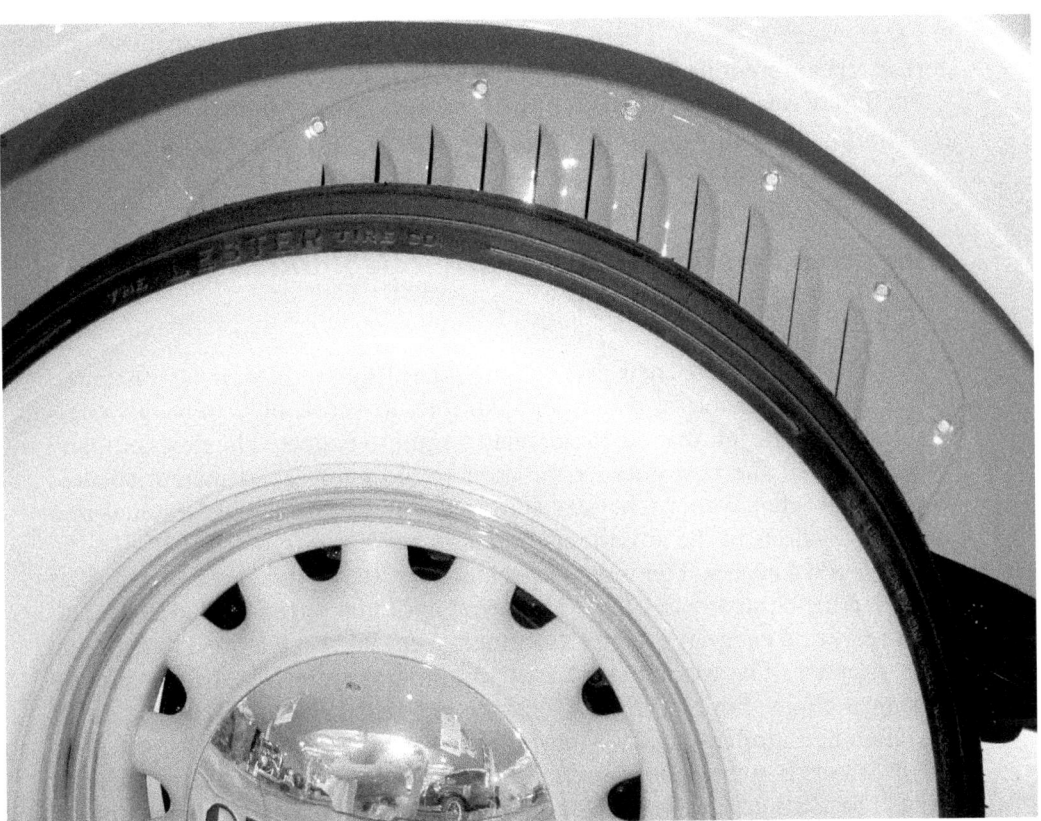

ENGINE COMPARTMENT SIDE HATCH—The Airflow structure started at the front bumper and flowed upward to the cowl at the base of the windshield. A side opening hood was out of the question and a front opening hood was required. When potential customers asked how simple engine adjustments were made to the side of the engine, they were told to remove this hatch. It was not quite that simple because the front tire had to be removed first and then the hatch removed from the wheel side. Customers would have nothing to do with this complex process for a simple task and it became another sales problem. This car is on permanent display at the Walter P. Chrysler Museum in Auburn Hills, Michigan.

notes, and he was bitter that the wide windshield of the Airflow (requiring a semi-unit body at that time) and aerodynamic shapes of the Airflow were softened when used by the main line of cars made by Chrysler Corporation. He was particularly bitter with manufacturing in not delivering cars at the start of 1934. He called it "too little, too late" as if he had nothing to do with the semi-unit body decision. However it happened, all Chrysler cars were made with the Airflow concepts in 1935.

There were 25,000 Airflows made in 1934, but only 11,000 were sold that year, 14,000 in 1935, 11,000 in 1936 and 5,000 in 1937. There were 2.8 million cars sold by Chrysler Corporation in these four years but only 55,000 of them were Airflows. There is no question it was the largest financial failure in the automobile business until the $250 million Edsel failure in the late '50s. There was never an accounting of the Airflow cost within Chrysler Corporation. The Airflow legacy lived on because by the late '30s, every car was made to the Airflow concept except for the semi-unit body.

Chrysler Firsts: The Company Lifeblood Under Walter Chrysler

Up until the 1920s, new cars were an adventure for the new car customer. They were unreliable and not very durable; in short, they were not engineered to do the job that customers had a right to expect. The first company that delivered the customer expectation would enjoy good market success and that is what Walter Chrysler and ZSB set out to do. This resulted in a number of firsts in the automobile industry.

The 1924 engine. The most important Chrysler first was the engine that founded the company in 1924. Most companies that were founded in the late teen years and twenties used the Continental engine that was made by an outside supplier. The tooling cost for an engine was so high that there was no practical choice but to use the Continental engine. Even Durant had to do so when he founded Durant Motors, although he had access to capital from Wall Street. It was a good, serviceable engine, but undistinguished in any way. The ZSB engine was breakthrough and was superior to any engine on the market. G.M. and Ford had good engines and the independents, Hudson Nash, Willys, Studebaker and Packard, had good engines, but any new car customer could not ignore the new Chrysler engine that was better than any of them.

Hydraulic Brakes—1924. Hydraulic brakes were not a Chrysler first; they had been used on the Duesenberg. It was Chrysler, however, that turned a concept by Lockheed into a practical design.

Mechanical brakes had been around since the beginning of the industry. Mechanical links, in some way, would work levers to apply the brakes. The problem was that the force at each wheel was never the same and when the brakes were applied, the car would pull right or left. It was foolish to apply the brakes without a firm grip on the steering wheel. If the rear wheel brakes applied differently, the car would pull one way or the other. If the front brakes applied differently, the steering wheel could be snapped out of the driver's hands as the car headed off the road. Bad as it was most of the time, it was impossible on an icy road. The very best mechanical system could be adjusted, with great care, so that the linkage travel at all wheels would be exactly the same. Because the distance to each of the wheels was different, the friction was different and therefore the force was different at each wheel. Mechanical brakes could not deliver the same brake force to all four wheels. Changes in temperature, humidity, dirt buildup and other problems would make even the best mechanical system perform differently each day or each month, usually to the surprise of the driver.

Hydraulic brakes use the principle that the pressure in a liquid is the same in all directions. It does not make any difference if the liquid is shaped like a bucket or long tubes in several directions. A pressure applied at one point in the liquid (the master cylinder) will be the same at all other points (the wheel cylinders). The concept was patented by the Lockheed Company and Walter Chrysler decided to use it on the new 1924 Chrysler. ZSB started to develop the design and found that it was an unproven concept that was not ready for production. The fluid was not worked out and would freeze in the winter and, in the long term would attack the seals and leak. A new concept had to be invented for both the fluid and the seal material. A reliable seal for the tubes had to be invented. The Chrysler work was so important that Lockheed let Chrysler use the brake system without a fee if Lockheed could use the Chrysler redesign as they sold the brake system to other customers.

Replaceable element oil filter—1924. Oil filters were widely used as an aftermarket product but ZSB wanted something that was easy to change and developed a replaceable version. They also required an air cleaner on their new engine and a temperature gauge on the instrument panel. These were not Chrysler firsts, but did show a concern that the new engine would be equipped for long term durability.

Enclosed rubber engine mounting—1926. Most engines were rigidly mounted to the frame and, in fact, were sometimes a major strength element in the early cars. All sounds and vibrations of the engine were transferred to the driver. ZSB had a research project that showed that a car was much quieter if the engine was isolated from the frame. They expanded on an earlier development by Nash Motors to bond rubber to steel. The result was a very successful system for mounting an engine in a car.

Full range crankshaft impulse neutralizer—1928. The first Chrysler was known for the smooth way the flow of power was applied. ZSB continued their research into the subject and developed a vibration damper to further the feeling of a smooth flow of power. All cars of today have crankshaft vibration dampers.

Bonderite paint process—1929. Along with the revolution of the paint process came the need to have a low cost way to prepare the metal for the Duco paint. The Bonderite process would remove the oil that was on the steel as a required part of the stamping process. The labor required to prepare a car body for paint was greatly reduced.

Downdraft carburetors—1929. Cars of the day used an updraft carburetor. They tended to feed the middle cylinders but starve the end cylinders. When added fuel was needed to accelerate the car, most of it would fall to the ground before the engine speed would pick up so the air would carry more fuel up to the engine. A downdraft carburetor reversed the process.

More fuel could be dumped into the engine for an immediate engine response and acceleration. This was the system used on every car made until recent times, when the industry changed to a fuel injection system.

Fully automatic spark control, centrifugal and vacuum—1931. Centrifugal spark control had been developed as a way to automatically advance the ignition spark as the engine ran faster. The problem was that at car speeds, the engine was slow to accelerate because the spark would not advance to get more power until the engine speed increased. When the throttle opened, the engine vacuum would drop and that could advance the spark, but the amount of advance could cause the engine to "knock" and lose power. ZSB developed a way to have the amount of spark depend on both speed and engine vacuum to accurately meet the needs of the engine. The performance results were excellent with the already introduced downdraft carburetors in combination with the new spark advance system. It was not long before every car made used the Chrysler-developed system.

"Floating Power" engine mounting system—1931. This was one of the great tactical events of the market of the early '30s. The 1929 Chevrolet 6, "a six at the price of a four," was a watershed event in the low priced market. It caught Henry Ford flat-footed with his new 1928 Model A as an obsolete design. Walter Chrysler recognized the seriousness of the problem and knew what to do, but had to design and tool a new six cylinder engine to have the volume needed to replace four cylinder production capacity. Chrysler could not tool a new six cylinder engine until 1932.

ZSB had been involved with development work in engine mount systems that would reduce noise and vibration. The system that was developed by Owen Skelton would allow the engine to vibrate around its center of gravity and not transmit vibration to the car frame and therefore to the driver. It did not eliminate vibration, just kept it from the driver. The advertising line was "the smoothness of an eight with the economy of a four." This was a master stroke in confusing the customer. What the customer really wanted was a six cylinder engine, but Plymouth did not have one for sale.

The car went into production on May 1, 1931, and Walter Chrysler was so proud of it that he took an early production car along with him to a scheduled meeting with Henry Ford. It was a stroke of bravado to bring Zeder, Skelton and Breer and meet with Henry Ford, Edsel Ford and Charles Sorenson for lunch at the Ford Headquarters. The lunch went very well and Chrysler showed Ford the new "Floating Power" Plymouth. He left the car with the Fords and the Chrysler group took a taxi back to their offices.

The luncheon meeting took place on July 10, 1931, and after the Chrysler group left, Sorenson expressed interest in the new engine mounting system, but Henry Ford said he had no interest and that was the end of any development by FMC. The most galling part of the Chrysler visit was that the new engine mount system was applied to an engine that entered production in 1915 as a Maxwell and was made in a 1909 building (Building 108 at the

FLOATING POWER—Chevrolet introduced a six cylinder to the low priced market in 1929 and it became the standard of the market. Chrysler would need two years to tool a six to respond to the Chevrolet challenge. "Floating Power" on a four cylinder engine was a stopgap measure for 1931. The front of the engine was mounted just below the fan and water pump. The engine was free to roll around its own center and reduce the vibration transferred to the car. While the market wanted a six, Plymouth four with "Floating Power" increased sales until a six was available in 1932. This engine is on permanent display at the Walter P. Chrysler Museum in Auburn Hills, Michigan.

Chrysler Highland Park Plant). The now-obsolete Ford Model A engine was new three years earlier in 1928.

The Chrysler visitors did not know that the pressure was mounting on Henry Ford to do something about the Chevrolet 6. His Model A did well in 1930, but for 1931 the Chevrolet 6 was starting to outsell the four cylinder Ford Model A. Further, his old employee, William Knudsen at Chevrolet, and Alfred Sloan at G.M. had dropped the Chevrolet 6 price for 1931, but Ford had to maintain the Model A four cylinder prices because of costs. The old Ford market plan of dropping prices did not work anymore. Worse, the new Plymouth with "Floating Power" that Walter Chrysler had brought to

Henry Ford on that July day was easily as good looking as the new 1932 Ford Model B that would to enter production in only four more months.

Roller bearing universal joints—1932. Many cars used a flexing tire carcass as a universal joint on the propeller shaft to the rear axle as a low cost method of delivering power to the rear axle. The "cross type" steel design worked well but was costly. Chrysler Engineering developed a roller bearing universal joint design that worked as well as the cross type but cost less. The Chrysler design was later used by all manufacturers.

Tungsten alloy exhaust valves—1932. The Chrysler engines were excellent for durability and valve life. But where added life was needed, the simple addition of high alloy exhaust valves was all that was required to give the customer exceptional durability.

All helical geared transmission—1933. Transmissions of the day used spur gears, particularly on first and reverse. The spur gears made a tick sound as each gear tooth engaged and because there were so many gear teeth, the result was a "loud whine." Helical gears have part of a tooth engaged at all times with matching teeth that slid by each other with only a little sound. All helical geared transmissions were quiet.

Scientific weight distribution—1934. This was the "Airflow" and was, by any measure, a breakthrough concept that changed every car that has been made since 1934.

Automatic overdrive—1934. This was used on the Imperial Airflow cars and was a way that the car would shift into a fourth gear at highway speeds. It also allowed the car "free wheel" on coasting and that greatly improved the fuel economy. It also made the car difficult to stop because there was no engine braking. It was dropped when several states outlawed the feature.

One piece curved windshield—1934. The development of the Airflow showed that a rounded windshield would greatly reduce wind drag. Chrysler tried to develop the needed curved glass but the shape was difficult to achieve and to match to the curve of the windshield opening. When first tried in production, every windshield would break as the car was being built. Most Airflow cars were retooled to use flat windshields and the curved windshield was used only on the Imperial. Installation of the curved windshield was still difficult in production, even at low Imperial volume.

Amola steel (high strength carbon molybdenum steel)—1934. The use of high strength steel in the structural development of the Airflow was an industry first.

Body providing most of the structural strength—1934. The Airflow "semi-unit" body construction was a step along the way to the first true unit body of an American car, the 1940 Nash. A wooden body had no strength and automotive engineers had no choice but to have the body sit on a frame that provided all the strength. With the development of all-steel bodies, primarily by Dodge Division, engineers started to look at having the body carry a portion of the needed strength of the car, thereby reducing the weight of the car. The

Europeans were first to explore this possibility because of the high European fuel prices and the need of better fuel economy that would result from a lighter weight.

The Airflow used a full length light frame that bolted to the bottom of the full length body. Carl Breer, in his notes, said that the Airflow was 150 pounds lighter as a result of its semi-unit construction. That may have been the engineering goal, but the actual car required so much body solder to repair the poor body fits that the production cars were at least 150 pounds over what a conventional car would have weighed.

The Airflow body design was not copied by any other manufacturer. Everyone agreed the 1936 Lincoln Zephyr unit body design had a construction superior to that of the Airflow.

Fully isolated rubber body mounts—1937. Chrysler Engineering continued their research into better noise isolation, and the introduction of rubber body mounts were the next step.

Safety padded rear seat backs—1937. Chrysler did some impact testing in the '30s and one of the simple things that could be done with a major benefit to the customer would be to pad the back of the front seat to make it safer in case of an accident.

Rubber isolated steering gear—1937. This was one more step in the Chrysler Engineering project to make Chrysler cars quieter than competitive cars.

Superfinish—1938. This was a significant improvement in machining quality and precision manufacturing. It made the Chrysler engine and machined parts have a better fit and lower friction than more conventional machining methods.

Fluid coupling—1938. The development of a fluid coupling was an essential step toward a fully automatic transmission. When the car stopped, the engine had to be separated from the drive wheels so the engine could continue to run. This was done with a manual clutch that had to be pushed down. Chrysler Engineers learned that they could use a fluid coupling that would do the same thing without any movement by the driver. The coupling would pump very little fluid at 500 rpm or idle speed, and the car could sit still with the engine running. When the engine was accelerated, the fluid coupling would pump enough fluid so that the car would accelerate smoothly. Throughout the 1940s every automatic transmission used a form of a fluid coupling.

Power convertible top—1939. Plymouth developed a power top for the convertible for 1939. Almost every convertible since that date has had a power top as either standard or optional equipment.

Two leading shoe front brakes—1940. Engineers noticed the conventional hydraulic brake system would show wear on the front shoes of the two-shoe wheel brakes. The reason was that the front shoe would wrap into the forward spinning motion of the brake drum. The rear shoe would be resisted by the spinning drum and would be far less effective than the front shoe. A standard brake system would have four leading shoes and four trailing shoes whether the car was going forward or backward. Chrysler engineers developed a brake system in which the front wheel brake had separate top and bottom wheel cylinders so that both front brake shoes were leading shoes. The result was that there were six leading shoes to stop the car when driving forward and two leading shoes when driving backward. Since most driving was in a forward direction, the brake wear was on six leading shoes rather than four, as in a conventional system. The brake system was more effective in stopping the car going forward. All customers had improved brake lining life, but for taxi companies this was vital.[35]

CHRYSLER ENGINEERING

During the '20s and '30s Chrysler Engineering was at the top of its form. Since the 1926 Walter Chrysler statement of engineering philosophy and the 1928 ZSB engineering organization, Chrysler had the best engineering in the business. They had brought to market a line of cars that grew from 335,000 in 1928 to 850,000 in 1940, the year Walter Chrysler died. In addition to the line of very competitive cars, the above listed "Chrysler Firsts" were introduced to the public. Most of the "Chrysler First's" were standard equipment with each of the new model cars. This was in keeping with Walter Chrysler's approach to the market that new features would be added for the customer, but serious cost control in the manufacturing side of the business would result in no greater cost and therefore price to the customer.

Each of the chief engineers was expected to be a world leader in his field and they were. Any new automotive feature or item of interest was bought by the corporation and torn down and analyzed. Chrysler had an open account with book and magazine publishers around the world to buy anything that was published in a very broad field of interests. That collection still exists and is the basis of the archives of the DaimlerChrysler Historical Collection.

One of the areas that Engineering was not a leader in was automatic transmission development. The fluid coupling was a Chrysler first but the related automatic transmission was a G.M. development. The Chrysler engineers felt that the hydraulic control system would be too complex for successful manufacturing or maintenance in customer hands. The hydraulic valving was very precise in manufacture and complex in assembly. Dirt or machining chips would ruin the valve body and transmission. The transmission had four forward speeds and the shifts were under load. The timing of the release of a set of bands or clutches and the application of other bands or clutches had to be exact to make a smooth shift. To their credit, G.M. persisted in the development and introduced the Hydromatic transmission on Oldsmobiles in 1937. Later it was combined with the Chrysler-developed fluid coupling to be the modern automatic transmission.

Chrysler developed a four speed transmission with first and second gear in a low range and third and fourth in a high range. The first/second shift and third/fourth shift were made automatically by lifting the throttle foot and taking the power off the transmission. A solenoid would make the shift with a "clunk" sound. The shift from low to high range was done in the conventional way with the clutch and shift lever. A Chrysler product could idle with the fluid coupling and then accelerate in third gear (slowly) and make the clunk shift into fourth gear at highway speeds. It worked, but the G.M. cars were excellent performers that used all four speeds and made the shifts between speeds under engine power. It would be over a decade before Chrysler Engineers would become serious about developing a true automatic transmission.

Styling: Walter Chrysler's Special Interest

Harley Earl was hired by Alfred Sloan to improve the appearance of the G.M. line of cars. His design philosophy was clear for anyone to see. He wanted cars to be longer, lower and wider. The cars of the mid–'20s were typified by the Model T. Design-wise, it was a high box at 7 feet (the body), with a small box in front (the engine hood) with winglike fenders hanging in all directions and hung-on headlamps, tail lamps, a trunk and a spare tire. Harley Earl devoted over 20 years of his life to getting all the parts to appear as an overall design.

His first design for G.M. was the 1927 LaSalle. It was to be priced between a Buick and a Cadillac and was built to appeal to a more youthful buyer than would buy a Cadillac. Earl lowered the belt line (just below the windows) and raised the hood so the car had a long horizontal shape that extended from the front grille to the rear bumper. The car was beautiful and an instant success. Harley Earl's next new project was the 1928 Chevrolet where he did the same thing in getting the hood and belt line to line up in a long, horizontal form that made the car look long and low. While Edsel Ford no doubt understood what Harley Earl was doing, he was not able to influence his father. The new Model A Ford had a hump at the cowl that made the car look old even if brand new. It was not until the Model B in 1932 that the long hood-to-body form looked as up to date as the 1928 Chevrolet.

Ray Dietrich was one of the great designers during the classic era of great designers. His designs for LeBaron and others were among the best ever. In 1932, he was out of work as the custom car market shrank to nothing and he wrote Fred Zeder and asked for a job. Zeder answered that he was laying people off. That was no doubt true, but it did not answer the question Dietrich was asking. Here was a "star quality" designer, but Zeder did not want any "stars" in his organization, no matter how good they were.

Walter Chrysler found out about the Dietrich situation and responded

1932 Ford V8—The 1932 Ford Model B had the appearance of the 1928 Chevrolet but still had a four cylinder engine and was uncompetitive. Plymouth was to introduce a six cylinder engine in 1932. Henry Ford was undecided as to what to do. At the last moment he decided to make a V8 engine an option on the Model B. This photograph is of a Model B V8 on the road at the 2002 Old Car Festival at Greenfield Village, Dearborn, Michigan.

with direct action. Walter Chrysler was a master of working with his people and using his expert knowledge of all parts of the automobile business in getting what he wanted from those people. He could have done that with Fred Zeder, but he chose to hire Ray Dietrich as his own personal employee and place him in the middle of Engineering Division. ZSB had built an organization of solid engineering talent and a stylist in the middle would be a thorn. It was all right if he picked paint colors or styled ornaments, but to change the shape of future cars was trouble. The strong, engineering-directed style of the Airflow had made Walter Chrysler realize that professional styling help was needed and Ray Dietrich was one of the best in the industry, but having him report directly to Walter Chrysler was a real and ongoing problem to ZSB.

Harley Earl continued on his predictable styling path and in the mid–'30s the trunk and spare were inside the car and out of sight. By the late '30s, the hood and fenders were a broad shape that had the headlights, and at the rear of the car, tail lamps in a smooth shape. The grille changed from a vertical to horizontal design. In the 1940s the fenders flowed into the doors and the car was now so low that running boards were no longer needed and were either covered or dropped completely. Ray Dietrich did an excellent job of seeing that the Chrysler cars were up to date with the new cars that Harley Earl was introducing at G.M. The Ford cars always seemed to be slightly out of date, in spite of Edsel Ford and his excellent sense of car style. The Ford cars of the '40s did not have the front fenders flowing into the front doors and were the last cars to cover or eliminate the running boards. Both G.M. and Chrysler had moved to new looking, lower car shapes.

In spite of Ray Dietrich and his "thorn like" position in the company, he was effective. In 1935 he was able to style a single body that could be used across all lines of cars, except for the Airflow. This achievement saved the company from the Airflow disaster. That continued until 1939 when he was able to retool only the roof and cowl area and use a V-shaped windshield in the carryover common body. The appearance change was so different that most observers thought it was a new car. In 1926, Walter Chrysler had said that interchangeability was the essence of cost control. That may be true, but it is also necessary to market a line of different looking cars. Dietrich had been doing that in the 1934 through 1939 line of cars with great success. In 1939, in addition to the vee windshield, Dietrich came up with his strongest theme that could be used for the four brands and still not reveal that the whole line of car originated from only one body. The 1939 designs stand as a high point of Ray Dietrich's genius, but on May 26, 1938, Walter Chrysler became seriously ill and withdrew from any company affairs. Dietrich's brilliant design for 1939 cars was only a few months from introduction when Fred Zeder fired Ray Dietrich and the "thorn" was removed from Engineering Division.

Non-Automotive: Endless Curiosity

In the 1920 and 1930s Chrysler Corporation moved in several non-automotive directions and this reveals a great deal about Walter Chrysler.[36]

Marine and industrial engines—1927. Walter Chrysler lived on Long Island and commuted to Manhattan by speed boat with a short walk to his office. He owned several yachts and was interested in marine engines. Automobile engines were unsuited for marine applications because they did not have any durability. The Chrysler engines were developed to run a 50 hour wide open throttle test and not show any defects. The result was that the engine would reach maximum temperature and test the engine cooling and engine lubrication systems. If it passed this test, it would have years of service in an automotive application.

1939 DODGE—Ray Dietrich was head of Styling at Chrysler Corporation and did a good job of keeping the Chrysler cars up to date with the new cars from General Motors. Interchangeability was the watchword at Chrysler and his challenge was to keep appearance different for each of the car brands. In 1939 he created what appeared to be a new car, but it came from a single carryover body shell. This car, a Hayes coupe, was as up to date as any in the 1939 market. This car is on permanent display at the Walter P. Chrysler Museum in Auburn Hills, Michigan.

Marine service is very demanding since the engine has to run at 80 or 90 percent of its power for hours at a time. A car application is a light duty use because after several minutes of full power, the car is going so fast as to exceed any speed limit. The power needed to hold a constant road speed is 15 to 20 hp and the full power of the engine is needed only to accelerate up to those road speeds. Unlike other passenger car engines, the Chrysler engines needed only a small improvement in the valve durability to be used successfully in marine or industrial applications.

Walter Chrysler started a marine and industrial division, not just to make a profit but as a testimonial to the durability that was built into every Chrysler engine. A particularly successful venture was the combination with Chris

Craft. Boat designers would develop a boat and install an engine, but there was little thought to the match. The Chris Craft–Chrysler engine marriage of 1927, the Cadet, was the first step in giving a customer an engineered combination, and with a low-cost but durable automotive based engine.

Chrysler Building.[37] There is no connection between the Chrysler Building and Chrysler Corporation. Both were efforts of the same man, Walter Chrysler. Chrysler Corporation rented space in the building but that was the only business connection.

In 1928, Walter Chrysler expressed interest in a New York skyscraper building project that had failed because of lack of funding. Chrysler was interested in a semi-retirement project for himself and a future business for his sons, Walter Jr. and Jack Chrysler. The building as planned had a flat dome roof. Chrysler changed everything above the 61st floor. He always had a good eye for style, as evidenced in the cars that he brought to market. For his new building, he wanted the tallest building in the world with some kind of "point or crown." The Chrysler Building stands today as not just a fine example of art deco style, but as one of the most beautiful buildings in the world. It was all due to Walter Chrysler and his architect, William Van Alen.

Once the project got started, Chrysler approached it the same way he did everything else in his life. He was curious and into everything. He picked the marble, the wood, the designs; he was everywhere and must have driven Van Alen crazy. One of his pet issues was the elevator speed. The City Code for elevator speed was 750 feet per minute, but Walter Chrysler determined that this speed in the highest of all buildings would take too long. If more elevators were added to move people in and out of the building, then the lower floors would be an almost solid bank of elevators and there would no room for commercial space. He proposed 1,000 feet per second of elevator speed for his new building. It became the standard for the City Code and is still used today. Walter Chrysler made his mark on the building as only he could. At the Thirtieth floor, the brickwork had car running boards and brickwork wheels and chrome hub caps. There were the polished steel wings of Mercury, as used on the Chrysler car hood ornament. On the sixtieth floor there were eight steel gargoyles and above that the famous steel spire. The steel was chrome nickel stainless that was tested at Chrysler Engineering in Detroit.

The building was completed and opened on May 27, 1930, and in spite of the Depression had a good occupancy level. It was the tallest building in the world for only one year. The Empire State Building was opened and with its dirigible mast on the top of the building, it stole the honors.

Amplex Division—1930. Chrysler Engineering developed a way of using cintered metal and of having oil in the small spaces within the metal, thereby resulting in a self-lubricating bearing. Cintered metal was not new and was powdered copper, tin and graphite in various combinations that were pressed to a final shape with different amounts of pressure. With a great deal of pressure, a part could be formed with similar strength as a machined part, but the process formed a complete part with no added machining directly from the die. Small gears or small motor parts were a good application for the process. If a lower pressure was used, the part might have 30 percent open space, and if filled with oil under pressure and formed to the shape of a bearing, the result was a bearing that would provide its own oil under the pressure of use and the oil would flow back to the bearing when the use stopped. This was a self-lubricating bearing. Walter Chrysler felt that the invention was worth investment and authorized that the Amplex Division of Chrysler be formed in 1930 to make cintered metal products and Oilite bearings. Amplex Division was a solid money maker and a corporate bright spot during the depths of the Depression.

Airtemp Division—1934. The construction of the Chrysler Building had shown Chrysler that air conditioning was a future market, but making a product that was correctly engineered, self-contained and easy for the customer to install would be a challenge. On the other hand, the components were condensers and evaporators that were much like automotive radiators, compressors much like car engines and tubing similar to brake lines. Walter Chrysler had been on the G.M. Board when Frigidaire was added as a new business at General Motors by William Durant.

Chrysler saw Airtemp as a good future business for Chrysler Corporation and indeed it was. He could not have foreseen that Packard would develop an automotive air conditioning system in 1939 and that in another two decades, almost every car made in America would be air conditioned.

Railroad trucks—1938. Walter Chrysler never lost his interest in railroading and in fact served on the boards of directors of several railroad companies. Railroads started to lose freight and passenger business to trucks and buses in the late '30s. A train ride was rough for passengers, with a great deal of vibration and bounce. Carl Breer thought that the lessons of improving the ride of the Airflow might improve train travel. A major project was started at Chrysler Engineering to improve the ride of passenger trains. Breer succeeded and a company was formed to manufacture and sell the improved "trucks" that rail cars rolled on. Walter Chrysler saw to it that passenger cars were made with the new design and demonstrations were made across the country to railroad officials. The new trucks did work, and in fact improved the ride of freight cars to carry fragile freight. The reality was that rail transportation business was dropping so fast that an improved ride would do little or nothing to change the business. The Chrysler designed rail trucks were withdrawn.

A Time to Relax

At the peak of his abilities and after years of high stress and long working hours, Chrysler decided, in 1935, to turn over day to day operations to his handpicked successor, K. T. Keller. Keller was a manufacturing man like himself and knew how to control costs so that customer features could be standard on Chrysler cars and still sell at competitive prices. This continued the Walter Chrysler business practice. Chrysler said, "My work is done," and remained as Chairman of the Board. He lived on Long Island and loved the life of New York—Broadway, Wall Street, art, music and night clubs—and he took advantage of it all. He took a trip to Europe almost every year. He lived the life of one of the wealthiest men in America and he was.

His company was well managed under K. T. Keller as President. Sales were about 800,000 and well ahead of Ford for a firm second place in the industry. In 1938, Walter Chrysler had a stroke and began to have heart troubles. In late 1938, his wife, Della, died suddenly. He soon lacked the strength, and perhaps the desire, to walk very far and in his last year he was wheelchair bound. He died on August 18, 1940, at age 65.

Summary of a Business Life: An Automotive Polymath

Walter Chrysler was a master machinist, a manufacturing expert and head of all G.M. manufacturing, a company doctor, an expert on cost control and knowledgeable about everything having to do with the automobile business. His main strength was manufacturing and cost control. In addition, he knew accounting, business management, Wall Street financing, and automotive engineering, and had a good eye for automotive style. In 1920 John Willys said the following of Walter Chrysler: "Why is this man so valuable? Any employer can handle any number of specialists in single lines.... With somewhat more difficulty you can get men who are specialists in perhaps two subjects. With a still greater difficulty you can hire men who are not specialists, but who have the ability to manage other men. With a great deal more difficulty, you can find an occasional specialist who can handle men successfully. But the rarest man on earth is the man whom I have just described, who seems to be a specialist in nearly every subject and can also manage any kind of men. Such a man is worth practically any amount of money, for there is no limit to the amount of business he can direct.... Thereby you extend the power of your own hand."[38]

In 1947, Fred Zeder said this of Chrysler: "As a good manager, he had the ability to surround himself with men who knew their professions and trades supremely well; and yet every man who worked for him felt that Mr. Chrysler knew his subject as well as he did himself. But Mr. Chrysler never assumed the prerogative of doing the man's work for him. If one had the responsibility and the ability to act, he did so with confidence, realizing that his leader would depend on his judgment and would sustain it."[39]

What else can be said about one of the giants of the automobile industry? He was a leader who recognized that the customer did not actually want a car that was easy to repair, but rather an engineered car that did not need repair—in short, the modern automobile.

Epilogue: Four Business Lives

Career Goals and Commitment

All four men reached what could be called a career goal before becoming a part of the automobile industry. Henry Ford was the Chief Engineer of the Detroit Edison plant in Detroit. William Durant was president of Durant and Dort and a millionaire. Alfred Sloan was president of Hyatt Bearing Company and a millionaire, and Walter Chrysler was the Works Manager (V.P. of Manufacturing) at the American Locomotive Company in Pittsburgh, Pa.

All four were unshakable in their belief that the automobile market was boundless in size. Henry Ford proved the market was boundless every time he lowered prices and a flood of orders came in. Ford had another commitment to lower the price of cars so there would be personal transportation for anyone with a good job. His unique view was expressed at the Dodge Stockholders Trial when he said that a company has an obligation to its workers and the public. The suit proved there was no such obligation and Henry Ford bought out all the stockholders so he could continue to run the company according to his viewpoint.

Durant committed everything that he had at several different times. First, when he expanded G.M. beyond the cash position of the company in 1910. Secondly, when he took over G.M. in order to improve the shareholder value in 1915. Thirdly, when he put in place a manufacturing expansion in the late teens to be ready for the Roaring Twenties. He was right even if his stock purchases forced him out of G.M. in 1920.

As a supplier to the industry, Sloan saw the boundless increase in parts ordered by the industry. As head of G.M. he saw to it that there was a system that would meet expanding future sales growth, but with budgets that would maintain control so the company could prosper and meet even further future growth.

Walter Chrysler saw no bounds to the industry. Automobile sales passed 4 million units per year in the 1920s and hand wringers worried about "saturation." Walter Chrysler said that there was no such thing and except for short downturns, he was right.

The optimistic view of all four carried into the Depression when all four were wrong, but only for a short time for three of the four. William Durant's Durant Motors went bankrupt. Sloan fared the best because his system gave an early warning and he could react to keep General Motors profitable for the entire Depression. Chrysler fared well with cost cutting and lost money for the one year that a six cylinder engine was tooled for Plymouth so it could increase sales. Ford tooled two V8 engines and a V12 and survived the Depression as a break-even.

The Part of Luck

The luckiest of them all was Henry Ford. In 1902 he was out of work. The most prominent manufacturing man in Detroit, Henry Leland, was critical of his designs and his inventions. Ford had no money and had his family living in his father's home to save money. He had made the power structure of Detroit very angry at him, personally, and there was no more money for his automobile experiments.

Alexander Malcomson took a long gamble in funding $3,000 for Ford to build a prototype car. Henry Ford was a man that could raise $86,000 in 1899, and another $30,000 in 1901, but now, in 1903, only $28,000 would come forward. It was all from Malcomson's friends and business associates. In another piece of luck, the Dodge Brothers added $70,000 of their funds in tooling, labor cost and material cost to the new Ford Motor Company. The result was about $100,000 in luck to launch the Ford Motor Company.

William Durant had the luck of an optimist in a growing American economy. At every turn he could see a way to make money and did. Only when his optimism ran into a short term problem, a gamble, was he in trouble. Like a gambler, his losses happened as many times as he had made a fortune and his life ended modestly.

Alfred Sloan had the luck of a person who chose his parents very well. His father's support was critical to his success. His abilities in organization and management made him a success at Hyatt Bearing Company and were vital to the success of G.M. when he took over as president in 1923 and ran the largest industrial firm in the world for 33 years.

Walter Chrysler had the luck of the prepared mind. The idea that he could fund a new car development and that it would ever enter production would be unbelievable. At any time over a four year period, his large financial investment would be nothing but scrap paper. He was ready with a new car concept in 1924 to replace the failing Chalmers at Maxwell Motors. He was ready with a plan to solve the Dodge market and product problem. Although this was a problem he had created in 1928 with the DeSoto. When the Ford Model T went out of production in 1927, he was ready, one year later, with a new Plymouth. When the Depression surprised everyone, he was ready with a full featured Plymouth that would be responsible for getting his company out of the Depression.

Every American company is organized so that the company assets are leveraged with stock on the open market, bonds or debt outstanding so that money is made on a larger base than just the capital assets themselves. Such a company would have committees and a board of directors and everything would be approved in a formal way. The Dodge stockholder lawsuit proved Henry Ford's belief that a business had an obligation to employees and the public was wrong under the law. Henry Ford's view would have been correct for a nonprofit company, but his was a "for profit" corporation.

Henry Ford had a grammar school education as was usual for his generation, and his business experience was different from that of the other giants of the automobile industry. Durant founded a successful wagon company and with his Wall Street background knew how to found, raise capital and manage a business. Sloan's background was similar. Walter Chrysler took extensive correspondence courses and was a master of business management.

The Ford Motor Company was founded with $28,000 in invested capital. Another $70,000 was invested by the Dodge Brothers and while Ford would have been aware of their investment, it was not FMC money. What was unique was that the company was so successful, and so quickly, that added investment capital was not needed. New stock issues, corporate bonds or bank loans were not needed as the company grew to the largest industrial firm in the world. All parts of the company, including the Rouge, were paid for out of earnings. This experience gave Henry Ford a different viewpoint from other industrial leaders and he had no reason to change his beliefs, even after the loss of the Dodge lawsuit.

Any conventional business would have lowered cost as Henry Ford did, but what FMC did after that was unique. In 1910 and after, no other company chose to lower prices as Henry Ford did. Buick was making cost reductions under Walter Chrysler but Buick was increasing, not dropping, prices. It is doubtful that any conventional company would have done what Ford did. Would they have lowered prices almost every year for 19 years? Would they have doubled workers' pay (to $5.00 a day)? The evidence is that none did. Such proposals would never have made it to the board level for discussion, much less approval. Henry Ford's ideas were original and with his 58 percent ownership of the stock, without any corporate bonds outstanding and with no debt, his decisions did not need any other approval.

Henry Ford put into practice the populist ideas of the day, even if they were not the thrust of corporate law. In 1918, Theodore Roosevelt said he wanted to find a way for workers to share in the profits and stock of their employers.[1] These were the same ideas Henry Ford expressed at the Dodge lawsuit trial of 1917. Without a Henry Ford and his unique approach to business, American society would never have been lucky enough to develop the way it did. That event put the world on wheels.

The automobile industry was certainly the favorite child of the capitalist system in rewarding the major producers of the automobile industry with pre-tax earnings that were of the level of Microsoft or Intel of the late 1990s. Unlike the late 1990s, in this case that earnings level went on for several decades. General Motors, which has an accounting system like the companies of today, had an average pre-tax earnings on sales of 15.5 percent from 1923 to 1942. These were the years that Alfred Sloan was president of the company and before World War II, which distorted financial results. Walter Chrysler's company also had an accounting system that was like the companies of today and made an average of 6.6 percent pre-tax earnings on sales from the start of the company in 1925 to the end of Chrysler's life in 1940. Chrysler made less in earnings on sales than General Motors because it made less content per car than did General Motors. Chrysler, however, had a better return on assets than General Motors for the same reason. These earnings are remarkable in that these years included the Depression. Ford did not have a financial system that could be compared to today's, but the company was rewarded by the market by earning all the funds needed to grow from the initial capitalization of $28,000 into a giant without public stock offerings, corporate bonds or bank debt.

Notes

Chapter 1

Henry Ford left a huge collection of primary material for the modern researcher. When he died in 1947 his home, Fairlane, and his office at Ford Motor Company had tons of paper notes and material that he had saved throughout his life. It ranged from contracts and un-cashed checks to turn of the last century notes to give someone a raise in pay and notes to pick up groceries for his wife, Clara, on his way home from work. It took archivists several years to organize this collection. It became the basis of the archives of Henry Ford Museum and Greenfield Village in Dearborn, Mich. The primary work from this collection is the three volume *Ford: The Times, The Man, The Company* by Allan Nevin and Frank Hill (Charles Scribner and Sons, 1962).

Ford's image was so overwhelming as one of the greats of the 20th century that it is difficult to find a more critical viewpoint of his life for some balance. Two works provide some balance to the Ford halo: *Ford: the Man and the Machine* by Robert Lacy (Little, Brown, & Company, Boston and New York, 1986), and *The Fords—An American Epic* by Peter Collier and David Horowitz (Summit Books, New York and London, 1987).

Prices and detailed information on specific cars came from *The Standard Catalog of American Cars 1805–1942* by Beverly Rae Kimes and Henry Austin Clark, Jr. (Krause Publications, Iola, Wis, 1989).

Sales and Production information came from *Automobiles in America* by the Automobile Manufacturers Association, Inc., Wayne State University Press, Detroit, Mich., and "New Car Registrations, 1923–1972, *Financial and General Facts Book*, Chrysler Corporation, 1972.

The archives at Henry Ford Museum and Greenfield Village are available to the modern researcher and were extensively used as a source of primary material by the author.

Cited sources are as follows:

1. *Birth of a Giant*, by Richard Crabb. Chilton Book Company, Philadelphia, 1969.

2. *The Road Is Yours*, Reginald M. Cleveland and S. T. Williamson. The Greystone Press, Chicago, 1965.

3. *Men, Money and Markets*, by Dean Russell. Privately printed by Atwood Vacuum Machine Company, 1959.

4. *Men, Money and Motors* by Theodore F. McManus and Norman Beasley. Harper & Row, New York and London, 1929.

5. *Young Henry Ford—A Picture History of the First Forty Years*, by Sidney Olson. Wayne Stare University Press, Detroit, Mich., 1963.

6. *My Life and Work*, by Henry Ford with Samuel Crowther. Doubleday, Garden City, N. Y., 1923.

7. "Ransom Eli Olds, The Man Behind The Marque" by Beverly Rae Kimes. *Automobile Quarterly*, Vol. 41, No. 4, Kutztown Publishing, Kutztown, Pa.

8. "Ford's Automobile Has New Fea-

tures and is a Novel Machine," *The Detroit Journal*, Saturday, July 29, 1899.

9. *Detroit Automobile Company Catalog*, Product Literature Collection, Archives of the Henry Ford Museum and Greenfield Village, Dearborn Mich.

10. Quote from *The Life of John Wendell Anderson* by Milo M. Quaife, p. 81, privately printed, Detroit, 1950.

11. "Ford's Automobile Has New Features and is a Novel Machine," *The Detroit Journal*, Saturday July 29, 1899.

12. Quote from volume *Ford: The Times, The Man, The Company*, by Allan Nevin and Frank Hill, p. 210. Charles Scribner and Sons, 1962.

13. *The Road Is Yours*, Reginald M. Cleveland and S. T. Williamson. The Greystone Press, Chicago, 1965.

14. Leland quote from "General Motors—The First 75 Years of Transportation Products," p. 26, *Automobile Quarterly*, printed by General Motors, Detroit, Mich., 1983.

15. "Ford's Automobile Has New Features and is a Novel Machine," *The Detroit Journal*, Saturday, July 29, 1899.

16. "Swifter than a Race Horse, It Flew Over the Icy Streets," *Detroit News-Tribune*, February 4, 1900.

17. "The Dodge Brothers, the Automobile Industry, and Detroit Society in the Early Twentieth Century," by Dr. Charles Hyde. *The Michigan Historical Review*, Vol. 22, No. 2, Fall 1996.

18. *Monopoly on Wheels*, by William Greenleaf. Wayne State University Press, 1961, Detroit, Mich.

19. "I Invented the Automobile," by Robert Scott. *Automobile Quarterly*, Vol. 7, No. 3, Kutztown Publishing, Kutztown, Pa.

20. Box List, "Columbia." Archives of the DaimlerChrysler Historical Collection, Detroit, Mich.

21. Box List, "Oversize Books, Dodge Brothers Payroll Ledger," Archives of the DaimlerChrysler Historical Collection, Detroit, Mich.

22. Quote from June 4, 1903, letter from John Anderson to William Anderson, *The Life of John Wendell Anderson*, by Milo M. Quaife, p. 98, privately printed, Detroit, 1950.

23. "The Benjamin Briscoe Story," by Beverly Rae Kimes. *Automobile Quarterly*, Vol. 17, No. 2, Kutztown Publishing, Kutztown, Pa.

24. "U.S. Motor, Ben Briscoe's Shattered Dream," by Anthony Yanik. *Automobile Quarterly*, Vol. 36, No. 2, Kutztown Publishing, Kutztown, Pa.

25. *The Ford Agency: A Picture History*, by Henry L. Dominguez. Motor Books International, Osceola, Wis., 1981.

26. "Low Cost Breakthrough," *The Detroit News*, January 5, 1906.

27. Quote from *Made in Detroit* by Norman Deasley and George Stark, p. 141. G. P. Putnam and Sons, New York, 1957.

28. *The Model T Ford—the Car That Changed the World*, by Bruce W. McCalley. Krause Publications, Iola, Wis., 1994.

29. Quote from *Detroit Is My Home Town*, by Malcolm W. Bingey. The Bobbs-Merrill Company Publishers, Indianapolis and New York.

30. "Building an Industry: The Architecture of Albert Kahn," by Joshua Markel. *Automobile Quarterly*, Vol. 34, No. 1. Kutztown Publishing, Kutztown, Pa.

31. *From the American System to Mass Production 1800–1932*, by David A. Hounshell. The Johns Hopkins University Press, Baltimore and London, 1984.

32. "Ford Motor Company Income 1903–1921," Martindale Papers, Archives of the Henry Ford Museum and Greenfield Village, Dearborn, Mich.

33. Quote from *Made in Detroit*, by Norman Deasley and George Stark, p. 216. G. P. Putnam and Sons, New York.

34. "Affordability Index," by Comerica Bank, Detroit, Mich.

35. *The Ford Agency: A Picture History* by Henry L. Dominguez. Motor Books International, Osceola, Wis., 1953.

36. *Automobile Franchise Agreements*, by Charles Mason Hewitt. Indiana University School of Business, Richard D. Irwin, Inc., Homewood, Ill., 1956.

37. Box list "Dodge Brothers Box 1," Archives of the DaimlerChrysler Historical Collection, Detroit, Mich.
38. *The Triumph of an Idea—The Story of Henry Ford*, by Ralph H. Graves. Garden City, New York, Doubleday, Doran and Company, 1935.
39. *The Ford Farm Tractors*, by Randy Leffingwell. MBI Publishing Company, 1998, ISBN 0-7603-0337-1.
40. *The Life of John Wendell Anderson*, by Milo M. Quaife, privately printed, Detroit, 1950.
41. *Henry's Attic*, by Ford R. Bryan. Ford Books, Dearborn, Mich.
42. *Ford: The Man and the Machine*, by Robert Lacy. Little, Brown, & Company, Boston and New York, 1986.
43. *The Lincoln Motor Car: Sixty Years of Excellence*, by Thomas E. Bonsall. Bookman Dan, Baltimore Md., 1984.
44. *The Cars Of Lincoln/Mercury*, by George Dammann and James Wagner. Crestline Publishing.
45. *The Model T Ford—The Car That Changed the World*, by Bruce W. McCalley. Krause Publications, Iola, Wis., 1994.
46. *The Ford Model A*, by George DeAngelis, Edward P. Francis and Leslie R. Henry. Motor Cities Publishing Company, South Lyons, Mich., 1971.
47. "8 for the Price of a 4: Ford's Fabulous Flathead," by Mike Mueller. *Automobile Quarterly*, Vol. 36, No. 1, Kutztown Publishing, Kutztown, Pa.
48. *The Turning Wheel: The Story of General Motors through Twenty Five Years, 1908–1933*, by Arthur Pound. Doubleday, Doran & Company, Garden City, N.Y., 1934.
49. *The Cast Iron Wonder*, by Doug Bell. Floyd Clymer Publications, Los Angeles, California, 1961.
50. *The Ford V8*, by George DeAngelis, Edward P. Francis and Leslie R. Henry. Motor Cities Publishing Company, South Lyons, Mich.
51. *Knudsen* by Norman Beasley. Whittlesey House–McGraw Hill Book Company, Inc., New York and London, 1947.
52. *The Whiz Kids*, by John A. Byrne. Published by Doubleday, New York, 1971.
53. Quote from *The Whiz Kids*, by John A. Byrne, p. 171. Published by Doubleday, New York, 1971.
54. Quote from *Detroit Is My Home Town*, by Malcolm Bingey, p. 51. The Bobbs-Merrill Company, Indianapolis and New York, 1946.
55. *From the American System to Mass Production 1800–1932*, by David A. Hounshell. The Johns Hopkins University Press, Baltimore and London, 1984.
56. *The Machine That Changed the World*, by James P. Womack. Ransom Associates, New York, 1990.
57. Box List, "WWII—Bofors." Archives of the DaimlerChrysler Historical Collection, Detroit, Mich.
58. Box List, "Educational Orders Act." Archives of the DaimlerChrysler Historical Collection, Detroit, Mich.
59. *The Lincoln Motor Car: Sixty Years of Excellence*, by Thomas E. Bonsall. Bookman Dan, Baltimore Md., 1987.
60. "Zephyr, Edsel's West Wind," by Kit Foster. *Automobile Quarterly*, Vol. 40, No. 4. Kutztown Publishing, Kutztown, Pa.
61. *The Cars Of Lincoln/Mercury*, by George Dammann and James Wagner. Crestline Publishing.
62. "Genesis of Mercury, Ford's Medium—Priced Advantage, by James K. Wagner. *Automobile Quarterly*, Vol. 35, No. 1, Kutztown Publishing, Kutztown, Pa.

Chapter 2

There is very little primary material available to the modern researcher about William Durant. He started an autobiography but got no further than the introduction. He did affect a great many lives and they have reported parts of his life.

Alfred Sloan knew Durant as a customer that he called on while at Hyatt

Bearing Company and knew him as a boss from 1916 to 1920. He did write extensively and covered William Durant's life extensively. Sloan's insights are a basic source of material on Durant. They are *Adventures of a White-Collar Man* by Alfred P. Sloan, Jr., and Boyden Sparks (Doubleday, Doran & Company, Inc. New York, 1941) and *My Years with General Motors* by Alfred P. Sloan, Jr., edited by John McDonald with Catherine Stevens (Doubleday & Company, Inc., 1964).

Prices and detailed information on specific cars came from *The Standard Catalog of American Cars 1805–1942*, by Beverly Rae Kimes and Henry Austin Clark, Jr., Krause Publications, Iola, Wis., 1987.

Sales and production information came from *Automobiles in America* by the Automobile Manufacturers Association, Inc. Wayne State University Press, Detroit, Mich., and "New Car Registrations, 1923–1972," *Financial and General Facts Book*, Chrysler Corporation, 1972.

Cited sources are as follows:

1. "Billy Durant: Hurrah for the Little Man" by Beverly Rae Kimes. *Automobile Quarterly*, Vol. 40, No. 3, Kutztown Publishing, Kutztown, Pa.

2. "Wouldn't You Rather be a Buick," by Beverly Rae Kimes. *Automobile Quarterly*, Vol. 7, No. 1, Kutztown Publishing, Kutztown, Pa.

3. *The Turning Wheel: The Story of General Motors through Twenty-Five Years, 1908–1933*, by Arthur Pound. Doubleday, Doran & Company, Garden City, N.Y., 1934.

4. *Birth of a Giant*, by Richard Crabb. Chilton Book Company, Philadelphia, 1969.

5. *The Road Is Yours*, Reginald M. Cleveland and S. T. Williamson. The Greystone Press, Chicago, 1965.

6. "Birth of the Bowtie: The Car That Made General Motors," by Joseph S. Freeman. *Automobile Quarterly*, Vol. 34, No. 4, Kutztown Publishing, Kutztown, Pa.

7. *The Dream Maker: William C. Durant, Founder of General Motors*, by Bernard A. Weissberger. Little, Brown & Company, Boston and Toronto, 1979.

8. Quote from *My Years with General Motors*, by Alfred P. Sloan, Jr., edited by John McDonald with Catherine Stevens, p. 25. Doubleday & Company, Incorporated, 1964.

9. *Plungers and Peacocks*, by Dana L. Thomas, Putnam, New York, 1967.

10. *Automotive Giants of America—Men Who Are Making Our Motor Industry*, by B. C. Forbes and O. D. Foster. B. C. Forbes Publishing Company, New York, 1926.

11. "Ten Great Years with Boss Kettering," by Louis Ruthenberg. *Ward's Auto Report*, 1969.

12. *Automotive Giants of America—Men Who Are Making Our Motor Industry*, p. 47, by B. C. Forbes and O. D. Foster. B. C. Forbes Publishing, New York, 1926.

13. *The Automobile Industry: The Coming of Age of Capitalism's Favorite Child*, by Edward D. Kennedy. Reynal & Hitchcock, New York, 1941.

14. *Motor Memories: a Saga of Whirling Gears*, by Eugene W. Lewis. Alved Publications, Detroit, 1947.

Chapter 3

In one sense there is not the wealth of primary research material about Alfred Sloan that there is for Henry Ford. In another sense, the business changes that Sloan made at General Motors constitute a complete public record of his entire business career.

He did write extensively, and that is a basic source of material: *Adventures of a White-Collar Man* by Alfred P. Sloan, Jr., and Boyden Sparks (Doubleday, Doran & Company, Inc., New York, 1941) and *My Years with General Motors* by Alfred P. Sloan, Jr., edited by John McDonald with Catherine Stevens (Doubleday & Company, Inc., 1964).

Every idea that Sloan had was recorded and published by Peter Drucker in *Concept of a Corporation* (John Day Company, 1946). Peter Drucker was allowed to attend General Motors corporate meetings and record the management discussions and decision process from within the company. This book was required reading for every Ford manager and executive for a time under Henry Ford II. It could be said that the business career of Alfred Sloan was completely recorded by Peter Drucker, and that it is the core of the modern business school course of study.

Reference to the post–World War II G.M. and Toyota manufacturing methods are from *The Machine That Changed The World*, by James P. Womack (Rawson Associates, New York, 1990).

Prices and detailed information on specific cars came from *The Standard Catalog of American Cars 1805–1942*, by Beverly Rae Kimes and Henry Austin Clark, Jr. (Krause Publications, Iola, Wis., 1989).

Sales and production information came from *Automobiles in America* by the Automobile Manufacturers Association, Inc. Wayne State University Press, Detroit, Mich., and "New Car Registrations, 1923–1972," *Financial and General Facts Book*, Chrysler Corporation, 1972.

Cited sources are as follows:

1. Quote from *The Road Is Yours—The Story of the Automobile and the Men Behind It*, by Reginald M. Cleveland and S. T. Williamson. The Greystone Press, New York, 1951, p. 37.

2. Quote from *My Years with General Motors*, by Alfred P. Sloan, Jr., edited by John McDonald with Catherine Stevens. Doubleday & Company, Inc. 1964, p. 87.

3. *Ibid.*, p. 53.
4. *Ibid.*, p. 98.
5. *Ibid.*, p. 156.
6. *The Machine That Changed the World*, by James Womack, Daniel T. Jones and Daniel Roos. Rawson Associates, New York, 1990.

Chapter 4

There are only two studies of Walter Chrysler: *Life of an American Workman*, by Walter P. Chrysler, in collaboration with Boyden Sparks (Curtis Publishing Company, New York, 1937), and *Chrysler, the Life and Times of an Automotive Genius* by Vincent Curcio (Oxford University Press, New York, 2000).

In 1972, Carl Breer wrote his notes on his recollection of the early days of Chrysler Corporation. The original is at the archives of the DaimlerChrysler Historical Collection, Detroit, Mich. It is used as a source for this book and was also used for *The Birth of Chrysler Corporation*, by Carl Breer, as edited by Anthony Yannick, SAE International, Warrendale, Pa.

Another source of material is the archives of the DaimlerChrysler Historical Collection, Detroit, Mich. The author spent three years in organizing and researching the collection. The new material that gives an insight into Walter Chrysler is from that source.

Prices and detailed information on specific cars came from *The Standard Catalog of American Cars, 1805–1942*, by Beverly Rae Kimes and Henry Austin Clark, Jr., Krause Publications, Iola, Wis., 1989.

Sales and production information came from *Automobiles in America* by the Automobile Manufacturers Association, Inc. Wayne State University Press, Detroit, Mich., and "New Car Registrations, 1923–1972," *Financial and General Facts Book*, Chrysler Corporation, 1972.

Cited sources are as follows:

1. Quote from *Life of an American Workman*, by Walter P. Chrysler, in collaboration with Boyden Sparks, p. 111. Curtis Publishing Company, New York, 1937.

2. *Automotive Giants of America—Men Who Are Making Our Motor Industry*, by B. C. Forbes and O. D. Foster. B. C. Forbes Publishing Co., New York, 1926.

3. Quotes from *Automotive Giants of America—Men Who Are Making Our*

Motor Industry, by B. C. Forbes and O. D. Foster, pp. 37 and 38. B. C. Forbes Publishing Co., New York, 1926.

4. "Climbing His Own Ladder: The Elevation of Charles Nash," by Karla A. Rosenbuch, *Automobile Quarterly*, Vol. 35, No. 3, Kutztown Publishing, Kutztown, Pa.

5. Box List, "The Miller Collection," the Archives of the DaimlerChrysler Historical Collection, Detroit, Mich.

6. Box list, "Dodge plant and Maxwell plant," the Archives of the DaimlerChrysler Historical Collection, Detroit, Mich.

7. Quote from *Chrysler: the Life and Times of an Automotive Genius* by Vincent Curcio, p. 251. Oxford University Press, New York, 2000.

8. Quote from *Life of an American Workman,* by Walter P. Chrysler, in collaboration with Boyden Sparks, p. 166. Curtis Publishing Company, New York, 1937.

9. "John North Willys: His Magnetism, his Millions, his Motor Cars," by Beverly Rae Kimes. *Automobile Quarterly*, Vol. VII, No. 3, third quarter 1979, Kutztown Publishing, Kutztown, Pa.

10. "One for All and All for One, Chrysler's Three Engineers," by Karla A. Rosenbusch. *Automobile Quarterly*, Vol. 37, No. 3, Kutztown Publishing, Kutztown, Pa.

11. Box List "ZSB," "The Origin of Chrysler Corporation and the First Chrysler Car," by Owen Skelton, the Archives of the DaimlerChrysler Historical Collection, Detroit, Mich.

12. Box list, "ZSB," "Memoirs of Tobe Couture," the Archives of the DaimlerChrysler Historical Collection, Detroit, Mich.

13. Box List, "The Miller Collection," the archives of the DaimlerChrysler Historical Collection, Detroit, Mich.

14. *Ibid.*

15. "The Chrysler Six: The First Modern Automobile," by Mark Howell, *Antique Automobile*, Vol. XXXVI, No. 1, January–February 1972.

16. Box List, "Maxwell Corporation, Board of Directors Minutes, May 1923," the Archives of The DaimlerChrysler Historical Collection, Detroit, Mich.

17. *Motor Memories,* by Eugene Lewis. Alved Publishers, Detroit, 1947.

18. "The New York Automobile Show," *Motor Vehicle Magazine*, February 1924.

19. Quote from *Life of an American Workman,* by Walter P. Chrysler, in collaboration with Boyden Sparks, p. 184. Curtis Publishing Company, New York, 1937.

20. "Chrysler, The Early Years," by Cullen Thomas. *Automobile Quarterly*, Vol. 1, No. 1 summer 1967, Kutztown Publishing, Kutztown, Pa.

21. "The New Chrysler/Dealer Contracts," *Business Week*, February 14, 1938.

22. Quote from "Reducing Manufacturing Costs," by Walter P. Chrysler. *Industrial Management*, May 1926.

23. *The Dodges,* by Jean Maddern Pitrone. Icarus, South Bend, Ind., 1981.

24. Box List, "1928 Dodge Facts Books," the Archives of the DaimlerChrysler Historical Collection, Detroit, Mich.

25. Quote from *Life of an American Workman,* by Walter P. Chrysler, in collaboration with Boyden Sparks, p. 193. Curtis Publishing Company, New York, 1937.

26. Box list "Dodge papers 1928," the Archives of the DaimlerChrysler Historical Collection, Detroit, Mich.

27. "Of Arms and Automobiles," *Fortune*, XXII, December 1940.

28. "Streamlining America," Henry Ford Museum and Greenfield Village, 1987.

29. Quote from "Chrysler outlines Traffic Needs," *Detroit News*, March 10, 1928, p. 5.

30. *The Road Is Yours—The Story of the Automobile and the Men Behind It*, by Reginald M. Cleveland and S. T. Williamson. The Greystone Press, New York, 1951.

31. Box list "Airflow, boxes 1–6," the

archives of the DaimlerChrysler Historical Collection, Detroit, Mich.

32. "Automobile Aerodynamics, Form and Fashion," by Karl Ludvigsen. *Automobile Quarterly*, Vol. IV, No. 2, Fall 1967, Kutztown Publishing, Kutztown, Pa.

33. "The Slippery Shapes of Paul Jaray," by Jerry Sloniger. *Automobile Quarterly*, Vol. VIII, No. 3, 1975, Kutztown Publishing, Kutztown, Pa.

34. Box list "Airflow, boxes 1–6," the archives of the DaimlerChrysler Historical Collection, Detroit, Mich.

35. Box list, "Chrysler Firsts," the Archives of the DaimlerChrysler Historical Collection, Detroit, Mich.

36. "Chrysler," *Fortune*, August 1935.

37. "I Like to Build Things," by Steven Fox, *Invention and Technology*, Summer 1999.

38. Quotes from "The More People You Can Direct—The More You Are Worth," *The American Magazine*, August 1920. Walter Chrysler is not mentioned by name but there is no other person that fits the description. From *Chrysler, the Life and Times of an Automotive Genius*, by Vincent Curcio, p. 267. Oxford University Press, New York, 2000.

39. "Leadership, A message to America," by Fred Zeder. A tribute to Walter Chrysler delivered at a dinner of the Newcomen Society of England, Mayflower Hotel, Washington D. C., published by the Princeton Press, 1947. From *Chrysler, the Life and Times of an Automotive Genius*, by Vincent Curcio, p. 325. Oxford University Press, New York, 2000.

Epilogue

1. "Is Today's New Investor Tomorrow's New Populist?" by Jim Yardley. *New York Times*, July 14, 2002, section 4, p. 5.

Index

AC Spark Plug Company 83
Albert Champion Company 73
Allison Engine Division 108
American Locomotive Company 112, 134, 172
American Manufacturing System 61
American Motors 134
Anderson, John 9, 17, 18, 20, 42
A. O. Smith Co. 116, 136
Arsenal of Democracy 61
Association of Licensed Automobile Manufacturers (ALAM) 16, 17, 18, 19, 20, 70
Autocar 4, 16
Autolight 81, 136
Automotive franchises 64
Automotive industries 123

Bendix Corporation 108
Bennett, Sloan and Company 84
Blair and Company 128
BMW 101
Bofors anti-aircraft gun 61
Borg Warner 81, 136
Brady, Anthony 18, 72
Brady, James 127
Brady, Nicholas 127

Brayton cycle engine 16, 19
Breech, Earnest 56
Breer, Carl 118, 120, 128, 153, 154, 156, 160, 170
Briggs Body Co. 82, 136
Briscoe, Benjamin 69, 73
Briscoe, Frank 69
Brown, Donaldson 90
Brown and Sharpe Company 10
Bryant, Milton 9
Budd Company 82, 136, 139, 142
Buffalo 28
Buick 28, 34, 37, 45, 62, 63, 67, 68, 69, 70, 73, 74, 78, 82, 83, 87, 93, 94, 101, 104, 113–117, 128, 134–136, 143, 149, 165, 174
Buick, David 69
Buick and Sherwood Plumbing Company 69
Buick Model B 70
Buick Model C 70
Buick Model 10 73, 74, 75

Cadillac 4, 11, 17, 23, 28, 31, 44, 45, 73, 74, 85, 86, 89, 94, 101, 103, 106, 165
Cadillac 60 Special 105
Carter Carburetor Company 136
Cartercar 74, 83

Cass Avenue 27
Chalmers 125, 173, 141
Chalmers Motor Company 120, 121, 126
Chase Bank 128, 130
Chevrolet Cars 49, 50, 63, 65, 92, 95–102, 104, 107, 137, 138, 147
Chevrolet Division 48, 49, 57, 58, 76, 77, 79, 81, 92, 101, 106, 116, 143, 144, 148, 150, 165
Chevrolet Six 50, 55
Chicago & Great Western Railroad 111
Chicago 1908 Auto Show 112
Chicago Tribune 42, 46
Chris Craft–Chrysler 169
Chrysler, Della 171
Chrysler, Walter 34, 67, 71, 78, 79, 81, 82, 87, 89, 90, 93, 97, 99, 103, 109, 110, 112–122, 125–131, 134–137, 140–143, 145, 147, 148, 152, 155, 156, 158–159, 164, 165–168, 170–172, 175; and Henry Ford 143
Chrysler Auditing Department 134
Chrysler Building 111, 169, 170
Chrysler cars 106, 135, 137, 154, 157, 165; Chrysler Airflow 62, 131, 150–153, 155, 156, 158, 162, 163, 167;

Chrysler Airstream 132, 162, 163, 167;
Chrysler, first car 123, 124, 130–133;
Chrysler, first car—Willys 119, 120;
Chrysler Plymouth 143, 144
Chrysler Corporation 17, 57, 61, 69, 71, 72, 106, 109, 115, 131, 133, 135, 136–138, 142, 143, 145, 147, 149, 150, 151, 156, 157–159
Chrysler Engineering 134, 135, 137, 150, 162–164, 169
Chrysler firsts 158–164
Chrysler Motors Division, Willys Corp. 118, 122, 127–129
Cleveland 28
Colorado and Southern Railroad 110
Columbia 16, 17, 19, 20, 28
Comerica Bank in Detroit 34
Commodore Hotel 129, 130
Continental Engine Co. 81
Cousins, James 20, 22, 26, 42
Crapo, Henry 67

Daimler Benz 17
DaimlerChrysler 71
DaimlerChrysler Corporate Historical Collection 17, 61, 98, 111, 115, 119, 125, 128, 129, 164
DaimlerChrysler Technical Center 111
Dealership franchises 37
Delco Electric Company 78, 88
Delco Research Labs. 91
DeSoto 106, 135, 138, 140, 141, 143, 144, 149, 152, 154, 173

Detroit Automobile Company 7, 8, 9, 11, 39, 65
Detroit Edison Company 7–9, 172
Detroit Yacht Club 69
Dietrich, Raymond 165–168
Dillon and Read 138, 141
Dodge, Horace 15
Dodge, John 15
Dodge Brothers 13, 14, 15, 17, 18, 20, 22, 23, 38, 39, 42, 44, 60, 70, 94, 98, 115, 135, 138–141, 155, 173
Dodge Division—Chrysler Corp. 143
Dodge lawsuit 41, 64, 65, 172, 174
Dort, Dallas 68, 69, 78
Drucker, Peter 108
Duco Paint 97, 98
duPont, E. I. 80, 89, 90, 95, 96, 98
duPont, Pierre 90
Durant, William 19, 28, 45, 67, 70, 71, 73–83, 87, 88, 89, 93, 99, 102, 104, 116, 117, 121, 122, 170, 172–174
Durant and Dort Carriage Company 68, 69, 70, 73, 82, 83, 90, 172
Durant Motors 81, 83, 100, 173
Duryea 4, 28

Earl, Harley 50, 103, 105, 165–167
Eaton Spring Co. 82, 136
Edison, Thomas 66
Educational Orders Act of 1938 61
Electric Vehicle Corporation (EVC) 16, 17, 72
Elizabeth, N.J., plant 81, 118, 119, 121, 125, 129
Elmore 74
Erskine, Albert 127

Evansville, Indiana 135
Evens, Oliver 60
Everett 23
Ewing 74

Fairlane 36
Fiat 4
Fields, Joseph 134
Fisher Body Corporation 78, 88, 93, 94, 117, 142, 155
Flanders, Walter 23
Flanders car 23
Flint car 81, 122
Floating Power 145, 150, 160, 161
Flowers Machine Shop 3, 9
Foch, French General (WWI) 61
Forbes 120, 129
Ford, Clara Bryan 3
Ford, Edsel 3, 42, 62, 160, 165
Ford, Henry 3–5, 7, 8–15, 19, 20, 22, 24, 28, 31, 33, 36, 37, 41, 42, 44, 46, 49, 50, 53, 54, 56, 59, 62, 63, 65–67, 70, 71, 73, 83, 95, 97, 99, 100, 115, 143, 150, 155, 158, 160, 162, 172–175; and Walter Chrysler 143
Ford, Henry II 57, 63, 66
Ford, William 11
Ford accounting 55, 65
Ford cars 132, 143; Edsel 106; Ford Model A 1903 4, 11, 15; Ford Model A 1928 49, 50, 51, 54, 55–57, 97–99, 100, 104, 109, 143, 161, 165; Ford Model B 1904 22 Ford Model B 1932 52, 53, 56, 162, 165, 166; Ford Model K 22, 74; Ford Model N 24, 25, 28, 40, 60, 74; Ford Model R 25,

74; Ford Model S 25, 74; Ford Model T 24, 25, 32, 37, 38, 40, 46–48, 54, 60, 74, 76–78, 95–100, 107, 109, 138, 143, 143, 165, 173; Ford 1935 155, 156
Ford dealership 36
Ford engineering 44
Ford Manufacturing Company 22, 39
Ford Motor Company 11, 1315, 17, 19, 20, 22, 25, 26, 32, 39, 49, 42, 45, 49, 57–59, 61–63, 65, 71, 73, 87, 89, 97–99 104, 106, 108, 115, 136, 143, 145, 154, 155, 158, 160, 164, 173;
Ford V8 50, 53, 56, 104, 173
Ford V8-60 55
Fordism 59–61
Fordson 39–41
Fortune (December 1940) 146, 147
Franklin 16, 91
French 75 60
Frigidaire 170

General Motors 19, 34, 49, 56, 57, 61, 67, 68, 71, 73–93, 95, 97, 98–102, 104–109, 114, 128, 132, 133, 135, 136, 138, 141, 143, 147, 150, 154, 155, 158, 165–167, 170, 172, 173, 175
General Motors Building 79, 80, 88
General Motors Parts Divisions 136
GMAC 97, 99
GMC Truck 74, 83
Grand Central Palace 129
Gray, John 20, 42
Great Depression 51, 52, 104, 143, 148, 149, 154, 170, 173, 174
Grosse Pointe 36

Harrison Radiator Company 88
Hayes Apperson 16
Henry Ford and Son Company 39
Henry Ford Company 9–11, 39, 46, 65
The Henry Ford Museum 43, 44
Highland Park (Ford plant) 26–28, 29, 33–35, 38, 76
Highland Park (Chrysler plant) 138, 161
Holley, George 49
Hoover, Herbert 66
Hudson 106, 158
Hudson Essex 100
Hutchinson, B.E. 134
Hutchinson Parkway 148
Hyatt Bearing Company 10, 78, 83, 84, 86, 87, 88, 117, 172
Hydromatic 164

Indiana 28
Intel 108
International 16
Ireland 40

Jefferson, Thomas 30
Joy, Henry 18, 34, 35

Kahn, Albert 26, 27, 115
Kahn, Julius 27
Kansas 109, 112
Keller, K. T. 134, 140, 170, 171
Kelvinator 134
Kettering, Charles 91
Kings Point (Long Island) 130
Klaxton Company 88
Knox car 16
Knudsen, William 31, 32, 49, 59, 92, 161

Land speed record 11
LaSalle 103
Lee and Higginman 75
Leland, Henry 10–11, 12, 23, 30, 31, 44, 46, 86, 173
Leland Machine Shop 10
Lexus 101
Liberty engines 45
Life of an American Workman 129, 141
Lincoln 45, 46, 62, 101
Lincoln, Abraham 45
Lincoln Continental 62
Lincoln V12 62, 173
Lincoln Zephyr 62, 163
Lockheed hydraulic brakes 158, 159
Locomobile 16, 81, 112
Loewy, Raymond 149
Long Island Parkway 148
Lumber barons 6

Malcomson, Alexander 13, 14, 20, 22, 39, 173
Marquette 74
Marr, Walter 69
Mason, George 134
Maxwell, Jonathan 69
Maxwell Briscoe Corporation 69, 73
Maxwell Chalmers 17
Maxwell Motor Company 17, 23
Maxwell Motor Corporation 17, 98, 115, 120, 121, 125–128, 133, 134, 141
Mercedes 4
Mercury 62, 63, 106
Merritt Parkway 148
Metsger car 23
Microsoft 108
Midland Steel Co. 136
Milton, Bryant 9
Morgan, J. P. 73, 80, 89
Motor Age 16
Mott, C. S. 87
Murphy, William 7

Nash 106, 114, 116, 134, 148, 158
Nash, Charles 87, 114, 116
Nash Kelvinator 134
New Castle, Indiana 135

New Departure Bearing Company 78, 88
New Process Gear Co. 136
New York Automobile Show 1923 92
New York Automobile Show 1924 128
North American Aviation 108

Oakland 73, 74, 92, 98, 101, 102, 138
Olds, Ransom 6, 7, 11, 28, 72, 73
Oldsmobile 4, 7, 10, 13, 16, 52, 62, 63, 92, 94, 101, 104, 149, 164, 165
Oldsmobile, curved dash 4, 7, 8, 11, 28, 72, 73
Otto cycle engine 16, 19

Packard 4, 16, 23, 34, 44, 45, 106, 158, 170
Peerless 4, 16
Pennsylvania Turnpike 148
Perlman Rim Company 88
Philco Radio Co. 136
Pierce 4, 16
Piquette Plant 22, 23, 26, 27, 60
Pliny Olds Machine Shop 6
Plymouth 52, 55, 63, 97, 106, 132, 135, 137, 143, 147, 150, 160, 161, 163, 173, 174
Plymouth Assembly Plant 146, 147
Pontiac 73, 94, 98, 101, 102, 104, 137, 141–143, 145,
Pope Company 16

Quadricycle 3, 4, 7

Rackham, Horace 18, 20, 42
Rambler 4, 13
Randolph 74
Rapid 74
Reliance 74
Remy Electric Company 88
Renault 4
REO 72, 73
Ricardo, Sir Harry 123, 124
Richards, Eugene 69
Rolls-Royce 4
Roosevelt, Theodore 174
Rouge manufacturing complex 46, 57, 59, 83, 135

Sampson 78, 102
Santa Fe Railroad 109
Searchmont 16
Selden, George 16
Selden patent 15, 16, 18, 72
Seligman 75
Silver Dome 124
Skelton, Owen 118, 156, 160
Sloan, Alfred P., Jr. 10, 49, 78, 81–87, 89, 90, 91, 93, 95, 96, 97, 99–102, 103, 104, 106, 108, 133, 135, 137, 141, 161, 172, 173, 175
Sloan, Alfred P., Sr. 84
Smith, Samuel 6, 7, 72, 73
Sorenson, Charles 160
Star car 81
Stevens 17
Studebaker Corporation 23, 106, 118, 121, 127, 128, 158

Terry, Eli 30, 60
Terry Clock 30
Thomas car 17
Thornton, Tex 57, 59, 63
Timkin Axle Co. 82, 136
Toyoda, Eiji 107
Toyota 107
TV's 26

United Motors 78, 88, 136
U.S. Long Distance 16
United States Motors 17, 23, 88
Universal Products Co. 136

Van Alan, William 169
VCR's 26

Wall Street 79, 82, 83, 89, 103, 128, 142
Wall Street Journal 34
Waltham Watch Company 28, 30
Wayne County sheriff 46
Welch 74
Weston Mott Company 73, 83
White Brothers 121, 125
Whiting, James 69
Whitney, William 15, 16, 17, 72
Whiz Kids 57
Wills, C. Harold 87
Willys, John 117, 118, 121, 127, 171
Willys Corporation 117, 121, 129, 142, 158
Winton 4
Winton car 16, 17, 18
Wisconsin 28
Woolson, Harry 120
World War II 61, 64

Zeder, Fred 118–120, 125–127, 156, 160, 165–167, 171
Zeder car 125
Zeder, Skelton and Breer (ZSB) 118–130, 133, 134, 137, 55, 158–160
Zenith 49